Artistic Duplicity

Artistic Duplicity

The Fiction and Poetry of Juliana Horatia Ewing

— WILLIAM B. DILLINGHAM —

FOREWORD BY REGENIA GAGNIER

Sacristy
Press

Sacristy Press
PO Box 612, Durham, DH1 9HT

www.sacristy.co.uk

First published in 2020 by Sacristy Press, Durham

Sacristy Limited, registered in England & Wales, number 7565667

British Library Cataloguing-in-Publication Data
A catalogue record for the book is available from the British Library

ISBN 978-1-78959-063-0

This book is dedicated with deep and lasting appreciation to "My Editor."

Foreword

There is a heritage of heroic example and noble obligation, not reckoned in the Wealth of Nations, but essential to a nation's life; the contempt of which, in any people, may, not slowly, mean even its commercial fall.

Juliana Horatia Ewing, Jackanapes (1879)

Juliana Horatia Ewing's (1841–85) fiction and poetry counted among their admirers thousands of children and the parents who read to them but also John Ruskin, Henry James, Arnold Bennett, and Rudyard Kipling. William B. Dillingham, Charles Howard Candler Professor of American Literature, Emeritus, Emory University, convincingly speculates that her *Jackanapes* influenced Herman Melville's masterpiece *Billy Budd* (1924), and her way of seeing locally, in contrast to the conspicuous tourism fashionable during her time, appears to have much in common with Henry David Thoreau's "discipline of looking always at what is to be seen . . . The perception of surfaces will always have the effect of miracle to a sane sense" at Walden Pond. *Aunt Judy's Magazine* (1866–85), the popular organ of children's literature edited first by her mother Margaret Gatty and then by Ewing and her sister, Horatia K. F. Eden, also published the nineteenth century's preeminent illustrators Randolph Caldecott and George Cruikshank and writers Hans Christian Andersen and Lewis Carroll.

Dillingham attributes the discriminating esteem in which Ewing was held to her "artistic duplicity," or her creation of symbols comparable to Wordsworth's "spots of time" that go so deeply into the conscious and unconscious minds of even the most sophisticated readers that they are moved beyond the ability to understand why. What the mighty river was in Ewing's favourite novel *Huckleberry Finn* (1884), the meadow is in a minor scale in her *Mary's Meadow* (1883–84). This artistic duplicity means that Ewing, like Mark Twain, consistently and invariably reaches both young and mature readers simultaneously, each at their own level.

The main reason Ewing's symbols—of topaz-eyed toads, noble soldiers, gardeners who gratuitously sow flower seeds throughout the countryside, obsessive gift-givers, and deluded little girls and their mamas—work themselves deep into our memories is due to her realism, her meticulous observation of everyday life among common people and their environments on the Yorkshire moors, what she called "small facts" that Dillingham believes influenced the reliably observant narrators in Kipling. *Realism* is one way of putting the kind of attention Ewing brought to her people and their environments; another is *Aesthesis*, or sensory experience and feeling distinct as a body of knowledge from abstract ideas. Ewing represents sensuous human and nonhuman activity in all its forms: sowing, growing, harvesting, caring, holding, labouring, fighting, worrying, praising. Like her devoted Kipling, a self-professed anti-aesthete, who saw the Aesthetes as a self-centred clique, she avoided Naturalism (the School dealing with humans in their biological capacities—humans as animals, she called it) and the Fleshly School of Poetry, but sensuous human activity and the sensible world are nonetheless central to her aesthetic. One could easily say of her, but say it differently from what one said of Théophile Gautier—say it "slant" as Dillingham cites Emily Dickinson's "Tell all the truth but tell it slant"—she was one for whom the visible world existed.

In Ewing's *Mary's Meadow*, meticulously researched in John Parkinson's *Paradisi in Sole Paradisus Terrestris* (1629) and Alphonse Karr's *A Tour Round My Garden* (1855) as well as in her lifetime avocation of gardening, Ewing sketches many images of the Beautiful, what Kant critiqued as "the symbol of the morally good" that so aligns one with one's environment that one can feel (rather than merely cognize) what it would be like to live harmoniously with others, acting in such a way that one's actions could be the basis of universal action. Ultimately Ewing's senses were in the service of the soul.

The best contemporary critic of the period, Holbrook Jackson wrote in *The Eighteen-Nineties* (1913) that it was "singularly rich in ideas, personal genius and social will" whose "central characteristic was a widespread concern for the correct—the most effective, most powerful, most righteous—mode of living." Although Ewing tended to see herself as a writer of the micro, the local, the intimate, today we can hear her voice at a distance as one of the paradoxes of a most complex time and place, an empire of exploitation and violence in which ordinary Britain at home saw itself as a Christian society in which unselfishness would be the cornerstone of all its virtues, in which one would put one's body in the service of others unselfishly, in which, in short, it aspired to be the antithesis of possessive, competitive individualism. Today, the Transatlantic world that Ewing inhabited and wrote about may well acknowledge the lack of heroic example and noble obligation that worried her, not reckoned in the Wealth of Nations, but essential to a nation's life; the contempt of which might even mean its commercial fall.

One summer's evening in Devon, August 2018, the British Association for Victorian Studies (BAVS) brought together leading scholars of the period from around the world. Academics from Australasia, the Middle East, and the Americas as well as Britain and Europe were treated to an authentic Victorian Magic Lantern show performed by master lanternists Jeremy and Carolyn Brooker. Although many of us had attended literally hundreds of conferences on the period, and had been privileged to experience some cracking exhibitions (other magic lanterns, British Psychic Society, Ectoplasm, lightshow on the walls of Jerusalem, etc.), we concurred that we had never felt so uncannily close to the Victorians, or so reduced to child-like awe, as in the Brookers' magic lantern presentation, including a particularly powerful composition entitled "Death is not the End". I felt the same way reading *Artistic Duplicity: The Fiction and Poetry of Juliana Horatia Ewing*. We rarely come so close to the Victorians as here, with their tireless interrogation of the correct—the most effective, most powerful, most righteous—mode of living.

Regenia Gagnier
Devon, 2019

Preface and Acknowledgments

Juliana Horatia Ewing was and is a prominent author, but only in the field of children's literature. This book is a modest attempt to begin a movement not to remove her completely from the position in British literature that she has enjoyed for so long but to explore her works on another level, so that their appeal to an adult audience is also recognized. In that sense, this is a new approach that introduces a new Juliana Horatia Ewing, and to reflect that goal, I often refer to her throughout the book in a new way—as "Juliana Ewing" or simply as "Ewing." For my boldness in this respect, I apologize to those who know and in many instances who love her writings, who may expect all those who write about her always to use her full name as she did and as has been the custom in years past, and who may be offended by any other usage.

It is not, however, as if Juliana Ewing never had adult admirers who recognized that her writings were also for them, but they were silent admirers, not literary critics or professional reviewers. They were those countless parents and others who tended children and who, beginning in the 1860s, read to them stories and poems of hers published in the children's periodical, *Aunt Judy's Magazine*, edited by her mother, Margaret Gatty. This audience, mostly of women, found Ewing's works easily at hand, since they were published in a popular children's magazine. No doubt a good many of these readers to children recognized how different her stories and poems were from those of other popular children's writers of the time. We have no record of how they reacted to Ewing's works, but it seems safe to conclude that they must have been surprised at the degree of provocative probing in them.

The children, on the other hand, found their own level of enjoyment. They were undoubtedly pleased that many of the narrators in Ewing's works are themselves children, but they are children who are strikingly different. Little girls and little boys of various ages they are (as well as an assortment of talking animals and things), but they are always exceptional, quite distinct from ordinary children and in a way peculiarly articulate because their words often communicate one meaning to the child and the very same words another, deeper, meaning to the adult reading to her charge or to her own child.

These child narrators in Ewing's stories and poems are not little angels who are always presented as exemplars to other children of how to act. In one poem, "A Sweet Little Dear," for instance, the speaker is a deplorably spoiled little girl who must always have her way. The child who reads or listens to a reading of this poem will unquestionably get the point that he or she should not be like that little girl but should always try to be unselfish. To the adult doing the reading, however, another effect builds strongly, that of profound sadness that emerges from the loneliness of this little girl and the terrible frustration of her mother who wants above all else to be a good mother but who in the attempt to be just that is ruining her child as well as destroying her own health. It is a child's poem that is at the same time a work of deep pathos at its heart that strongly affects adults. For children, it is the story of a bad little girl; for adults, it is the story of a sad little girl. This is an example of what is referred to in various places of this book as "artistic duplicity," *artistic,* for while it may appear that what Ewing is accomplishing is merely a kind of multi-layering that is easy to bring off, in truth only a gifted artist could accomplish it. Again and again in many ways, Juliana Ewing was such a literary artist.

In the process of writing this book, I have profited immeasurably from having been furnished a quiet haven apart from the storm of life, namely a faculty study in Emory University's Woodruff Library devoid of disturbance and the winds of trivia. The research staff and others of that unusually friendly and cooperative library have been ever ready and able to assist me. Invaluable help in various ways also came my way from the person to whom this book is dedicated and to whom "I owe more than I can tell," as in his autobiography Rudyard Kipling wrote of Juliana Ewing.

I wish to express my thanks to Robert Langenfeld, editor of *English Literature in Transition 1880–1920,* for permission to reprint "Ruddy Kipling and His Aunt Judy," vol. 61, no. 1 (2018), which appears as "Introduction: Ruddy, His Aunt Judy, and *Six to Sixteen*" in this book. Thanks also to the Provincial Archives of New Brunswick (Canada) for permission to use the sketch by Juliana Ewing on the dust jacket of the book and the image of her that serves as the frontispiece.

A note on the texts of Juliana Ewing's writings included in this book

All texts are those of the Uniform Edition published by the Society for Promoting Christian Knowledge, London, which have no dates for the individual volumes nor are they numbered. Readers will notice instances of misuse of punctuation here and there and a few other minor errors. In an effort to be faithful to the source, no attempt has been made to correct these mistakes except in the most egregious instances.

Contents

Ruddy, His Aunt Judy, and *Six to Sixteen*

Juliana Horatia Ewing, known as "Aunt Judy" to her siblings and to those who read the popular nineteenth-century children's publication, *Aunt Judy's Magazine*, was the second of nine children (one died in infancy). Their grandfather was Alexander John Scott, former navy chaplain (Anglican) serving under Admiral Horatio Nelson, the hero of Trafalgar, and the admiral's close friend and private secretary. Both her father and mother were distinguished people. Her father, Alfred Gatty, was an author and the much-loved vicar of Ecclesfield in Yorkshire, a position he held for sixty-four years. Her remarkable mother, Margaret Gatty, edited the magazine of writings for children that she named for her daughter, *Aunt Judy's Magazine,* and composed stories for children herself—among others, the profound and brilliant *Parables from Nature*, which was read at least as much by adults as by children. In her excellent monograph, *Mrs. Ewing*, Gillian Avery states that "Queen Victoria and Gladstone read Mrs. Gatty's stories, Lord Tennyson admired them, and through them made her acquaintance, which later developed into a close friendship."[1] Margaret Gatty's interest and her fame, however, were not limited to the area of children's literature, for she collected and studied seaweed with such expertise and enthusiasm that she attracted the attention and respect of prominent marine biologists (including William Henry Harvey) with whom she regularly corresponded. She authored a two-volume work, *British Sea-weeds* (1863), that became a widely respected textbook on the subject.

When she was still quite young, Juliana, "Aunt Judy," became the chosen storyteller of the family, especially for her younger siblings. She was clearly the leader of the pack, and her gift for literary creativity and inventiveness even exceeded that of her extraordinary mother. Though she came from a much applauded and honored family and early conceived of herself as an inventor of tales and therefore developed a strong confidence in the quality of her mind and her writing, and even though she achieved during her lifetime (1841–85) a high degree of success as an author of children's literature, she no doubt would have been astonished to learn, even when she was at the height of her powers, that she was to become the mentor, not in person but strictly through what she had written, of one of the most famous authors in the world, the inimitable Rudyard Kipling, who won the Nobel Prize for Literature in 1907. The extent of Kipling's debt to Juliana Ewing, the subject of this introduction, has never been fully explored before. When it is, the remarkable depth and richness of Ewing's writings as they served to mentor Kipling become apparent.

◆ ◆ ◆

In 1871, before Rudyard Kipling had reached his sixth birthday, he, his parents, and his little sister traveled from India, where he was born, to England for the purpose of depositing the children for an undetermined period in the home of Captain and Mrs. Pryse Agar Holloway of Lorne Lodge, 4 Campbell Road (then named Havelock Park), Southsea, Portsmouth, Hampshire. Children of English parents did not as a rule fare well in India where the intense heat of the summers and the year-round threat of diseases put them in constant danger. Alice and John Lockwood Kipling were loving and conscientious parents who were keenly aware not only of this peril but also of the advantages of their children's being exposed in their early and most formative years to English culture rather than the radically different environment of India.

The Holloways advertised themselves as willing and highly capable of boarding, nurturing, and sending to school the children of English parents stationed in India. Reacting to this advertisement, the Kiplings decided that this respectable middle-class family sounded as if it were just what they were looking for to take tender care of their precious two children; so, they engaged them to do just that. In 1874, however, Captain Holloway, who had been kind to the little boy, died, leaving Ruddy and Alice or Trix, as she was called, in the care of Sarah Holloway and her young son. From that point on, young Ruddy's quality of life went into a downward spiral.[2]

What Kipling encountered in the Holloway home particularly after the death of Captain Holloway, the one person that had seemed to care for him, has been thoroughly documented, starting with Kipling himself, who in his autobiography graphically described the horrors of what he called "the House of Desolation."[3] His sister, Trix, was treated fairly well, but Sarah Holloway, her mind and disposition narrowed and distorted by her obsession with straight-laced religiosity, felt that she must take this active and precocious Rudyard in hand and teach him with frequent bouts of punishment the virtues of strict obedience and humility. In his autobiography, he states: "I was regularly beaten."[4] Such beatings were always accompanied by her dire warnings that eternal damnation awaited him for lying, and he was accused of lying frequently. Until he came under the care of Sarah Holloway, he had no idea what "eternal damnation" meant, for he had never heard of hell. She soon made him acquainted with its unspeakable torments, however. Her ally, indeed, her disciple, in this plan to break the haughty spirit of the child she had taken in for a fee to help bring up, was her son, Harry, who was six or seven years older than Rudyard. The younger boy had the dubious privilege of sleeping in the same room with the older boy, who took delight in reporting to his mother the ostensible sins—mostly fabricated or highly exaggerated—of his roommate. Punishment always followed.

Apparently, part of the understanding that Sarah Holloway had with the Kiplings was that she would teach the children to read. She did, and that was the most fortunate development during this desolate time in Rudyard's life. Reading opened up a new and bright world to him, and his imagination began to develop and lend to his generally miserable day-to-day existence a degree of pleasure and excitement. It was a mixed blessing, however, for when Mrs. Holloway discovered how much delight the boy took in reading, she knew that she had found a new and highly effective form of punishment to inflict on him: taking away his reading material, which she did with missionary zeal, in an effort to reform the young sinner.

Nevertheless, he progressed with startling speed in his reading, consuming what there was to read in the Holloway home. In one of his letters to his parents, probably written with the aid of Mrs. Holloway, he informed them of his ability to read, and they, pleased with what they interpreted as the excellent training he was receiving, began to send him various kinds of children's literature commensurate with, as far as they could determine, his age and the stage of his education. Only by reconstructing the context of misery in which young Kipling learned to read and by taking close notice of the fact that it was this pleasure—reading—that was forbidden to him as punishment is it possible to understand adequately the deep and lasting impression that what he did read in these early years in Lorne Lodge had on him. Those writings became more deeply etched on his memory and were more dear to his heart than anything that he read later in his life. One author and one work in particular by that author remained more vivid in his memory and impressed him more than all the rest. This one he wrote about in the last year of his life as having had a profound and continuing influence on him that lasted all of his days:

> There were not many books in that house, but Father and Mother as soon as they heard I could read sent me priceless volumes. One I have still, a bound copy of *Aunt Judy's Magazine* of the early 'seventies, in which appeared Mrs. Ewing's *Six to Sixteen*. I owe more in circuitous ways to that tale than I can tell. I knew it, as I know it still, almost by heart. Here was a history of real people and real things.[5]

The above statement has been quoted here and there in commentaries on Juliana Ewing and in various studies of Rudyard Kipling, but not nearly as often—particularly in biographies of Kipling—as its importance would dictate. Wherever it has been quoted, the manner in which it is handled is nothing less than astonishing. Those who have quoted it, strange to say, do not seem to have been much affected by the remarkable information it gives, information, one would think, that should carry a tremendous impact. Generally, the statement is given as Kipling's kind tribute to a writer that he read as a child, praising the author because he felt that she dealt with real life rather than with fantasy. Since the passage appears in the first chapter of *Something of Myself*, "A Very Young Person," it is one of many statements that deal with early experiences, and that may be one reason that it has not been given the careful attention it deserves but is often considered only in the context of Kipling's childhood as if it has little relevance to his later years as a writer. I have never seen it discussed for what it undeniably is: a stunning revelation that should produce such utter amazement as to cause one to read it over and over to make sure it says what it appears to say. It should cause shock and wonderment to every reader who has even a modicum of interest in Kipling, for it tells much about a prime influence on him and about how and from whom the very fundamentals of his writings may have been formed.

Kipling could pay no higher compliment to any author—in this case, Juliana Horatia Ewing—than to indicate that he had practically memorized her novel, *Six to Sixteen*. Given his remarkably high praise of the book and the substantial influence it had on his writing and his thinking about writing, it seems obvious that he read it repeatedly, especially in view of the fact that at the time he wrote his autobiography, the last year of his life, he still had a copy of the novel. He indicated "I have it still." *It* was perhaps the very same copy that he read as a child when his parents sent it to him while he was at Lorne Lodge—the novel included serially in a bound copy of *Aunt Judy's Magazine* for 1872. If we are to believe him, then, this bound copy of *Aunt Judy's Magazine*, in which appeared for the first time *Six to Sixteen*, accompanied him on his long journey through life. That being true, it follows that his knowing the novel "almost by heart" resulted not from a single reading of it as a child but from later readings as well, perhaps long after he left the House of Desolation.

Thus, the extent of his admiration for and devotion to *Six to Sixteen*, which was written by a woman whose reputation rests upon her stories and poems for an audience of children, appears unbounded. He could not find the words, he wrote, to express the depth of his debt to *Six to Sixteen* and therefore to its author. He could no doubt have written a more explicit statement about the nature of that debt, for he is a prime example of the conscious artist, but he was not inclined to do so. He was prepared to indicate only that he owed what he owed "in circuitous ways," which for him was another way of saying that what he learned from Juliana Ewing is so complex and far reaching that he simply could not go into it in this rather brief and modest autobiography. He does not have the space or the inclination to do so. What is certainly evident from his terse explanation that he now, at the end of his life and looking back on his career, owes "more in circuitous ways" to *Six to Sixteen* than it is possible for him to articulate—what is evident is that he not only read the book as a child and found it appealing but also kept rereading it and that it had a tremendous influence on his writings. That is precisely the nature of the debt: Aunt Judy was his mentor.

The reason *Six to Sixteen* had such a strong and immediate appeal to Kipling is probably that from the first he identified with the narrator, Margery Vandaleur, who spent her first few years in India, just as did Kipling, and who was largely in the care of an affectionate ayah there as was Kipling. Margery and Ruddy were both children of British fathers stationed in India—Margery the daughter of a captain in the British army and Kipling the son of an English art teacher and museum curator in India.

The first and second chapters of *Six to Sixteen* contain so many parallels to Kipling's own childhood experiences that it is no wonder he took so readily to the novel and that it meant so much to him. Perhaps the similarity most striking in the experience of the two children is that the narrator of *Six to Sixteen* loses both her parents when she was about the same age as was Ruddy when he, in a sense, lost his parents, that is, when they left him at Lorne Lodge and returned to India not to see him again for a little more than five years. As he read about what Margery went through emotionally when she became an orphan at six years of age, he was drawn to the book and to its heroine. His sympathy went out to Margery Vandaleur, and his allegiance to her creator, Aunt Judy, was established. Thereafter, she was *his* Aunt Judy. She had made her way into his heart. Many years later, Kipling, his wife Carrie and daughter Elsie visited the illustrious Lady Gregory for lunch. Lady Gregory recorded in her journal: "Rudyard Kipling came to lunch with his wife and daughter and I liked him; he was friendly and unaffected." They spoke of the importance of what one had read in early life, and he told Lady Gregory that "He had loved Aunt Judy's Magazine."[6]

That he identified with the narrator is a major reason that Kipling was taken with *Six to Sixteen* and felt that he owed the author a great debt, but there were other reasons as well. The novel introduced to him certain subjects and attitudes that became increasingly congenial to him. For example, it is likely that Juliana Ewing was the first author he read who wrote of the military service. She treated the soldiers who play a part in *Six to Sixteen* with fondness and respect. She married a member of the British army, but even before she met Major Alexander Ewing, she obviously admired those who served their country, giving their very lives, if necessary, in its defense. Her grandfather had served his country with distinction in the British navy. Her treatment of such characters as Major Buller in *Six to Sixteen*, who takes the orphan Margery Vandaleur into his home and treats her as if she were his own daughter, and Lieutenant George Abercrombie who loves, understands, and comforts her from the time she is very young—these and other representatives of the military in *Six to Sixteen* embody the nobility that she associated with soldiers. It would perhaps be too much to claim that Rudyard Kipling's lifelong support of and admiration for the military was the result of his simply having read *Six to Sixteen* and perhaps other works by Juliana Ewing that appeared in *Aunt Judy's Magazine*, such as "The Story of a Short Life" and "Jackanapes," but it is certainly reasonable to assume that Ruddy's early reading of Aunt Judy's works preconditioned him to value what she valued, in this instance, those who served in the British military forces.

Ewing's highly favorable treatment of the characters in her stories who serve in the military is one manifestation of a wider, more inclusive theme that is present in one form or another in nearly everything she wrote: her conviction that unselfishness is the root of all virtue. Although *Six to Sixteen* is not a didactic book, the idea of putting others first reverberates throughout. Unselfishness is the most prominent trait of both Margery Vandaleur and her close friend, Eleanor Arkwright, and it is the characteristic that marks them both as two of Ewing's most admirable heroines. From Eleanor's mother, they periodically receive instructions in the necessity of "sympathy," that is, for acceptance of others and the need to resist any tendency to rudeness. Speaking of Eleanor's mother, Margery writes in Chapter 26: "Her mother—who reasoned with us far more than she commanded—convinced us of how much selfishness there was in this, as in all acts of discourtesy."[7]

One of the most impressive passages in *Six to Sixteen* is the lecture that Eleanor's mother gives the girls on the selfishness of cliques, which she terms "the petty pride of clique." For her, "pride" is synonymous with self-interest and the opposite of self-abnegation. She introduces the subject by indicating: "I do not know which is the worst . . . a religious clique, an intellectual clique, a fashionable clique, a moneyed clique, or a family clique. And I have seen them all." She then relates her experience with cliques and elaborates on their perniciousness:

> I have a vivid remembrance of a man belonging to an artistic clique, to whose house I once went with some friends. . . . This man talked the shibboleth of his craft over one's head to other members of the clique with a defiance of good manners arising more from conceit than from ignorance of the ways of society; and with a transparent intention of being overheard and admired which reminded me of the little self-conscious conceits of children before visitors. He was one of a large family with the same peculiarities, joined to a devout admiration of each other. Indeed, they combined the artistic clique and the family clique in equal proportions. From the conversation at their table you would have imagined that there was but one standard of good for poor humanity, that of one "school" of one art and absolutely no one who quite came up to it but the brothers, sisters, parents, cousins, or connections by marriage of your host. Now, I honestly assure you that the only other man really like this one that I ever met, was what is called a "self-made" man in a commercial clique. Money was *his* standard, and he seemed to be as completely unembarrassed as my artist friend by the weight of any other ideas than his own, or any feeling short of utter satisfaction with himself. Their contempt for the conventionalities of society was about equal. (pp. 259–60)

The cruciality of unselfishness reverberates through the writings of Juliana Ewing, including *Six to Sixteen*. Young Kipling could not have avoided being repeatedly exposed to it. He may not have understood her statement on selfish cliques when he first read *Six to Sixteen*, but it is precisely the kind of passage that meant a great deal to him as he grew older, for unselfishness, or as he called it "service," became a strong recurrent theme in his writings as it was in the works of Ewing. In his system of values, as in that of Ewing's, nothing was more important than service to others.[8] It may well be that he was first exposed to the virtue of service not by Sarah Holloway but by his Aunt Judy.

At the end of his "seven years hard" on newspapers in India, Kipling departed for England in 1881 only to encounter after he had been there but a short while one of the "artistic cliques" that he had read about in *Six to Sixteen*. His reaction to this clique, the "Aesthetic Movement," was essentially the same as that of Eleanor's mother in *Six to Sixteen*. Its members are, he wrote,

> . . . long haired things
> In velvet collar-rolls,
> Who talk about the Aims of Art,
> And "theories" and "goals."[9]

Kipling's pronounced opposition to this circle of art-for-art's-sake enthusiasts, which he made known not only in "In Partibus" but also in other writings, was based on his perception that they were self-serving, arrogant, and artificial. He knew what they were like long before he actually encountered them, for Aunt Judy had enlightened him.[10]

Kipling's remarkable tribute in *Something of Myself* to *Six to Sixteen* and its author names two specific and important aspects of the novel that continued to impress him and that served to remind him of what to shoot for as he created his own characters and placed them in a narrative framework. "Here," he wrote, referring to *Six to Sixteen*, is a "history of real people and real things." In other words, the narrative itself, the events of the story line, have the stamp of actual history on them—believable, not fanciful—and the people of the novel are three dimensional rather than mere pasteboard figures. *Six to Sixteen*, therefore, illustrated to him two of the most basic lessons to be learned about the craft of fiction.

As he grew older and more adept at his own craft, his appreciation of Ewing's creative skill as exhibited in *Six to Sixteen* must have increased greatly. His own lifelong drive was for originality, and if, indeed, he continued to read Ewing, his perception of this quality in her writing could not fail to have impressed itself upon him, for the narrative structure of *Six to Sixteen* is highly original and effective. It is a novel, but it has all the trappings of an autobiography. The success of this genre pretense—the illusion of autobiography—is attributable to a number of ingenious authorial maneuvers. From the very first pages of the book, for example, Ewing deftly communicates the impression that what she is writing is not fiction but an autobiography written by a sixteen-year-old girl—herself—as her part of an agreement with her friend, Eleanor, namely that they both write the stories of their lives so far and then read each other's work. Skillfully, Ewing creates a situation in which the autobiography itself is enclosed within a frame narrative written in the first person that begins: "Eleanor and I are subject to fads" (p. 11). At this point, the narrator has not given her name, but since the dedication of the book is obviously the product of the author herself and she begins with the words "My dear Eleanor" (to whom the book is dedicated), the early impression is inescapable that the actual person Eleanor and the Eleanor with which the narrator has the agreement that they both write their autobiographies are one and the same person. Later we learn that is not the case, but the seed is planted early that this book is not fantasy but, as Kipling himself put it, "a history of real people and real things."

Throughout *Six to Sixteen*, Ewing expertly employs what may be termed "the art of the actual" to anchor the work in what Margery, the narrator, calls "the trivialities of our everyday lives" so that it would not be taken, as the dedication indicates, "as a vehicle for theories" (v) or for preaching on transcendent subjects, which Ewing was determined to avoid. On the first page, Margery mentions a disagreement she and Eleanor had over the question of whether their autobiographies would be worthwhile. Margery argues that their autobiographies, unlike Samuel Pepys' diary, would record merely the boring "trivialities of our everyday lives." She continues: "Mr. Pepys lived in stirring times, and amongst notable people. *His* life was like a leaf out of English history, and his case quite different to the case of obscure persons living simply and monotonously on the Yorkshire moors." To this Eleanor, in this instance the spokesperson for the author, responded that "the simple and truthful history of a simple mind from childhood would be as valuable, if it could be got, as the whole of Mr. Pepys' Diary from the first volume to the last" (pp. 11-12). Thus, the strong argument for employing the art of the actual, in this case the facts, the details, even the "trivialities" of everyday life, is established.

What goes into creating the illusion of the actual in fiction is a good deal more than the simple details of the everyday life of the characters. In *Six to Sixteen* it is made up as well of Ewing's countless references to real people, events, and works of music, history, and literature. These are what Margery calls "small facts" when immediately after she has recorded the discussion that she and Eleanor had over the importance of their respective autobiographies, she gives away what will be an important aspect of her practicing the art of the actual when she writes that "my biography [will be] . . . a record of small facts" (p. 12). Shortly after Margery refers to her dealing in small facts, she begins to do so. She alludes to Mrs. Nickleby, a character in Charles Dickens' *Nicholas Nickleby* (1839), and a few lines below that mentions the eerie wind that blows over Deadmanstone Hill, which is not an imaginary site but an actual mountain in Yorkshire, an outcrop of rock through which a natural tunnel runs and about which numerous legends have been circulated. On the next page, the "Ladybrig murder"[11] is mentioned, and a little further on, a certain Italian dictionary, the *Della Crusca,* followed closely by a reference to Dante's "Divina Commedia." This pattern of allusions continues through the novel, never creating the impression of authorial showing off, never appearing strained or artificial, but always keeping the story from floating aloft into the realms of fancy.

Juliana Ewing, like her ardent admirer, Rudyard Kipling after her, was so determined to get all of her "small facts" right that she impressed everyone who knew her as something of a fanatic in that regard. Her sister, Horatia K. F. Eden, described her insistence upon corroborating her facts when she was writing "A Great Emergency":

> In 1874 Julie wrote "A Great Emergency" as a serial for the Magazine [*Aunt Judy's Magazine*], and took great pains to corroborate the accuracy of her descriptions of barge life for it. I remember our inspecting a barge on the canal at Aldershot, with a friend who understood all its details, and we arranged to go on

an expedition in it to gain further experience, but were somehow prevented. The allusions to Dartmouth arose from our visit there, of which I have already spoken, and which took place whilst she was writing the tale; and her knowledge of the intricacies of the Great Eastern Railway between Fenchurch Street Station and North Woolwich came from the experience she gained when we went on expeditions to Victoria Docks, where one of our brothers was doing parochial work under Canon Boy.[12]

Horatia Eden gives numerous examples to fortify her point that her sister would not let a story go to press without first being certain that every allusion, every reference, every "small fact," no matter how seemingly trivial, was accurate. According to Eden, when Juliana was writing "Father Hedgehog and His Friends" (1876), she

> spared no trouble in trying to ascertain whether Hedgehogs *do* or do not eat pheasants' eggs; she consulted *The Field,* and books on sport, and her sporting friends, and when she found that it was a disputed point, she determined to give the Hedgehog the benefit of the doubt. Then the taste for valerian, and the fox's method of capture, were drawn from facts, and the gruesome details as to who ate who in the Glass Pond were equally well founded![13]

In a letter to her sister, Horatia Eden, Juliana summarizes a story she was at that time writing and revising, "The Land of Lost Toys," and she expresses her regret that "old Dr. Fisher" has passed away because she no longer can gather details from him that she needs to include in her story. "I very much wanted" she wrote, "some statistics about toy-making." Then she wonders if her sister can help her in this regard: "You never read anything about the making of common Dutch toys, did you?"[14] So concerned with technical detail was Ewing, according to her sister, on occasion it obscures the intended focus of the story.[15]

From the time that Rudyard Kipling began writing, he was conscious of the need to ground his stories in what Aunt Judy had called "small facts." In his autobiography, he uses a term much like Ewing's "small facts." What counts in trying to paint "mental pictures," he writes, "is the seasonal detail of *small things* and doings (such as putting up fly-screens and stove-pipes, buying yeast cakes and being lectured by your neighbors)."[16] He followed closely in the footsteps of Aunt Judy by sometimes going to extreme lengths to make sure that his facts were accurate. While he was writing *Captains Courageous*, he relied heavily on his friend Dr. James Conland, who in his youth had been a New England cod fisherman, to supply him with adequate details about that occupation. Together they went to Gloucester, Massachusetts, so that Kipling could get first-hand details from cod fishermen themselves. From there they moved on to "the old T-wharf of Boston Harbour." He describes in *Something of Myself* the extent of their information gathering trip:

> We assisted hospitable tug-masters to help haul three-and four-stick schooners of Pocahontas coal all round the harbor; boarded every craft that looked as if she might be useful. . . . Charts we got—old and new—and the crude implements of navigation such as they used off the Banks, and a battered board-compass . . . Conland took large cod and the appropriate knives . . . and demonstrated anatomically and surgically so that I could make no mistake about treating them in print. Old tales, too, he dug up, and the lists of dead and gone schooners whom he had loved, and I revelled in profligate abundance of detail . . .

Even that much detail, he felt, was not enough for *Captains Courageous*; so, he gathered more:

> I desired that some of my characters should pass from San Francisco to New York in record time, and wrote to a railway magnate of my acquaintance asking what he himself would do. That most excellent man sent a fully worked-out time-table with watering halts, changes of engine, mileage, track conditions and climates, so that a corpse could not have gone wrong in the schedule. My characters [in the novel] arrived triumphantly.[17]

A crucially important fact about the influence of Juliana Ewing on Kipling, one that has never been pointed out before, is that he not only read *Six to Sixteen* when he was a child and probably continued to read it and other of her stories as he grew older, but also that sometime either in 1887 or later he acquired a copy of the book quoted earlier, that written by Juliana's sister, *Juliana Horatia Ewing and Her Books* by Horatia H. K. Eden. It is listed in Kipling's personal library in his home, Bateman's, in a long inventory assembled in 1940 of his books. The year of publication of Eden's book is given in the inventory as 1887. In the first half of the book, Kipling found a splendid if somewhat brief account of Juliana Ewing's life and her writing career from the perspective of one very close to the author. In the second half are many of her personal letters that reveal her personality and much about her philosophy of composition. What he had enjoyed as a child in her writing was now magnified and made clearer than it ever had been before. After reading Eden's book, he no doubt became strongly aware of how much he had learned from Ewing and how he continued to be indebted to her "in circuitous ways."

A passage in Eden's book relating how Juliana had not been satisfied until she thoroughly researched the question of whether hedgehogs eat pheasants' eggs is strikingly reminiscent of an event in Kipling's own life, which he describes in *Something of Myself* and then adds his admonition that getting facts straight in writing is of the utmost importance. He tells of how his friend, Sir John Bland-Sutton, then Head of the College of Surgeons, came to visit him for the express purpose of corroborating a fact that he wished to include in a lecture he was to deliver on the subject of "gizzards." He would not be satisfied until he, taking Kipling with him, ran down one of the chickens on Kipling's property and then a rooster so that he could place his ear to the correct spot to determine if there was, indeed, a click in the animal's gizzard. Though this may seem a somewhat extreme measure to authenticate a detail one wishes to use in a lecture, Kipling makes the following case for Bland-Sutton's wisdom and then advises all would-be writers to follow his example: "There are always men who by trade or calling know the fact or the inference that you put forth. If you are wrong by a hair in this, they argue: 'False in one thing, false in all.'"[18]

Examples abound that reveal how meticulous Kipling was in following the example of Aunt Judy by making sure that facts and references were accurate, but his reason for doing this went beyond the desire to escape the kind of criticism that he mentions in that quotation from *Something of Myself*. The greater reason was that he, like Juliana Ewing, was insistent that the narrative voice in a work of fiction must come across as both truthful and authoritative if the work is to be convincing. The art of the actual requires that the author convey the impression that he or she is something of an authority on whatever the subject at hand may be. In her dedication section to *Six to Sixteen*, Ewing states that the book illustrates "a belief in the joys and benefits of intellectual hobbies" (p. vi). Although "intellectual hobbies" may seem an odd label for sketching, sewing, flower gardening, and "natural science collecting," these are the endeavors that the narrator of the novel speaks of frequently and with such specific detail, at least in the case of the first three,[19] that the author conveys the message that she knows what she is writing about, and that impression is important in creating the aura of the actual. For example, late in the novel Eleanor's mother instructs the girls, her daughter and Margery, in sewing. Margery details how she and Eleanor went about making dresses for themselves from patterns they had obtained:

> Our first work was to lay these patterns upon the new stuff, with weights on them, and so to cut out our new bodies. . . . When these and the sleeves were accomplished (and they looked most business-like), we began upon the skirts. We cut the back and the front breadths, and duly "sloped" the latter. Then came the gores. We folded the breadths into three parts; we took a third at one end, and two-thirds at the other, and folded the slope accordingly. It became quite exciting. (p. 274)

To be sure, it is not "exciting" to readers who know nothing about sewing, to whom "bodies," "sloped," and "gores" are terms with which they have absolutely no acquaintance, but the technical details, nevertheless, function precisely as Juliana Ewing intended, namely to convey the impression that while the reader may know nothing about sewing, the author of this novel surely does. And if she knows what she is writing about when she gives the details of how to make a dress, she must be reliable in other matters.

Details about the "intellectual hobby" of sketching run through the novel. Even when the topic is something else, Ewing refers to sketching as a metaphor, especially for writing. For example, in the dedication, she indicates that the novel was meant "as a *sketch* of domestic life" (p. v). When Eleanor is sketching for the drawing master at the boarding school that she and Margery attend, her comments reveal her knowledge of how to sketch various trees:

> "Oak branches are all elbows . . . So different from willows and beeches . . . Willows are nice to do . . . and the bark is prettier than oak, I think, and easier with these long points. My mother says branches of trees should be done from the tips inwards; and they do fit in better, I think. Only willow branches seem as if they ought to be done outwards, they taper so. Beech trunks are very pretty, but the leaves are difficult, I think; Scotch pines are easy." And Eleanor left the beech and began upon the pine, fitting the horizontal branches under the foliage groups with admirable effect. (pp. 161–2)

As for Ewing's treatment of gardening and flowers especially, one has to begin by stating that flowers were her first and her most enduring love. She was ever making herself acquainted with those she had not seen before and ever learning more about those with which she was already familiar and making sketches of them. They play a significant role not only in *Six to Sixteen* but also in a great many of her other works. When she wrote about them, it was often to identify them and to describe their beauty and fragrance, but they also serve to project her favorite theme of unselfishness and as metaphors for the end-product of the literary imagination. Juliana Ewing's flowers are in this sense her writings, which are given unselfishly to others and have been nourished by her creative imagination and grown in the garden within her. Horatia Eden writes:

> One of the causes which helped to develop my sister's interest in flowers was the sight of the fresh ones that she met with on going to live in New Brunswick after her marriage. Every strange face [flower] was a subject for study, and she soon began to devote

a notebook to sketches of these new friends, naming them scientifically from Professor Asa Gray's *Manuel of the Botany of the Northern United States.*[20]

When in *Six to Sixteen*, Margery returns from boarding school to Eleanor's home in northern England, she is struck with the variety of flowers described here with notable detail as in many other places in the novel:

> It was midsummer . . . Huge rose-bushes—literal *bushes*, not "dwarfs," or "standards"—the growth of many years bent under their load of blossoms. The old "maiden's blush," too rare now in our bedding plant gardens, the velvety "damask," the wee Scotch roses, the prolific white, and the curious "York and Lancaster," with monster moss-rose trees, hung over the carriage road. The place seemed almost overgrown with vegetation, like the palace of the Sleeping Beauty. (p. 191)

The fascination that Ewing had for flowers and her ever-present interest in incorporating them in her fiction is made evident in a letter she wrote to her mother on 1 May 1870:

> I have got some work into my head which has been long seething there, and will, I think, begin to take shape. It is about *flowers*— the ancestry of flowers; whether the flowers will tell their own family records, or what the *plot* will be I have not yet planned, and it will take me some time to collect my data, but the family histories of flowers which came originally from Old Mexico in the days of Montezuma, and the floating gardens, and the warriors who wore nosegays, and the Indians who paddled the floating gardens on which they lived up the waters of that gorgeous city with only vegetables for the chiefs—would be rather weird! And then the strange fashions and universal prevalence of Japanese gardening. The wisteria rioting in the hedges, and the great lilies wild over the hills. Ditto the camellias. With all the queer little thatched Japanese huts that always have lumps of *iris* on the top,

which the Japanese ladies use for bandoline. Then the cacti would have queer legends of South America, where the goats climb the steep rocks and dig them up with their horns and roll them down into the valley, and kick and play with them till the *spines* get rubbed off, and then devour them at leisure. I give you these instances in case anything notable about flowers comes in your way, "when found to make a note of for me."[21]

By the time that Kipling had read these words of Juliana Ewing in his copy of her sister's *Juliana Horatia Ewing and Her Books*, he had long since, under her very influence, formed his allegiance to facts, for his belief in the essentiality of getting them right is apparent even in his earliest work. It is tempting to conclude that his devotion to hard facts had its beginning in some advice that Mark Twain gave him when Kipling visited him in Elmira, New York, in 1889. "Get your facts, first," the older writer forcefully advised his young visitor.[22] Rather than being enlightened by the dictum, however, he simply agreed with it since he was already totally convinced of its correctness from the repeated examples in the writings of Aunt Judy, his mentor, whose novel he first read years previously and who always took "some time to collect" her "data" before she put pen to paper. It is more than likely that it was Juliana Ewing, not Mark Twain or any other person, that made Kipling so acutely aware of the importance of establishing trust in readers by showing them that you know what you are talking about. So important was collecting his data and especially checking it for accuracy that he arrived at the conclusion that doing so acts as a stimulus to the creative imagination, which he referred to frequently as his daemon. "Take nothing for granted if you can check it," he writes in *Something of Myself*. "Even though that seems waste-work, and has nothing to do with the essentials of things, it encourages the Daemon."[23] In another rather startling statement, Kipling seems to attribute much of his success as a writer and the kindness directed to him by readers to the factual accuracy of his writings. Recounting his trip to New Zealand, he writes: "Everyone generally put aside everything for my behoof, instruction, amusement, and comfort. So, indeed, it has always been. For which reason I deserve no credit when my work happens to be accurate in detail."[24]

The "circuitous ways" that Kipling owed a debt to Juliana Ewing, especially *Six to Sixteen*, become not so circuitous when it comes to the ideas that he got from her for characters and plots that he used in his own writings. The most outstanding example, though certainly not the only one, is his use of a character in *Six to Sixteen* as his model for Mrs. Lucy Hauksbee, who appears in no less than eight of Kipling's stories.[25] Charles Allen has called Mrs. Hauksbee "one of the most engaging female characters in English fiction."[26] Andrew Lycett finds that she is "One of Rudyard's most intriguing and alluring fictional characters."[27] Harry Ricketts indicates that as time passed, Mrs. Hauksbee "soon became one of his [Kipling's] best-known characters."[28]

These same biographers and critics who extol the achievement represented in the characterization of Mrs. Hauksbee generally agree that her portrait is that of a woman whom Kipling knew in India, Isabella Burton, or a composite of Mrs. Burton and his mother, Alice Kipling. Allen seems totally convinced that it could have been no one else but Mrs. Burton who served as Kipling's model for Mrs. Hauksbee: "If any single person inspired Mrs. Hauksbee, it could only have been . . . Isabella Burton."[29] Lycett's research led him to believe likewise, that is, that the source for Mrs. Hauksbee was "the fiery Irish-born wife of an intelligence officer attached to the 1st Bengal Lancers." She was "a petite woman with a darting, original intelligence," his description of Isabella Burton.[30] According to Harry Ricketts, Mrs. Hauksbee "was based on his [Kipling's] own mother and partly on Mrs. Isabella Burton."[31] His assessment appears to agree with that of Angus Wilson: "Yet despite the fact that Mrs. Hauksbee is now known to have been much modelled on a friend, Mrs. Burton, the old tradition that Alice Kipling was one of the models seems to me sound."[32] Apparently representing the current consensus of the Kipling Society in this matter, John McGivering states in his excellent notes to "Mrs. Hauksbee Sits Out" on the Society's website that Mrs. Hauksbee "was almost certainly based on Mrs. Isabella Burton (the wife of Major F. C. Burton), who was a friend of young Kipling."[33] With this same degree of assurance that has become typical of those commenting on the source of Mrs. Hauksbee, Martin Seymour-Smith writes that "the famous Mrs. Hauksbee" was "certainly modelled on his [Kipling's] sharp-tongued mother but also more precisely, on another woman, Mrs. F. C. Burton."[34] Others, for example, David Gilmour, follow suit, confidently identifying the model for Mrs. Hauksbee either as Isabella Burton (the favorite), as Kipling's mother, or as both.[35]

Many who know a great deal about Kipling have thus seemingly closed the door to any new candidates for the position of model for Mrs. Hauksbee. Thus, it may seem presumptuous if not foolish to try to sing over this loud chorus of confidence and question the appropriateness of those who have peremptorily been identified for the position and suggest a new name. Yet certain questions remain, questions about 1) whether Kipling would have chosen one of his friends whose sophistication and sensitivity he greatly appreciated and who had aided him in various ways in his writing, a woman for whom he had the highest regard and whom he certainly would not want to offend, and 2) whether he would have chosen his own mother whose feelings he was always aware of and careful to avoid hurting as a model for a character who is in some ways admirable but who in certain stories in which she appears is delineated in a somewhat negative fashion—indeed, described in such a way as to be insulting to both Isabella Burton and Alice Kipling if he modelled Mrs. Hauksbee on either of them or both.

In "The Education of Otis Yeere," Mrs. Hauksbee is portrayed as a person who lives for a certain egocentric sensation, the exciting sense of personal power that comes from molding a person into a new, outgoing version of himself. She tutors Otis Yeere, who is a nobody in the Bengal Civil Service and is going nowhere, enabling him to acquire self-confidence so that he can ask for a better position. She is denied the sought-after satisfaction of having created a vital and successful man out of a flop, however, because to her dismay, he forces their relationship into a direction that shocks her: he falls in love with her. Instead of understanding and being kind in her refusal of him, she becomes angry because her scheme has gone awry and in a highly agitated state summarily turns him away. In her motivation for "helping" him as well as in her fury because of his love for her, she is not a character that either Isabella Burton or Alice Kipling would have liked to think was modeled on her.

Kipling described Mrs. Hauksbee's physical appearance and mentioned some of her less attractive traits in the first story in which she is a character, "Three and –an Extra": "She was a little brown, thin, almost skinny, woman with big, rolling, violet-blue eyes . . . [She was] possessed of many devils of malice and mischievousness. She could be nice, though, even to her own sex. But that is another story." It is no wonder that she was known as the "Stormy Petrel."[36] Andrew Lycett, who is in the forefront of those who are convinced that Isabella Burton is the woman on whom Kipling's Mrs. Hauksbee was patterned, has described the actual person, Mrs. Burton, not as "a little brown, thin, almost skinny woman" but as "petite" with "a darting, original intelligence" and with a rounded face with its full lips, largish nose and flashing violet eyes."[37] Not only does the actual physical appearance of Isabella Burton as Lycett has described her fail to fit well with the physical appearance of Mrs. Hauksbee as Kipling has described her, but Lycett himself points out another area in which the assumed model and the fictional character are quite different: "In real life she [Mrs. Burton] was more cultured and better read than the often crudely manipulative Mrs. Hauksbee . . . [Mrs. Burton] liked to discuss philosophy and ideas."[38]

More than likely, the unforgettable Mrs. Hauksbee is not a version of any actual woman that Kipling knew while he was working in India. He was already familiar with the type that she represents before he ever met Isabella Burton, the type of woman who stood out as a kind of dominant figure among the wives of military officers and civil service workers in the English community of India at the time. He made her acquaintance in that book he first read as a child and then reread to the extent that he felt he knew it almost by heart. In *Six to Sixteen*, which carries the subtitle *A Story for Girls*, this boy met Mrs. Minchin, the unforgettable Mrs. Minchin, so like the unforgettable Mrs. Hauksbee that it is all but obvious that she, not Isabella Burton or Alice Kipling, was Kipling's inspiration for that character as she makes her way through eight of his short stories.

One of the dominant traits of both Mrs. Hauksbee and Mrs. Minchin is the deep-seated desire to have influence over others. In *Six to Sixteen*, the narrator mentions that Mrs. Minchin possessed a "love of managing other folks' matters" (p. 50). That characteristic is one of the strongest of Mrs. Hauksbee's motivations. After a brief spell of humiliation in "A Second-Rate Woman" when she does not live up to her expectations of herself, she "began to direct the affairs of the world as before."[39] With each woman, this desire to lead, control, and in a sense help others, especially those younger and less knowledgeable in the ways of the world, assumes the form of becoming a guide and mentor. Mrs. Minchin "takes up" the younger woman, Mrs. Seymour, who is commonly known as "the bride" (p. 36). Mrs. Hauksbee similarly takes May Holt (as well as young Mr. Hawley) "under her wing" in "Mrs. Hauksbee Sits Out."[40] To be "taken up" by Mrs. Minchin or "taken under the wing" of Mrs. Hauksbee is but a temporary foot-up in the complex world of the British community in India. For it is not unusual for both of the older women to quarrel with their young apprentices and reject them. "To be hotly taken up by Mrs. Minchin," writes the narrator of *Six to Sixteen*, "meant an equally hot quarrel at no very distant date. The squabble with the bride was not slow to come" (p. 36). Mrs. Hauksbee quarrels with her understudy Otis Yeere and immediately takes him from under her wing.

Their marital status (both women married to important husbands who are stationed elsewhere); their ages; their social prominence; their "sway" over a host of women among whom they circulate; the quickness with which they take offence and quarrel with others; their tendency to meddle in the lives of people, particularly young people who interest them; their reputations as women whom "trouble" follows—these traits that the two fictional characters have in common would probably be more than adequate to conclude that Mrs. Minchin, a prominent character in the book that Kipling so admired, was what he started with, what he had in mind when Mrs. Hauksbee emerged from his imagination and into the pages of those eight stories. But there is one episode involving Mrs. Minchin in *Six to Sixteen* that was followed so closely by Kipling in one of his stories about Mrs. Hauksbee that the close similarity of the two occurrences should settle the question of who the model was for Kipling's unforgettable Lucy Hauksbee.

When writing *Six to Sixteen*, Ewing must have reached a point in her characterization of Mrs. Minchin when she realized that her portrayal so far was a bit one-sided. What with Mrs. Minchin's penchant for controlling and for quarreling, she was becoming simplistic and predictable. The fact that one of the major characters, the noble Major Buller, thoroughly disliked her merely added to the fact that something had to be done to make Mrs. Minchin a more complex figure by having her do something that would surprise and at the same time add a new dimension to her so as to make her a more interesting and believable figure. The result was a remarkable episode in *Six to Sixteen* in which Mrs. Minchin takes upon herself the mission of helping a woman care for her child who has become quite seriously ill, even promising the mother that she—Mrs. Minchin—would pull the sick child through. In this section of the novel, Mrs. Minchin is no longer selfish and self-serving but a kindly angel of mercy dramatically and forcefully contrasted in her nobility with Mrs. Seymour, "the bride":

> The truth is, Mrs. Minchin, though a gossip of the deepest dye, was kind-hearted after a fashion. Her restless energy, which chiefly expended itself in petty social plots, and the fomentation of quarrels, was not seldom employed also in practical kindness towards those who happened to be in favour with her. She was really interested—for good or for evil—in those with whose affairs she meddled, and if she was a dangerous enemy, and a yet more dangerous friend, she was neither selfish nor illiberal. The bride, on the other hand, had no real interest whatever in anybody's affairs but her own, and combined in the highest degree those qualities of personal extravagance and general meanness, which not unfrequently go together. (pp. 48–9)

When the quartermaster's children became ill during the voyage from India back to England, "neither her kindness of heart nor her love of managing other folks' matters would permit Mrs. Minchin to be passive then. She made the first advances, and poor Mrs. Curling gratefully responded" (p. 50). Consequently, Mrs. Minchin rolls up her sleeves, declares herself a more than adequate "sick nurse," and promises Mrs. Curling: "If you keep up your heart we'll pull them all through before we get to the Cape" (p. 50). With all her hard work and genuine devotion, however, little Arthur Curling dies when they are near the Cape: "How Mrs. Minchin contrived to keep her own feet and to nurse the poor boy as she did was a marvel. He died on her knees" (p. 51). For her failure to save this child she is profoundly humbled and grieved, though she struggles mightily to hide her sorrow and humiliation.

Kipling faced the same problem with Mrs. Hauksbee that Ewing faced with Mrs. Minchin, that is, having revealed so much of her negative side in stories that came before "A Second-Hand Woman," when he was composing that story, he realized that he needed to include some incident that would show that she, like Mrs. Minchin, was a more complex personality than previously delineated, that she was not merely a "Stormy Petrel" but a woman of deep and sympathetic feeling and self-sacrificing nobility. The incident he chose to reveal this side of Mrs. Hauksbee indicates strongly that he was again following his Aunt Judy. In "A Second-Rate Woman," the child of the Dancing Master and his wife, Mrs. Bent, becomes very ill, as in the case of Arthur Curling, and Mrs. Hauksbee comes to their aid as did Mrs. Minchin when Mrs. Curling and her child needed her. The ailment in this instance is diphtheria, and since it is contagious, the mother and child must be isolated. Mrs. Hauksbee, though holding no love for Mrs. Bent, takes her and the child to her quarters and cares for the child as if it were her own. Though nobly giving all her attention to the child, however, she, like Mrs. Minchin, is not able to save her patient. The child survives but only because another woman, Mrs. Delville, happens to be present at a time when the little girl is choking to death, and the "second-rate woman" knows precisely what to do in such an emergency whereas Mrs. Hauksbee does not and is helpless. The child survives, but Mrs. Hauksbee, like Mrs. Minchin in *Six to Sixteen,* is filled with self-reproach, which takes her a while to work through. One episode is much like the other, both included to make the point that there is something good and decent about the two women. So perhaps the greatest part of the debt that Kipling owed to *Six to Sixteen* was in its furnishing him with a model of an unusual and fascinating type of woman and then showing him a way of developing that character so that she transcends the type and becomes a complex and three-dimensional individual.

Exactly when Kipling first conceived the idea of writing about a boys' boarding school is difficult to determine, but it is natural to assume that *Stalky and Company* grew out of his looking back on the days when he himself attended such a school, the United Services College at Westward Ho! It may be that the idea was planted in his mind long before that, for a long section of *Six to Sixteen*, Chapters 13–18, deals with a trio of friends who attend a girls' boarding school, Bush House. In this section of the novel, the main character, Margery Vandaleur, plays a part suggestive of Beetle in *Stalky and Company,* and her friend Eleanor is even more strongly suggestive of the many faceted character Stalky. She possesses that rather remarkable quality of commanding the respect of both her teachers and her fellow students. She is strong-willed and not above challenging one of her instructors, the drawing master, because she believes his talent is suspect. As in *Stalky and Company*, the Head of the school is a highly sympathetic figure who wins Eleanor's respect even though she does not hesitate to lecture Eleanor when she is clearly out of line. As in *Stalky and Company*, the end of the term brings the students together one last time and as they say goodbye to go their separate ways, a sense of camaraderie and questions about what the future may bring permeate both episodes. To be sure, there is no absolute proof that this section of *Six to Sixteen* was the seed planted in the imagination of Kipling that in time grew and flowered as *Stalky and Company*, but given Kipling's sense of profound gratitude to Ewing's book for what it meant to his developing career as a writer, the possibility naturally arises.

In one of the books of the Apocrypha, Ecclesiasticus, Kipling found lifelong encouragement and support for his personal weltanschauung. In his autobiography, he wrote: "I earnestly commend to the attention of the ambitious young a text in the thirty-third chapter of Ecclesiasticus which runs: '*So long as thou livest and hast breath in thee, give not thyself over to any.*'"[41] From an early age, Kipling was determined to keep true to himself, to preserve his independence. When challenges to that independence came along, Ecclesiasticus often was, as he once wrote in a letter to his friend Rider Haggard, "my refuge."[42] His first exposure to Ecclesiasticus, to which he was drawn and which played an important part in his life, was most likely through his initial reading and later rereadings of *Six to Sixteen*. He became curious about it and fascinated with it because in the novel, it is one of the two favorite books of Eleanor Arkwright, the most attractive and most admirable character of the story. She brought it with her to the girls' boarding school, Bush House, and she and Margery Vandaleur read from it aloud to each other. She reads the following lines from Ecclesiasticus, the prayer of the Son of Sirach, before their house-mistress, known simply as "the Madam" since she is French, walks in on them and confiscates the book:

> When I was yet young, or ever I went astray, I desired wisdom openly in my prayer. I prayed for her before the temple, and will seek her out even to the end. Even from the flower till the grape was ripe hath my heart delighted in her; my foot went the right way; from my youth up I sought after her. I bowed down mine ear a little, and received her, and got much learning . . . Draw near unto me, ye unlearned, and dwell in the house of learning . . . Put your neck under the yoke, and let your soul receive instruction: she is hard at hand to find. Behold with your eyes, how that I have had but little labour, and have gotten unto me much rest. Get learning. (p. 179)

At this point, "Madam" intrudes and takes away the copy of the Apocrypha as Mrs. Holloway was wont to deprive Ruddy of his reading. Later, one of the other girls in the school describes Eleanor's search for wisdom through her reading as "greedy" reading, at which Eleanor laughs, "and quoted a verse from one of her favourite chapters: 'They that eat me shall yet be hungry, and they that drink me shall yet be thirsty.'"[43] The very fact that it is Eleanor who is taken with the book of Ecclesiasticus was enough to draw Kipling to it especially as he grew older with *Six to Sixteen* and began to read the work of Jesus the Son of Sirach on his own.

In his statement of gratitude citing Aunt Judy for her invaluable assistance "in circuitous ways," Kipling mentioned no other work of hers that he read and found provocative and useful in his own writing other than *Six to Sixteen*, but there is ample evidence that there were others. The most obvious is Juliana Ewing's "Mary's Meadow," which was serialized in *Aunt Judy's Magazine*, November 1883 through March 1884, with book publication in 1886. What Kipling thought of the author and especially "Mary's Meadow" is echoed in the words of McKnight, a character in Kipling's story "Fairy-Kist": "'Juliana Horatia Ewing,' said he. 'The best, the kindest, the sweetest, the most eenocent tale ever the soul of a woman gied birth to.'"[44]

It is not too much to claim that without "Mary's Meadow," Kipling's intricate and artistically sophisticated story "Fairy-Kist" would not exist.

Kipling did not merely read "Mary's Meadow": he read it Eleanor-style: "greedily," for the manner in which he used it in "Fairy-Kist" suggests that he probed its depths. It was not just a child's story to him, but— typical of Aunt Judy's stories—written in that extraordinary style that appears on the surface as simplicity itself and thus appealing to the bright child, particularly when the central character is a child, but awakeningly stunning to those adults who recognize that the profoundest truths are trapped in those absorbing words in the way that deeply below the surface of the earth water of purity and abundance is trapped in absorbent rock, the hidden ocean. At some point, Kipling made what was for him a colossal discovery. He recognized that she practiced a rare art, a way of writing which appealed so strongly to him that he deeply desired to master it, and he did. The result was widespread but certainly included those unforgettable little masterpieces in the two *Jungle Books*, his later dog stories, and the *Just So Stories*. His Aunt Judy awakened him to a gift he shared with her, artistic duplicity—writing in such a way that it is clear and simple enough for a child but deep enough to thrill the greedy reader.

When Kipling was in his second year at the United Services College, during holidays he visited the "three ladies," as he calls them in his autobiography, and took advantage of their invitation to read anything he pleased in their personal library. One selection was a multi-volume work written by Juliana Ewing's mother, Margaret Gatty, *Parables from Nature* (1855). Even at his early age, he recognized that these stories, or "parables," though they were marketed as children's literature, were also appealing to a more mature audience. At this point in his life, as he put it, "the tide of writing had set in," so he tried his hand at imitating the artistic duplicity that he was impressed with in *Parables from Nature*.[45] The results at the time pleased him, but it did not take him long to realize that he was not ready to practice this remarkable method of writing that he found in a work by the mother of the author of the book he so cherished, *Six to Sixteen*.[46] With time, and with the help of Aunt Judy, however, he mastered the technique of artistic duplicity. It was not the least of what he owed "in circuitous ways" to her.

Kipling's "The Last of the Stories" (1888) smacks of experimentation and originality although it relies in a general way on the long tradition of visits to hell established by Dante's fourteenth-century poetic masterpiece, the *Inferno,* the first part of the three-part work, *The Divine Comedy.* The title of Kipling's story signifies two "lasts": it was the last story that he was to write for the *Week's News* in Allahabad, a literary supplement to the newspaper, the *Pioneer.* It also suggests that this story may be the last that he will write inasmuch as he comes to believe that so far, he has mostly botched all his attempts at characterization.

What is different about Kipling's hell, at least the circle or level of it that he visits in the story, is that unlike Dante's inferno, this hell, known as the Limbo of Lost Endeavour, is populated by the victims of bad writing, the characters of literary endeavor who are not able to stand on their own feet. All of Kipling's characters that he created up to 1888 are there, maimed and crippled in various ways but none of them whole and complete. They all tell Kipling that he did not understand them. The implication is that an author cannot create a three-dimensional character unless he or she understands that character. He, the visitor, therefore, is the sinner, not those in the Limbo of Lost Endeavour. Consequently, this is a story of authorial self-blame. The characters Kipling created are suffering because he did not understand how to make them whole and real. He returns from his visit full of guilt and anger, anger that what has been revealed to him does not instruct him as to how to understand and create true-to-life characters. In its departures from the model of Dante, especially in his concept of the Limbo of Lost Endeavour and the reason those who are doomed must spend eternity there, Kipling's "The Last of the Stories" is strikingly original.

Or is it? Actually, it is another one of those "circuitous ways" in which Kipling owes Juliana Ewing a great debt, a debt the nature of which up to now has never been specified much less repaid by her receiving the credit she deserves. In this instance, Kipling's "The Last of the Stories" is in concept so much like Ewing's "The Land of the Lost Toys" that to conclude Kipling got the idea for his story from reading Ewing's story is inescapable. In both stories, a narrator has a vision or dream, which is the account of that person's journey to hell. In both, the narrator meets a guide (in one instance, a talking beetle; in the other "the Devil of Discontent" who resides in an ink pot). Both narrators are escorted through the surface of the earth downward: in Ewing's story through a hole at the base of a great tree; in Kipling's story, through the floor of a building. The two stories use the word "Lost" in ways that have thematic significance. Most importantly, what the narrators find in the hellish places to which they are guided is very much alike: in the one work, fictional characters that are in a sense the playthings of their author, who have been distorted and maimed by their owner or creator. They thus bear the crippling effects of this mistreatment. In the other work, we see the play-things or toys of their young owners who have mistreated and maimed them. They, too, are twisted, bruised, and damaged, as are the characters in the other story. Both "The Last of the Stories" and "The Land of the Lost Toys" depict in almost identical fashion the results of the narrator's vision or dream: they have been blamed for the first time for something that previously they did not know they were guilty of—in both instances, this blame laid upon them has a striking and even life-changing effect.

That Kipling read more widely in Ewing's published writings than has been previously recognized is clearly evident. For example, in "The Last of the Stories," the following exchange takes place after the narrator has been charged by the characters in all of his stories of not understanding them:

> Each one in passing told me the same tale, and the burden thereof was: "You did not understand." My heart turned sick within me. "Where's Wee Willie Winkie?" I shouted. "Little Children don't lie."
>
> A clatter of pony's feet followed, and the child appeared, habited as on the day he rode into Afghan territory to warn Coppy's love against the "bad men." "I've been playing," he sobbed, "playing on ve Levels wiv Jackanapes and Lollo, an' *he* says I'm only just borrowed. I'm *isn't* borrowed. I'm Willie Wi-*inkie*! Vere's Coppy?"[47]

The reference is to Juliana Ewing's *Jackanapes*, which was first published in *Aunt Judy's Magazine* in 1879. Lollo was his horse. Kipling, who obviously read *Jackanapes*, would have encountered on the last page of the story the following message to her homeland that she loved so dearly, a message with a hint of a warning. With all of its greatness, its prosperity, its distinguished past, its promise for the future, with all that in its favor, she pled to the "sons of what has deserved the name of Great Britain" not to forget the old verities, the truths by which they have always lived. It is a stirring reminder to her nation not to forget what it has stood for in the long history of its past; it is a plea for humility as the temptation for national arrogance arises:

> There is a heritage of heroic example and noble obligation, not reckoned in the Wealth of Nations, but essential to a nation's life; the contempt of which, in any people, may slowly mean even its commercial fall.
>
> Very sweet are the uses of prosperity, the harvests of peace and progress, the fostering sunshine of health and happiness, and length of days in the land.
>
> But there be things—oh, sons of what has deserved the name of Great Britain. Forget it not!—"the good of" which and "the use of" which are beyond all calculation of worldly goods and earthly uses: things such as Love and Honour, and the Soul of Man, which cannot be bought with a price, and which do not die with death. And they who would fain live happily EVER after, should not leave these things out of the lessons of their lives.[48]

Rudyard Kipling's famous poem, "Recessional," which stirred his nation, was published toward the end of Queen Victoria's Diamond Jubilee celebrations in 1891. Many consider it his best and certainly his most elevated expression of what should be his country's national purpose. In the search for possible influences, for sources, for what may have inspired the poem, the fruits have been neither plentiful nor appetizing. Some time ago, one critic stepped forward boldly to suggest that he had found "The Genesis of the Recessional," which was a sixteenth-century poem by Sir Thomas Wyatt (1503–42). That poem, "Forget not Yet the Tried Intent," is not an address to the speaker's nation with a warning and a plea for the right values as the country prospers and moves forward with ever more power, but a love song, a man addressing a woman.[49] When Kipling read those eloquent words of his Aunt Judy on the closing page of *Jackanapes*, he knew that someday, someway, somehow, he would turn them into a poem worthy of his mentor and his own genius. He did. The result was "Recessional."

C H A P T E R   1

Frowning Providence: *The Viscount's Friend*

A list of Juliana Ewing's works runs for six pages of small type in Eden's *Juliana Horatia Ewing and Her Books*.[1] In her account of Ewing's life, Eden is careful to point out that many of the works listed were written at a time when Juliana's health was problematic and later failing. If she had been a long-lived writer of children's stories and poems, works that were formulaic in nature and more simplistically moralistic than moralistically complex, this record of productivity would still be impressive, but given Ewing's relatively short life and the consistent evidence in her works of mature artistic skill and a rarely rich imagination that resulted in a high order of originality, what she achieved is nothing less than remarkable. At birth, she evidently was blessed with an enormous store of creative energy. Ideas did not slowly seep into her mind but flooded in upon her with such a deluge that she found it difficult to keep afloat. In this regard, Eden writes:

> Julie had often said how strange it seemed to her, when people who had a ready pen for *writing* consulted her as to what they should *write about*! She suffered so much from over-abundance of ideas which she had not the physical strength to put on paper. Even when she was very ill, and unable to use her hands at all, the sight of a lot of good German wood-cuts, which were sent to me at Bath, suggested so many fresh ideas to her brain, that she only longed to be able to seize her pen and write tales to the pictures.[2]

She wrote rapidly, then, as one driven by a haunting suspicion that she would not be able to write for long. Much like the noted author who claimed in his autobiography to having been greatly influenced by her— Rudyard Kipling—she did not spend hours tediously reviewing what she had written and making small changes in wording but practiced the art of "compression," as she called it, meaning that she simply deleted whole paragraphs or even sections from the writing she was currently working on.[3]

She mastered much of the craft that makes for the skillful writing of fiction and poetry, but perhaps her greatest strength, her finest talent, was in the area of characterization, and nowhere is that gift more in evidence than in one of her early short novels, *Monsieur the Viscount's Friend*, which was written when she was but nineteen years old.[4] It was among four stories—her first to be published—that appeared in 1861 in the *Monthly Packet*, a magazine founded in 1851 by Charlotte Mary Yonge (1823–1901). Its full title was *The Monthly Packet of Evening Readings for Younger Members of the English Church*. Yonge forcefully made clear as editor what was to be in the magazine. She indicated in her introductory letter accompanying the first volume of the *Monthly Packet* that the magazine was intended not for young children but for females fifteen to twenty-five years of age. And by the time Ewing published her early stories in the magazine, its readership had come to include a substantial number of adults, both male and female. Indeed, the very name of the periodical was changed in order to recognize its more mature readers: *The Monthly Packet of Evening Readings for Members* ["*Younger*" omitted] *of the English Church*.

It seems apparent, then, that Ewing did not have in mind an audience of small children when she began publishing, for she chose the *Monthly Packet*. Although the early pages of *The Viscount's Friend* focus on the protagonist as a young boy, it is difficult to imagine a child precocious enough to read this story with its mature level of diction or to perceive— even if the story is read to him or her—its meaning as it develops gradually as experiences tell upon the consciousness of the Viscount and force him to look deeply inward. What is likely to be even less accessible to children is the author's fondness for irony that sometimes reaches toward sarcasm. The first and second paragraphs of *The Viscount's Friend* are nothing less than masterful in their undercurrent of authorial questioning or even disapproval of what she appears to be praising with a "once upon a time" opening of what promises to be an idyllic tale but certainly is not:

It was the year of grace 1779. In one of the most beautiful corners of beautiful France stood a grand old château. It was a fine old building, with countless windows large and small, with high-pitched roofs and pointed towers, which in good taste or bad, did its best to be everywhere ornamental, from the gorgon heads which frowned from its turrets to the long row of stables and the fantastic dovecotes. It stood (as became such a castle) upon an eminence, and looked down. Very beautiful indeed was what it looked upon. Terrace below terrace glowed with the most brilliant flowers and broad flights of steps led from one garden to the other. On the last terrace of all, fountains and jets of water poured into one large basin, in which were gold and silver fish. Beyond this were shady walks, which led to a lake on which floated water-lilies and swans. From the top of the topmost flight of steps you could see the blazing gardens one below the other, the fountains and the basin, the walks and the lake, and beyond these the trees, and the smiling country, and the blue sky of France.

Within the castle, as without, beauty reigned supreme. The sunlight, subdued by blinds and curtains, stole into rooms furnished with every grace and luxury that could be procured in a country that then accounted itself the most highly-civilized in the world. It fell upon beautiful flowers and beautiful china, upon beautiful tapestry and pictures; and it fell upon Madame the Viscountess, sitting at her embroidery. Madame the Viscountess was not young, but she was not the least beautiful object in those stately rooms. She had married into a race of nobles who (themselves famed for personal beauty) had been scrupulous in the choice of lovely wives. The late Viscount (for Madame was a widow) had been one of the handsomest of the gay courtiers of his day; and Madame had not been unworthy of him. Even now, though the roses on her cheeks were more entirely artificial than they had been in the days of her youth, she was like some exquisite piece of porcelain. Standing by the embroidery frame was Madame's only child, a boy who, in spite of his youth, was already Monsieur the Viscount. He also was beautiful. His exquisitely-cut mouth had a curl which was the inheritance of scornful generations, but which was redeemed by his soft violet eyes and by an under-lying expression of natural amiability. His hair was cut square across the forehead and fell in natural curls behind. His childish figure had already been trained in the fencing school, and had gathered dignity from perpetually treading upon shallow steps and in lofty rooms. From the rosettes on his little shoes to his *chapeau á plumes*, he also was like some porcelain figure. Surely, such beings could not exist except in such a château as this, where the very air (unlike that breathed by common mortals) had in the ante-rooms a faint aristocratic odour, and was for yards round Madame the Viscountess dimly suggestive of frangipani![5]

So often is the word *beautiful* mentioned in these opening paragraphs that its overuse creates a tone of mockery of the sybaritic life. While ostensibly lauding the setting of the Viscount's château, Ewing inserts a sentence that subtly suggests a sense of arrogant elitism inherent in this way of life at this time among the French nobility. The château "stood (as became such a castle) upon an eminence, *and looked down*" (p. 134, italics mine). Indeed, so highly did such families regard themselves that from their lofty self-secure positions, there was no way to look but down upon the commonality. "The very air" in the rooms of such a place of the wealthy had "a faint aristocratic odour," which was "unlike that breathed by common mortals" (p. 136). The image that the author creates of the château is that of a "fine old building, with countless windows, large and small, with high-pitched roofs and pointed towers," but suddenly without warning, that image is infiltrated with details that blur what his tutor tells him about toads and about his need to learn about them. "Toads do not bite—they have no teeth," the tutor explains to his resisting pupil. "Neither do they spit poison" (p. 141). When he tells the boy, "You should study natural history," he is answered with a remark that reveals just how closed-minded the lad has become as a result of his culture, the culture of beauty, which has permeated his upbringing: "'That is what you always say,' interrupted the Viscount . . . 'but if I knew as much as you do, it would not make me understand why such ugly creatures need have been made'" (p. 143). Up to this point, the tutor, or "Monsieur the Preceptor," as he is alternately designated in the story, has been half appalled and half amused at the young Viscount's insistence upon destroying an innocent toad in the belief that it is dangerous. Now, however, he realizes that the boy by implication is denying that God is the Creator of all creatures on this earth. The angry Viscount is not questioning, as did William Blake when he wrote in his poem "The Tiger," "Did He who made the lamb make thee?" The Viscount does not have to ask that question using the toad instead of the tiger because he is convinced that such a creature of such supreme ugliness and thus such total evil as the toad could not possibly have been made by a benevolent god.

In response to the young Viscount's statement that he could not understand "why such ugly creatures need have been made," his tutor, who is also a priest, answers "firmly": "Nor is it necessary that you should understand it, particularly if you do not care to inquire [as, for example, did William Blake]. It is enough for you and me if we remember Who made them" (p. 143). With that, the tutor opens his breviary and walks away. The Viscount rejoins the group of children visiting him, and they all adjourn to the dining hall of the grand château. Soon the unpleasant experience with the disgusting toad is forgotten as the Viscount takes his place at the head of the table, his mother on his right hand and guests sitting around him with "the liveried lacqueys waiting his commands" (p. 144). What the priest, his tutor, has tried to teach him seems to have made no lasting impression, and he "forgot that anything had ever been made which could mar beauty and enjoyment" (p. 144). The author ends Chapter 1 on the same note that she began it, with a biting description of the world in which a young boy of noble birth belongs: "And so night fell over the beautiful sky, the beautiful château, and the beautiful gardens; and upon the secure slumbers of beautiful Madame and her beautiful son, and beautiful, beautiful France" (p. 144).

Throughout the first chapter, the author strongly emphasizes the formative influence that the culture of beauty has had upon the boy Viscount, molding him into the smug, arrogant hater of all that is ugly.

He believes that is the way to be; he believes that his father was that way and that his mother is that way now. He tells his tutor: "My mother would faint if she saw so hideous a beast [as a toad] among her beautiful flowers" (p. 142). And yet, Juliana Ewing, already wise for her young age in the ways of fictive creativity, subtly put the greedy reader on notice that this boy, from his birth suckled at the breast of beauty and knowing nothing else in his lofty life, was nevertheless deep down in the heart different from those whom the culture of beauty shaped and who never transcended this early training. When Ewing writes that the mouth of the young Viscount had a "curl," an inheritance from "scornful generations," she adds a highly significant qualification, for the curl "was *redeemed* by his soft violet eyes and by an under-lying expression of *natural* amiability" (p. 136, italics mine). The culture into which he was born has done its best to make of him the superficial young disciple of beauty who appears on the pages of the first chapter of the novel. Though it lay dormant within him, something innate "redeemed" him, and after undergoing a baptism of adversity, he emerges in the final chapter as a man noble in character as well as in title, his amiability by nature now taking the place of "the perverse folly of ignorance" that characterized him as a boy.[6]

The process through which this happens unfolds in Chapter 2. Thirteen years have gone by since the end of the first chapter, and the Viscount's environment has changed drastically: he has suddenly and rudely been snatched from his world of the beautiful and forced to enter an alien realm where beauty is absent, and ugliness is everywhere. His heaven has been invaded by the red terrors of hell, and he has to run for his life. The French Revolution is taking place, and the Reign of Terror proves to be the Viscount's personal experience in terror. Ewing's handling of the intense trauma that this horrible change of life causes in the Viscount's psyche is poignantly effective, unquestionably one of the most memorable aspects of this unforgettable novel that incises itself upon the memory like acid upon a metal plate.

As the Viscount, now no longer a child but a young man, first appears in the second chapter, he is literally starving, which metaphorically projects his frightful psychological condition: he has been cut off from the culture of beauty, which has nurtured him all of his life up to this point. It can no longer nurture him; it is no longer available to him. The man he encounters in his desperate search for nourishment is a scion of the ugly, a Jacobin whose "dress was not beautiful, [and] neither was he." In contrast, the Viscount's "face was beautiful still" (p. 145). This encounter of the Viscount with the Jacobin in which the former offers his watch to the latter in return for food has vital thematic implications. It is precisely at this point in the story where beauty passes out of the Viscount's life as the watch passes out of his possession. The beautiful watch, which belonged to his beautiful mother, evokes as a symbol the kind of multiplicity of suggestiveness that one finds only in the writings of the most gifted literary artists:

> It was a watch, a repeater, in a gold filigree case of exquisite workmanship, with raised figures depicting the loves of an Arcadian shepherd and shepherdess; and, as it lay on the white hand of its owner, it bore an evanescent fragrance that seemed to recall scenes as beautiful and as completely past as the days of pastoral perfection, when
>
> > All the world and love were young,
> > And truth in every shepherd's tongue. (p. 145)

Repeater watches with their delightful chimes have always been synonymous with wealth and noted for their beauty and the highest standard of workmanship. To own one has been and still is a mark of good taste and affluence. The appeal of this particular repeater watch is considerably enhanced by the raised figures of an Arcadian shepherd with a shepherdess, suggesting an idyllic world of the past when ugliness in any form did not exist, and all was true and beautiful. A fragrance lingers on the watch, the same fragrance that Ewing referred to in the second paragraph of the novel as that to be found in the ante-rooms of the château as "a faint aristocratic odour" (p. 136).

However, just as Ewing qualified her praise of the beauty-filled life in the first two paragraphs of the story with hints of artificiality, so does she do likewise here with her description of the watch. She quotes the two lines of poetry seemingly to sum up what the figures on the watch suggest, that is, a world of beauty where ugliness does not exist, but in reality, these lines do not suggest that at all but just the opposite as if again she is undercutting what she has just seemed to be praising. The quotation is from "The Nymph's Reply to the Shepherd," a satiric poem written by Sir Walter Raleigh and published in 1600 as a kind of realistic counterpunch aimed at Christopher Marlowe's highly romantic "The Passionate Shepherd to His Love" published the year before. The two lines that Ewing quotes have an entirely different meaning in Raleigh's poem from what they at first seem to have in *The Viscount's Friend* because they include a key word that Ewing no doubt intentionally omitted, the word "If": "*If* all the world and love were young, / And truth in every Shepherd's tongue . . . " But, as Raleigh's poem argues, all the world and love are not perpetually young but like everything else they grow old and fade. The speaker in the poem, the same nymph whom a shepherd addresses in Marlowe's "The Passionate Shepherd to His Love," is answering the shepherd's plea to "live with me and be my love." She is realistic and practical and knows that the life of lasting beauty and ease she is being offered exists only in the shepherd's folly-filled imagination. When Marlowe's "The Passionate Shepherd to His Love" and Raleigh's "The Nymph's Reply to the Shepherd" are placed side by side, the difference in worldviews between them is striking. It is, in a sense, the difference, psychologically and spiritually speaking, between the Viscount who wishes to kill a toad because it is ugly and the Viscount we see in Chapter 3 as an older and wiser man now enlightened dramatically and living what is a genuinely useful life in the final scene of the novel.[7]

The daughter of an Anglican clergyman, Juliana Ewing was herself a devoted Christian, and her writings reflect her spiritual orientation, but she was also a gifted, skillful writer of imaginative literature who abhorred preachy stories and poems. She was not interested in composing fiction without an uplifting moral message, but on the other hand, she did not write, and was not interested in writing, sermons. Therefore, the moral dimension of a work such as *The Viscount's Friend* tends to be more suggestive than apparent and obtrusive. Subtle but provocative, the central concern of the story is the working of divine providence in the life of an aristocratic Frenchman from his childhood to his death. Briefly defined, divine providence is God's care and protection of his children, and in caring and protecting, God often "moves in a mysterious way."[8] Such is the case in *The Viscount's Friend.*

On the most accessible level of meaning, the novel is about a man who, when a child, hates toads, such as the one that he discovers in his yard, but as an adult he learns to love a particular toad; indeed, it becomes his best friend. That understanding of *The Viscount's Friend* is like the first impression one has of a person who, when known better, appears excitingly more complex and more interesting than he or she seemed from merely a first contact. The germ of the novel's complexity and richness in meaning is the word—and the concept of—"friend."

Ordinarily, a friend is thought of as someone known and with whom a bond of affection is shared. In a more inclusive sense and in the theological context of *The Viscount's Friend*, a friend is an instrument of God in the working of Divine Providence. In this sense, the Viscount does not have just a single friend in the novel—namely, Monsieur Crapaud, the toad—but several. They are personally unlike, and they have varying attitudes toward the Viscount ranging from love to hatred, but they have one thing in common: whether or not they mean to, they all have a hand in saving him in one way or another and thus in playing a part in what he becomes, a man whose hard-won faith has taught him not only how to die but also how to live "an honourable, useful life" (p. 185). They are, then, "friends," instruments of God in the working of divine providence in the life of Louis Archambaud Jean-Marie Arnaud, Vicomte de B—.

His most obvious friend is a priest who is also his tutor, or, as he is frequently called, Monsieur the Preceptor, "a singular man" (p. 140). Different from all the elite residents of the château in that he has not been nurtured by the culture of beauty, he stands apart from their materialistic values and his very presence seems to call into question their validity:

> It was not only that he was wanting in the grace and beauty that reigned around him [in the château and its environs] but that his presence made those very graces and beauties to look small. He seemed to have a gift the reverse of that bestowed upon King Midas—the gold on which his heavy hand was laid seemed to become rubbish. In the presence of the late Viscount, and in that of Madame his widow, you would have felt fully the deep

> importance of your dress being à la mode, and your complexion
> à la strawberries and cream (such influences still exist); but let
> the burly tutor appear upon the scene, and all the magic died at
> once out of the brocaded silks and pearl-coloured stockings, and
> dress and complexion became subjects almost of insignificance.
> (p. 140)

His role in the novel is clearly that of the Viscount's savior. It is the "large heavy hand" of the Preceptor—which means "teacher"—that grasps the would-be slaying hand of the young and badly misled Viscount, who is intent on killing "the enemy," an innocent and harmless toad. Though he resents the Preceptor's stopping him, he will later remember the incident, and it will become a part of his movement toward enlightenment. The Viscount's first "friend," then, is his tutor. Standing out in the several descriptions of him in the story is his hand, the strong hand that saves his charge, the Viscount, from performing a senseless and despicable act, the hand of a man of God, constantly keeping his place in his breviary so that he will not lose his way in his devotion to doing God's will. Ewing repeatedly mentions the Preceptor's hand because he is the Viscount's "friend," and as such is an instrument of God. He is, in a sense, the hand of God in the work of divine providence in the novel. It is nothing short of providential that it is he who convinces Antoine, the jailer, to save the life of the Viscount by hiding him away in a remote lower level cell and not registering his name on the list of prisoners. It is providential that the cell assigned to the Viscount is that previously occupied by the Preceptor. And it is providential that the Preceptor, who while in that cell is not alone but visited by the same toad that providentially (and ironically) saves the Viscount from the torturous madness that is often the result of long periods of solitary confinement. Finally, just before he goes to his own death at the hands of the ungodly, the Preceptor sacrificially gives up something dear to him—a locket—and gives it to Antoine to assure the safety of the Viscount—an act of pure love. Though *The Viscount's Friend*, strictly speaking, is not an allegory, there are strong parallels between the Preceptor, who functions in the story as the hand of God and as teacher, and Jesus Christ.

Practically every character in the novel is the Viscount's "friend," and each has a hand in saving him. The Preceptor, his tutor, saves him; Antoine the jailer saves him; even the Jacobin saves him—though he hates him and sees to it that he is imprisoned—by putting on him the red hat that will allow him to pass unharmed through the threatening crowds. Valerie, whom he marries when he is no longer imprisoned, saves him from bitterness and teaches him the meaning of romantic love and domestic happiness. They are all instruments of God in this tale of divine providence. With a brilliant touch of irony it becomes clear by the end of the novel that the force that has been most intent on destroying him, the Reign of Terror, has also been an instrument of God and thus the Viscount's friend, because without having gone through that "sweet adversitie," to use Shakespeare's words from the quotation with which Ewing begins her novel, he never would have been taught how to die but "also how to live—an honourable, useful life" (p. 185).[9]

The Viscount's most important friend, however, is not a human being or even an historical event, but a toad. If the recurring image of a hand in the novel suggests the hand of God, that is, divine providence, the recurring image of eyes suggests a second aspect of God, omnipresence. The eyes watching over the Viscount while he sleeps in the prison of misery represent the eyes of God. In virtually every description of the toad, from the Viscount's first encounter with a toad in the garden of the château to his many visitations of the toad in his prison cell, the eyes of Monsieur Crapaud occupy center stage. The Viscount's gradual acceptance and then affectionate appreciation of those eyes, which are at first described—representing his point of view—as eerie and frightening and then as "golden," reflect his spiritual transformation from a complete lack of understanding of God and thus alienation from him to his loving those eyes, which becomes synonymous with the love of God. His best friend, then, of all who has had a hand in his spiritual enlightenment, the "Friend" referred to in the title of the novel, is God, who sometimes works wonders through mysterious ways, indeed, even through "frowning Providence," which hides a "smiling face."[10]

Monsieur the Viscount's Friend:
A Tale in Three Chapters

Sweet are the uses of adversitie
Which like the toad, ugly and venomous,
Weares yet a precious Jewell in his head.

As You Like It, 1623

Chapter I

It was the year of grace 1779. In one of the most beautiful corners of beautiful France stood a grand old château. It was a fine old building, with countless windows large and small, with high-pitched roofs and pointed towers, which in good taste or bad, did its best to be everywhere ornamental, from the gorgon heads which frowned from its turrets to the long row of stables and the fantastic dovecotes. It stood (as became such a castle) upon an eminence, and looked down. Very beautiful indeed was what it looked upon. Terrace below terrace glowed with the most brilliant flowers and broad flights of steps led from one garden to the other. On the last terrace of all, fountains and jets of water poured into one large basin, in which were gold and silver fish. Beyond this were shady walks, which led to a lake on which floated water-lilies and swans. From the top of the topmost flight of steps you could see the blazing gardens one below the other, the fountains and the basin, the walks and the lake, and beyond these the trees, and the smiling country, and the blue sky of France.

Within the castle, as without, beauty reigned supreme. The sunlight, subdued by blinds and curtains, stole into rooms furnished with every grace and luxury that could be procured in a country that then accounted itself the most highly-civilized in the world. It fell upon beautiful flowers and beautiful china, upon beautiful tapestry and pictures; and it fell upon Madame the Viscountess, sitting at her embroidery. Madame the Viscountess was not young, but she was not the least beautiful object in those stately rooms. She had married into a race of nobles who (themselves famed for personal beauty) had been scrupulous in the choice of lovely wives. The late Viscount (for Madame was a widow) had been one of the handsomest of the gay courtiers of his day; and Madame had not been unworthy of him. Even now, though the roses on her cheeks were more entirely artificial than they had been in the days of her youth, she was like some exquisite piece of porcelain. Standing by the embroidery frame was Madame's only child, a boy who, in spite of his youth, was already Monsieur the Viscount. He also was beautiful. His exquisitely-cut mouth had a curl which was the inheritance of scornful generations, but which was redeemed by his soft violet eyes and by an under-lying expression of natural amiability. His hair was cut square across the forehead and fell in natural curls behind. His childish figure had already been trained in the fencing school, and had gathered dignity from perpetually treading upon shallow steps and in lofty rooms. From the rosettes on his little shoes to his *chapeau a plumes*, he also was like some porcelain figure. Surely, such beings could not exist except in such a château as this, where the very air (unlike that breathed by common mortals) had in the ante-rooms a faint aristocratic odour, and was for yards round Madame the Viscountess dimly suggestive of frangipani!

Monsieur the Viscount did not stay long by the embroidery frame; he was entertaining to-day a party of children from the estate, and had come for the key of an old cabinet of which he wished to display the treasures. When tired of this they went out on to the terrace, and one of the children who had not been there before exclaimed at the beauty of the view.

"It is true," said the little Viscount, carelessly, "and all, as far as you can see, is the estate."

"I will throw a stone to the end of your property, Monsieur," said one of the boys, laughing; and he picked one off the walk and stepping back, flung it with all his little strength. The stone fell before it had passed the fountains, and the failure was received with shouts of laughter.

"Let us see who can beat that," they cried; and there was a general search for pebbles, which were flung at random among the flower beds.

"One can easily throw such as these," said the Viscount, who was poking under the wall of the first terrace; "but here is a stone that one may call a stone. Who will send this into the fish-pond? It will make a fountain of itself."

The children drew round him as, with ruffles turned back, he tugged and pulled at a large dirty looking stone, which was half-buried in the earth by the wall. "Up it comes!" said the Viscount, at length; and sure enough, up it came; but underneath it, his bright eyes shining out of his dirty wrinkled body—horror of horrors! —there lay a toad. Now, even in England, toads are not looked upon with much favor, and a party of English children would have been startled by such a discovery. But with French people, the dread of toads is ludicrous in its intensity. In France toads are believed to have teeth, to bite, and to spit poison; so my hero and his young guests must be excused for taking flight at once with a cry of dismay. On the next terrace, however, they paused, and seeing no sign of the enemy, crept slowly back again. The little Viscount (be it said) began to feel ashamed of himself, and led the way, with his hand upon the miniature sword which hung at his side. All eyes were fixed upon the fatal stone, when from behind it was seen slowly to push forth, first a dirty wrinkled leg, then half a dirty wrinkled head, with one gleaming eye. It was too much; with cries of, "It is he! He comes! He spits! He pursues us!" the young guests of the chateau fled in good earnest, and never stopped until they reached the fountain and the fish-pond.

But Monsieur the Viscount stood his ground. At the sudden apparition the blood rushed to his heart, and made him very white, then it flooded back again and made him very red, and then he fairly drew his sword, and shouting, "*Vive la France!*" rushed upon the enemy. The sword if small was sharp, and stabbed the poor toad would most undoubtedly have been, but for a sudden check received by the valiant little nobleman. It came in the shape of a large heavy hand that seized Monsieur the Viscount with a grasp of a giant, while a voice which only could have belonged to the owner of such a hand said in slow deep tones, "*Que faites-vous?*" ("What are you doing?")

It was the tutor, who had been pacing up and down the terrace with a book, and who now stood holding the book in his right hand, and our hero in his left.

Monsieur the Viscount's tutor was a remarkable man. If he had not been so, he would hardly have been tolerated at the château, since he was not particularly beautiful, and not especially refined, He was in holy orders, as his tonsured head and clerical costume bore witness—a costume which, from its tightness and simplicity, only served to exaggerate the unusual proportions of his person. Monsieur the Preceptor had English blood in his veins, and his northern origin betrayed itself in his towering height and corresponding breadth, as well as by his fair hair and light blue eyes. But the most remarkable parts of his outward man were his hands, which were of immense size, especially about the thumbs. Monsieur the Preceptor was not exactly in keeping with his present abode. It was not only that he was wanting in the grace and beauty that reigned around him, but that his presence made those very graces and beauties to look small. He seemed to have a gift the reverse of that bestowed upon King Midas—the gold on which his heavy hand was laid seemed to become rubbish. In the presence of the late Viscount, and in that of Madame his widow, you would have felt fully the deep importance of your dress being *a la mode*, and your complexion *a la* strawberries and cream (such influences still exist); but let the burly tutor appear upon the scene, and all the magic died at once out of the brocaded silks and pearl-coloured stockings, and dress and complexion became subjects almost of insignificance. Monsieur the Preceptor was certainly a singular man to have been chosen as an inmate of such a household; but, though young, he had unusual talents, and added to them the not more usual accompaniments of modesty and trustworthiness. To crown all, he was rigidly pious in time when piety was not fashionable, and an obedient son of the church of which he was a minister. Moreover, a family that fashion does not permit to be demonstratively religious, may gain a reflected credit from an austere chaplain; and so Monsieur the Preceptor remained in the château and went his own way. It was this man who now laid hands on the Viscount, and, in a voice that sounded like amiable thunder, made the inquiry, "*Que faites-vous?*"

"I am going to kill this animal—this hideous horrible animal," said Monsieur the Viscount, struggling vainly under the grasp of the tutor's finger and thumb.

"It is only a toad," said Monsieur the Preceptor, in his laconic tones.

"*Only* a toad, do you say, Monsieur?" said the Viscount. "That is enough, I think. It will bite—it will spit—it will poison; it is like that dragon you tell me of, that devastated Rhodes—I am the good knight that shall kill it."

Monsieur the Preceptor laughed headily. "You are misled by a vulgar error. Toads do not bite—they have no teeth; neither do they spit poison.

"You are wrong, Monsieur, said the Viscount; "I have seen their teeth myself. Claude Mignon, at the lodge, has two terrible ones, which he keeps in his pocket as a charm."

"I have seen them," said the tutor, in Monsieur Claude's pocket. When he can show me similar ones in a toad's head I will believe. Meanwhile, I must beg of you, Monsieur, to put up your sword. You must not kill this poor animal, which is quite harmless, and very useful in a garden—it feeds upon many insects and reptiles which injure the plants."

"It shall not be useful in this garden," said the little Viscount, fretfully. "There are plenty of gardeners to destroy the insects, and if needful, we can have more. But the toad shall not remain. My mother would faint if she saw so hideous a beast among her beautiful flowers."

"Jacques!" roared the tutor to a gardener who was at some distance. Jacques started as if a clap of thunder had sounded in his ear, and approached with low bows. "Take that toad, Jacques, and carry it to the *potager*. It will keep the slugs from your cabbages."

Jacques bowed low and lower, and scratched his head, and then did reverence again with Asiatic humility, but at the same time moved gradually backwards, and never even looked at the toad.

"You also have seen the contents of Monsieur Claude's pocket?" said the tutor, significantly, and quitting his hold of the Viscount, he stooped down, seized the toad in his huge finger and thumb, and strode off in the direction of the *potager*, followed at a respectful distance by Jacques, who vented his awe and astonishment in alternate bows and exclamations at the astounding conduct of the incomprehensible Preceptor.

"What is the use of such ugly beasts?" said the Viscount to his tutor, on his return from the *potager*. "Birds and butterflies are pretty, but what can such villains as these toads have been made for?"

"You should study natural history, Monsieur—" began the priest, who was himself a naturalist.

"That is what you always say," interrupted the Viscount, with the perverse folly of ignorance; but if I knew as much as you do, it would not make me understand why such ugly creatures need have been made."

"Nor," said the priest firmly, "is it necessary that you should understand it, particularly if you do not care to inquire. It is enough for you and me if we remember Who made them, some six thousand years before either of us was born."

With which Monsieur the Preceptor (who had all this time kept his place in the little book with his big thumb) returned to the terrace, and resumed his devotions at the point where they had been interrupted; which exercise he continued till he was joined by the Curé of the village, and the two priests relaxed in the political and religious gossip of the day.

Monsieur the Viscount rejoined his young guests, and they fed the gold fish and the swans, and played Colin Maillard in the shady walks, and made a beautiful bouquet for Madame, and then fled indoors at the first approach of evening chill, and found that the Viscountess had prepared a feast of fruit and flowers for them in the great hall. Here, at the head of the table, with Madame at his right hand, the guests around, and the liveried lacqueys waiting his commands, Monsieur the Viscount forgot that anything had ever been made which could mar beauty and enjoyment; while the two priests outside stalked up and down under the falling twilight, and talked ugly talk of crime and poverty that were *somewhere* now, and of troubles to come hereafter.

And so night fell over the beautiful sky, the beautiful château, and the beautiful gardens; and upon the secure slumbers of beautiful Madame and her beautiful son, and beautiful, beautiful France.

Chapter II

It was the year of grace 1792, thirteen years after the events related in the last chapter. It was the 2nd of September, and Sunday, a day of rest and peace in all Christian countries, and even more in gay, beautiful France—a day of festivity and merriment. This Sunday, however, seemed rather an exception to the general rule. There were no gay groups or bannered processions; the typical incense and the public devotion of which it is the symbol were alike wanting; the streets in some places seemed deserted, and in others there was an ominous crowd, and the dreary silence was now and then broken by a distant sound of yells and cries, that struck terror into the hearts of the Parisians.

It was a deserted bye-street, overlooked by some shut-up warehouses, and from the cellar of one of these a young man crept up on to the pathway. His dress had once been beautiful, but it was torn and soiled; his face was beautiful still, but it was marred by the hideous eagerness of a face on which famine has laid her hand—he was starving. As this man came out from the warehouse, another man came down the street. His dress was not beautiful, neither was he. There was a red look about him—he wore a red flannel cap, tricolour ribbons, and had something red upon his hands, which was neither ribbon nor flannel. The other stopped when he saw him, and pulled something from his pocket. It was a watch, a repeater, in a gold filigree case of exquisite workmanship, with raised figures depicting the loves of an Arcadian shepherd and shepherdess; and, as it lay on the white hand of its owner, it bore an evanescent fragrance that seemed to recall scenes as beautiful and as completely past as the days of pastoral perfection, when

> All the world and love were young,
> And truth in every shepherd's tongue.

The young man held it to the other and spoke. "It was my mother's," he said, with an appealing glance of violet eyes; "I would not part with it but that I am starving. Will you get me food?"

"You are hiding?" said he of the red cap.

"Is that a crime in these days?" said the other, with a smile that would in other days have been irresistible.

The man took the watch, shaded the donor's beautiful face with a rough red cap and tricolour ribbon, and bade him follow him. He, who had but lately come to Paris, dragged his exhausted body after his conductor, hardly noticed the crowds in the streets, the signs by which the man got free passage for them both, or their entrance by a little side-door into a large dark building, and never knew until he was delivered to one of the gaolers that he had been led into the prison of the Abbaye. Then the wretch tore the cap of Liberty from his victim's head, and pointed to him with a fierce laugh.

"He wants food, this aristocrat. He shall not wait long—there is a feast in the court below, which he shall join presently. See to it, Antoine! And you, *Monsieur, Mons-ieur!* Listen to the banqueters."

He ceased, and in the silence yells and cries from a court below came up like some horrid answer to imprecation.

The man continued—

"He has paid for his admission, this Monsieur. It belonged to Madame his mother. Behold!"

He held the watch above his head, and dashed it with insane fury on the ground, and bidding the gaoler see to his prisoner, rushed away to the court below.

The prisoner needed some attention. Weakness, and fasting, and horror had overpowered a delicate body and a sensitive mind, and he lay senseless by the shattered relic of happier times. Antoine, the gaoler (a weak-minded man whom circumstances had made cruel), looked at him with indifference while the Jacobin remained in the place, and with half-suppressed pity when he had gone. The place where he lay was a hall or passage in the prison, into which several cells opened, and a number of the prisoners were gathered together at one end of it. One of them had watched the proceedings of the Jacobin and his victim with profound interest, and now advanced to where the poor youth lay. He was a priest, and though thirteen years had passed over his head since we saw him in the château, and though toil and suffering and anxiety had added the traces of as many more, yet it would not have been difficult to recognize the towering height, the candid face, and, finally, the large thumb in the little book of—, Monsieur the Preceptor, who had years ago exchanged his old position for a parochial curé. He strode up to the gaoler (whose head came a little above the priest's elbow), and, drawing him aside, asked with his old abruptness, "Who is this?"

"It is the Viscount de B—. I know his face. He has escaped the commissaires for some days."

"I thought so. Is his name on the registers?"

"No. He escaped arrest, and has just been brought in, as you saw."

"Antoine," said the priest, in a low voice, and with a gaze that seemed to pierce the soul of the weak little gaoler; "Antoine, when you were a shoemaker in the Rue de la Croix, in two or three hard winters I think you found me a friend."

"Oh! Monsieur le Curé," said Antoine, writhing; "if Monsieur le Curé would believe that if I could save his life! But—"

"Pshaw!" said the priest, "it is not for myself, but for this boy. You must save him, Antoine. Hear me, you *must*. Take him now to one of the lower cells and hide him. You risk nothing. His name is not on the prison register. He will not be called, he will not be missed; that fanatic will think that he has perished with the rest of us (Antoine shuddered, though the priest did not move a muscle) and when this mad fever has subsided and order is restored, he will reward you. And Antoine—"

Here the priest pocketed his book, and somewhat awkwardly with his huge hands unfastened the left side of his cassock, and tore the silk from the lining. Monsieur le Curé's cassock seemed a cabinet of oddities. First he pulled from this ingenious hiding-place a crucifix, which he replaced; then a knot of white ribbon, which he also restored; and, finally, a tiny pocket or bag of what had been cream-coloured satin, embroidered with small bunches of heartsease, and which was aromatic with otto of roses. Awkwardly, and somewhat slowly, he drew out of this a small locket, in the centre of which was some unreadable legend in cabalistic-looking character, and which blazed with the finest diamonds. Heaven alone knows the secret of that gem, or the struggle with which the priest yielded it. He put it into Antoine's hand, talking as he did so partly to himself and partly to the gaoler.

"We brought nothing into this world, and it is certain we can carry nothing out. The diamonds are of the finest, Antoine, and will sell for much. The blessing of a dying priest upon you if you do kindly, and his curse if you do ill to this poor child, whose home was my home in better days. And for the locket—it is but a remembrance, and to remember is not difficult!"

As the last observation was not addressed to Antoine, so also he did not hear it. He was discontentedly watching the body of the Viscount, whom he consented to help, but with genuine weak-mindedness consented ungraciously.

"How am I to get him there? Monsieur le Curé sees that he cannot stand upon his feet."

Monsieur le Curé smiled, and stooping, picked his old pupil up in his arms as if he had been a baby, and bore him to one of the doors.

"You must come no further," said Antoine, hastily.

"Ingrate!" muttered the priest in momentary anger, and then, ashamed, he crossed himself, and pressing the young nobleman to his bosom with the last gush of earthly affection that he was to feel, he kissed his senseless face, spoke a benediction to ears that could not hear it, and laid his burden down.

"God the Father, the Son, and the Holy Ghost, be with thee now and in the dread hour of death. Adieu! We shall meet hereafter."

The look of pity, the yearning of rekindled love, the struggle of silenced memories passed from his face and left a shining calm—foretaste of the perpetual Light and the eternal Rest.

Before he reached the other prisoners, the large thumb had found its old place in the little book, the lips formed the old, old words; but it might almost have been said of him already, that "his spirit was with the God who gave it."

As for the Monsieur the Viscount, it was perhaps well that he was not too sensible of his position, for Antoine got him down the flight of stone steps that led to the cell by the simple process of dragging him by the heels. After a similar fashion he crossed the floor, and was deposited on a pallet; the gaoler then emptied a broken pitcher of water over his face, and locking the door securely, hurried back to his charge.

When Monsieur the Viscount came to his senses he raised himself and looked round his new abode. It was a small stone cell; it was underground, with a little grated window at the top that seemed to be level with the court; there was a pallet—painfully pressed and worn—a chair, a stone on which stood a plate and broken pitcher, and in one corner a huge bundle of firewood which mocked a place where there was no fire. Stones lay scattered about, the walls were black, and in the far dark corners the wet oozed out and trickled slowly down, and lizards and other reptiles crawled up.

I suppose that the first object that attracts the hopes of a new prisoner is the window of his cell, and to this, despite his weakness, Monsieur the Viscount crept. It afforded him little satisfaction. It was too high in the cell for him to reach it, too low in the prison to command any view, and was securely grated with iron. Then he examined the walls, but not a stone was loose. As he did so, his eye fell upon the floor, and he noticed that two of the stones that lay about had been raised up by some one and a third laid upon the top. It looked like child's play, and Monsieur the Viscount kicked it down, and then he saw that underneath it there was a pellet of paper roughly rolled together. Evidently it was something left by the former occupant of the cell for his successor. Perhaps he had begun some plan for getting away which he had not had time to perfect on his own account. Perhaps—but by this time the paper was spread out and Monsieur the Viscount read the writing. The paper was old and yellow. It was the flyleaf torn out of a little book, and on it was written in black chalk, the words—

> *Souvenes-vous du Sauveur.*
> (Remember the Saviour.)

He turned it over, he turned it back again; there was no other mark; there was nothing more; and Monsieur the Viscount did not conceal from himself that he was disappointed. How could it be otherwise? He had been bred in ease and luxury, and surrounded with everything that could make life beautiful; while ugliness, and want, and sickness, and all that made life miserable, had been kept, as far as they can be kept, from the precincts of the beautiful château which was his home. What were the *consolations* of religion to him? They are offered to those (and to those only) who need them. They were to Monsieur the Viscount what the Crucified Christ was to the Greeks of old—foolishness.

He put the paper in his pocket and lay down again, feeling it the crowning disappointment of what he had lately suffered. Presently, Antoine came with some food; it was not dainty, but Monsieur the Viscount devoured it like a famished hound, and then made inquiries as to how he came and how long he had been there. When the gaoler began to describe him, whom he called the Curé, Monsieur Viscount's attention quickened into eagerness, an eagerness deepened by the tender interest that always hangs round the names of those whom we have known in happier and younger days. The happy memories recalled by hearing of his old tutor seemed to blot out his present misfortunes. With French excitability, he laughed and wept alternately.

"As burly as ever, you say? The little book? I remember it, it was his breviary. Ah! It is he. It is Monsieur the Preceptor, whom I have not seen for years. Take me to him, bring him here, let me see him!"

But Monsieur the Preceptor was in Paradise.

That first night of Monsieur the Viscount's imprisonment was a terrible one. The bitter chill of a Parisian autumn, the gnawings of half-satisfied hunger, the thick walls that shut out all hope of escape but did not exclude those fearful cries that lasted with few intervals throughout the night, made it like some hideous dream. At last the morning broke; at half-past two o'clock, some members of the *commune* presented themselves in the hall of the National Assembly with the significant announcement:—"The prisons are empty!" and Antoine, who had been quaking for hours, took courage, and went with half a loaf of bread and a pitcher of water to the cell that was not empty. He found his prisoner struggling with a knot of white ribbon, which he was trying to fasten in his hair. One glance at his face told all.

"It is the fever," said Antoine; and he put down the bread and water and fetched an old blanket and a pillow; and that day and for many days, the gaoler hung above his prisoner's pallet with the tenderness of a woman. Was he haunted by the vision of a burly figure that had bent over his own sick bed in the Rue de la Croix? Did the voice (once so familiar in counsel and benediction!) echo still in his ears?

"*The blessing of a dying priest upon you if you do well, and his curse if you do ill to this poor child, whose home was my home in better days.*"

Be this as it may, Antoine tended his patient with all the constancy compatible with keeping his presence in the prison a secret; and it was not till the crisis was safely past, that he began to visit the cell less frequently, and reassumed the harsh manners which he held to befit his office.

Monsieur the Viscount's mind rambled much in his illness. He called for his mother, who had long been dead. He fancied himself in his own château. He thought that all his servants stood in a body before him, but that not one would move to wait on him. He thought that he had abundance of the most tempting food and cooling drinks, but placed just beyond his reach. He thought that he saw two lights like stars near together, which were close to the ground, and kept appearing and then vanishing away. In time he became more sensible; the château melted into the stern reality of his prison walls; the delicate food became bread and water; the servants disappeared like spectres; but in the empty cell, in the dark corners near the floor, he still fancied that he saw two sparks of light coming and going, appearing and then vanishing away. He watched them till his giddy head would bear it no longer, and he closed his eyes and slept. When he awoke he was much better, but when he raised himself and turned towards the stone—there, by the bread and the broken pitcher, sat a dirty, ugly, wrinkled toad, gazing at him, Monsieur the Viscount, with eyes of yellow fire.

Monsieur the Viscount had long ago forgotten the toad which had alarmed his childhood; but his natural dislike of that animal had not been lessened by years, and the toad of the prison seemed likely to fare no better than the toad of the château. He dragged himself from his pallet, and took up one of the large damp stones which lay about the floor of the cell, to throw at the intruder. He expected that when he approached it, the toad would crawl away, and that he could throw the stone after it; but to his surprise, the beast sat quite unmoved, looking at him with calm shining eyes, and, somehow or other Monsieur the Viscount lacked the strength or heart to kill it. He stood doubtful for a moment, and then a sudden feeling of weakness obliged him to drop the stone, and sit down, while tears sprang to his eyes with the sense of his helplessness.

"Why should I kill it?" he said bitterly. "The beast will live and grow fat upon this damp and loathsomeness, long after they have put an end to my feeble life. It shall remain. The cell is not big, but it is big enough for us both. However large be the rooms a man builds himself to live in, it needs but little space in which to die!"

So Monsieur the Viscount dragged his pallet away from the toad, placed another stone by it, and removed the pitcher; and then, wearied with his efforts, lay down and slept heavily.

When he awoke, on the new stone by the pitcher was the toad, staring full at him with topaz eyes. He lay still this time and did not move, for the animal showed no intention of spitting, and he was puzzled by its tameness.

"It seems to like the sight of a man," he thought. "Is it possible that any former inmate of this wretched prison can have amused his solitude by making a pet of such a creature? And if there were such a man, where is he now?"

Henceforward, sleeping or waking, whenever Monsieur the Viscount lay down upon his pallet, the toad crawled up on to the stone, and kept watch over him with shining lustrous eyes; but whenever there was a sound of the key grating in the lock, and the gaoler coming his rounds, away crept the toad, and was quickly lost in the dark corners of the room. When the man was gone, it returned to its place, and Monsieur the Viscount would talk to it, as he lay on his pallet.

"Ah! Monsieur Crapaud," he would say, with mournful pleasantry, "without doubt you have had a master and a kind one; but tell me, who was he, and where is he now? Was he old or young, and was it in the last stage of maddening loneliness that he made friends with such a creature as you?"

Monsieur Crapaud looked very intelligent, but he made no reply, and Monsieur the Viscount had recourse to Antoine.

"Who was in this cell before me?" he asked at the gaoler's next visit.

Antoine's face clouded. "Monsieur le Curé had this room. My orders were that he was to be imprisoned 'in secret.'"

Monsieur le Curé had this room. There was a revelation in those words. It was all explained now. The priest had always had a love for animals (and for ugly, common animals), which his pupil had by no means shared. His room at the château had been little less than a menagerie. He had even kept a glass beehive here, which communicated with a hole in the window through which the bees flew in and out, and he would stand for hours with his thumb in the breviary, watching the labours of his pets. And this also had been his room! This dark, damp cell. Here, breviary in hand, he had stood, and lain, and knelt. Here, in this miserable prison, he had found something to love, and on which to expend the rare intelligence and benevolence of his nature. Here, finally, in the last hours of his life, he had written on the fly-leaf of his prayer-book something to comfort his successor, and, "being dead, yet spoke" the words of consolation which he had administered in his lifetime. Monsieur the Viscount read that paper now with different feelings.

There is, perhaps, no argument so strong, and no virtue that so commands the respect of young men, as consistency. Monsieur the Preceptor's lifelong counsel and example would have done less for his pupil than was affected by the knowledge of his consistent career, now that it was past. It was not the nobility of the priest's principles that awoke in Monsieur the Viscount a desire to imitate his religious example, but the fact that he had applied them to his own life, not only in the time of wealth, but in the time of tribulation and in the hour of death. All that high-strung piety—that life of prayer—those unswerving admonitions to consider the vanity of earthly treasures, and to prepare for death—which had sounded so unreal amidst the perfumed elegances of the château, came back now with a reality gained from experience. The daily life of self-denial, the conversations garnished from Scripture and from the Fathers, had not, after all, been mere priestly affectations. In no symbolic manner, but literally, he had "watched for the coming of his Lord," and "taken up the cross daily"; and so, when the cross was laid on him, and when the voice spoke which must speak to all, "The Master is come, and calleth for thee," he bore the burden and obeyed the summons unmoved.

Unmoved!—this was the fact that struck deep into the heart of Monsieur the Viscount, as he listened to Antoine's account of the Curé's imprisonment. What had astonished and overpowered his own undisciplined nature had not disturbed Monsieur the Preceptor. He had prayed in the château—he prayed in the prison. He had often spoken in the château of the softening and comforting influences of communion with the lower animals and with nature, and in the uncertainty of imprisonment he had tamed a toad. "None of these things had moved him," and, in a storm of grief and admiration, Monsieur the Viscount bewailed the memory of his tutor.

"If he had only lived to teach me!"

But he was dead, and there was nothing for Monsieur the Viscount but to make the most of his example. This was not so easy to follow as he imagined. Things seemed to be different with him from what they had been with Monsieur the Preceptor. He had no lofty meditations, no ardent prayers, and calm and peace seemed more distant than ever. Monsieur the Viscount met, in short, with all those difficulties that the soul must meet with, which, in a moment of enthusiasm, has resolved upon a higher and a better way of life, and in moments of depression is perpetually tempted to forgo that resolution. His prison life was, however, a pretty severe discipline, and he held on with struggles and prayers; and so, little by little, and day by day, as the time of his imprisonment went by, the consolations of religion became a daily strength against the fretfulness of imperious temper, the sickness of hope deferred, and the dark suggestions of despair.

The term of his imprisonment was a long one. Many prisoners came and went within the walls of the Abbaye, but Monsieur the Viscount still remained in his cell; indeed, he would have gained little by leaving it if he could have done so, as he would certainly have been retaken. As it was, Antoine on more than one occasion concealed him behind the bundles of firewood, and once or twice he narrowly escaped detection by less friendly officials. There were times when the guillotine seemed to him almost better than this long suspense; but while other heads passed to the block, his remained on his shoulders; and so weeks and even months went by. And during all this time, sleeping or waking, whenever he lay down on his pallet, the toad crept up on to the stone, and kept watch over him with lustrous eyes.

Monsieur the Viscount hardly acknowledged to himself the affection with which he came to regard this ugly and despicable animal. The greater part of his regard for it he believed to be due to its connection with his tutor, and the rest he set down to the score of his own humanity, and took credit to himself accordingly; whereas in truth Monsieur Crapaud was of incalculable service to his master, who would lie and chatter to him for hours, and almost forget his present discomfort in recalling past happiness as he described the château, the gardens, the burly tutor, and beautiful Madame, or laughed over his childish remembrances of the toad's teeth in Claude Mignon's pocket; whilst Monsieur Crapaud sat well-bred and silent, with a world of comprehension in his fiery eyes. Whoever thinks this puerile must remember that my hero was a Frenchman, and a young Frenchman, with a prescriptive right to chatter for chattering's sake, and also that he had not a very highly cultivated mind of his own to converse with, even if the most highly cultivated intellect is ever a reliable resource against the terrors of solitary confinement.

Foolish or wise, however, Monsieur the Viscount's attachment strengthened daily; and one day something happened which showed his pet in a new light, and afforded him fresh amusement.

The prison was much infested with certain large black spiders, which crawled about the floor and walls; and, as Monsieur the Viscount was lying on his pallet, he saw one of these scramble up and over the stone on which sat Monsieur Crapaud. That good gentleman, whose eyes, till then, had been fixed as usual on his master, now turned his attention to the intruder. The spider, as if conscious of danger, had suddenly stopped still. Monsieur Crapaud gazed at it intently with his beautiful eyes, and bent himself slightly forward. So they remained for some seconds, then the spider turned round, and began suddenly to scramble away. At this instant Monsieur the Viscount saw his friend's eyes gleam with an intenser fire, his head was jerked forward; it almost seemed as if something had been projected from his mouth, and drawn back again with the rapidity of lightning. Then Monsieur Crapaud resumed his position, drew in his head, and gazed mildly and sedately before him; *but the spider was nowhere to be seen.*

Monsieur the Viscount burst into a loud laugh.

"Eh, well! Monsieur, said he, "but this is not well-bred on your part. Who gave you leave to eat my spiders? And to bolt them in such an unmannerly way, moreover."

In spite of this reproof, Monsieur Crapaud looked in no way ashamed of himself, and I regret to state that henceforward (with the partial humanness of mankind in general), Monsieur the Viscount amused himself by catching the insects (which were only too plentiful) in an old oyster-shell, and then setting them at liberty on the stone for the benefit of his friend. As for him, all appeared to be fish that came to his net—spiders and beetles, slugs and snails from the damp corners, flies, and wood-lice found on turning up the large stone, disappeared one after the other. The wood-lice were an especial amusement: when Monsieur the Viscount touched them, they shut up into tight little balls, and in this condition he removed them to the stone, and placed them like marbles in a row, Monsieur Crapaud watching the proceeding with rapt attention. After a while the balls would slowly open and begin to crawl away; but he was a very active wood-louse indeed who escaped the suction of Monsieur

Crapaud's tongue, as, his eyes glowing with eager enjoyment, he bolted one after another, and Monsieur the Viscount clapped his hands and applauded.

The grated window was a very fine field for spiders and other insects, and by piling up stones on the floor, Monsieur the Viscount contrived to scramble up to it, and fill his friend's oyster-shell with the prey.

One day, about a year and nine months after his first arrival at the prison, he climbed to the embrasure of the window, as usual, oyster-shell in hand. He always chose a time for this when he knew that the court would most probably be deserted, to avoid the danger of being recognized through the grating. He was, therefore, not a little startled at being disturbed in his capture of a fat black spider by a sound of something bumping against the iron bars. On looking up, he saw that a string was dangling before the window with something attached to the end of it. He drew it in, and, as he did so, he fancied that he heard a distant sound of voices and clapped hands, as if from some window above. He proceeded to examine his prize, and found that it was a little round pin-cushion of sand, such as women use to polish their needles with, and that, apparently, it was used as a make-weight to ensure the steady descent of a neat little letter that was tied beside it, in company with a small lead pencil. The letter was directed to *"The prisoner who finds this."* Monsieur the Viscount opened it at once. This was the letter—

> *In Prison, 24th Prairial, year 2.*
>
> *Fellow-sufferer, who are you? How long have you been imprisoned? Be good enough to answer.*

Monsieur the Viscount hesitated for a moment, and then determined to risk all. He tore off a bit of the paper, and with the little pencil hurriedly wrote this reply:—

> *In secret, June 12, 1794.*
>
> *Louis Archambaud Jean-Marie Arnaud, Vicomte de B., supposed to have perished in the massacres of September, 1792. Keep my secret. I have been imprisoned a year and nine months. Who are you? How long have you been here?*

The letter was drawn up, and he watched anxiously for the reply. It came, and with it some sheets of blank paper.

> *Monsieur, —We have the honour to reply to your inquiries, and thank you for your frankness. Henri Edouard Clermont, Baron de St. Claire. Valerie de St. Claire. We have been here but two days. Accept our sympathy for your misfortunes.*

Four words in this note seized at once upon Monsieur the Viscount's interest—*Valerie de St. Claire*; —and for some reasons, which I do not pretend to explain, he decided that it was she who was the author of these epistles, and the demon of curiosity forthwith took possession of his mind. Who was she? Was she old or young? And in which relation did she stand to Monsieur le Baron—that of wife, of sister, or of daughter? And from some equally inexplicable cause Monsieur the Viscount determined in his own mind that it was the latter. To make assurances doubly sure, however, he laid a trap to discover the real state of the case. He wrote a letter of thanks and sympathy, expressed with all the delicate chivalrous politeness of a nobleman of the old *regime,* and addressed it to *Madame la Baronne.* The plan succeeded. The next note he received contained these sentences:—"*I am not the Baroness. Madame mother is, alas! dead. I and my father are alone. He is ill, but thanks you, Monsieur, for your letters, which relieve the* ennui *of imprisonment. Are you alone?*"

Monsieur the Viscount, as in duty bound, relieved the *ennui* of the Baron's captivity by another epistle. Before answering the last question, he turned round involuntarily, and looked to whether Monsieur Crapaud sat by the broken pitcher. The beautiful eyes were turned towards him, and Monsieur the Viscount took up his pencil, and wrote hastily, "I am not alone—I have a friend."

Henceforward the oyster-shell took a long time to fill, and patience seemed a harder virtue than ever. Perhaps the last fact had something to do with the rapid decline of Monsieur the Viscount's health. He became paler and weaker, and more fretful. His prayers were accompanied by greater mental struggles, and watered with more tears. He was, however, most positive in his assurances to Monsieur Crapaud that he knew the exact nature and cause of the malady that was consuming him. It resulted, he said, from the noxious and unwholesome condition of his cell; and he would entreat Antoine to have it swept out. After some difficulty the gaoler consented.

It was nearly a month since Monsieur the Viscount had first been startled by the appearance of the little pincushion. The stock of paper had long been exhausted. He had torn up his cambric ruffles to write upon, and Mademoiselle de St. Claire had made havoc of her pocket-handkerchiefs for the same purpose. The Viscount was feebler than ever, and Antoine became alarmed. The cell should be swept out the next morning. He would come himself, he said, and bring another man out of the town with him to help him, for the work was heavy, and he had a touch of rheumatism. The man was a stupid fellow from the country, who had only been a week in Paris; he had never heard of the Viscount, and Antoine would tell him that the prisoner was a certain young lawyer who had really died of fever in prison the day before. Monsieur the Viscount thanked him; and it was not till the next morning arrived, and he was expecting them every moment, that Monsieur the Viscount remembered the toad, and that he would without doubt be swept away with the rest in the general clearance. At first he thought that he would beg them to leave it, but some knowledge of the petty insults which that class of men heaped upon their prisoners made him feel that this would probably be only an additional reason for their taking the animal away. There was no place to hide it in, for they would go all round the room; unless—unless Monsieur the Viscount took it up in his hand. And this is just what he objected to do. All his old feelings of repugnance came back; he had not even got gloves on; his long white hands were bare, he could not touch a toad. It was true that the beast had amused him, and that he had chatted to it; but after all, this was a piece of childish folly—an unmanly way, to say the least, of relieving the tedium of captivity. What was Monsieur Crapaud but a very ugly (and most people said a venomous) reptile? To what a folly he had been condescending! With these thoughts, Monsieur the Viscount steeled himself against the glances of his topaz-eyed friend, and when the steps of the men were heard upon the stairs, he did not move from the window where he had placed himself, with his back to the stone.

The steps came nearer and nearer, Monsieur Viscount began to whistle—the key was rattled in the lock, and Monsieur the Viscount heard a bit of bread fall, as the toad hastily descended to hide itself as usual in the corners. In a moment his resolution was gone; another second, and it would be too late. He dashed after the creature, picked it up, and when the men came in he was standing with his hands behind him, in which Monsieur Crapaud was quietly and safely seated.

The room was swept, and Antoine was preparing to go, when the other, who had been eyeing the prisoner suspiciously, stopped and said with a sharp sneer, "Does the prisoner always preserve that position?"

"Not he," said the gaoler, good-naturedly. "He spends most of his time in bed, which saves his legs. Come along, François."

"I shall not come," said the other obstinately. "Let the citizen show me his hands."

"Plague take you!" said Antoine, in a whisper. "What sulky fit possesses you, my comrade? Let the poor wretch alone. What wouldst thou with his hands? Wait a little, and thou shall have his head."

"We should have few heads or prisoners either, if thou hadst the care of them," said François, sharply. "I say that the prisoner secretes something, and that I will see it. Show your hands, dog of an aristocrat!"

Monsieur the Viscount set his teeth to keep himself from speaking, and held out his hands in silence, toad and all.

Both the men started back with an exclamation, and François got behind his comrade, and swore over his shoulder.

Monsieur the Viscount stood upright and still, with a smile on his white face. "Behold, citizen, what I secrete, and what I desire to keep. Behold all that I have left to secrete or to desire! There is nothing more."

"Throw it down!" screamed François; "Many a witch has been burnt for less—throw it down."

The colour began to flood over Monsieur the Viscount's face; but still he spoke gently, and with bated breath. "If you wish me to suffer, citizen, let this be my witness that I have suffered. I must be very friendless to desire such a friend. I must be brought very low to ask such a favour. Let the Republic give me this."

"The Republic has one safe rule for aristocrats," said the other; "she gives them nothing but their keep till she pays for their shaving—once for all. She gave one of these dogs a few rags to dress a wound on his back with, and he made a rope of his dressings, and let himself down from the window. We will have no more such games. You may be training the beast to spit poison at good citizens. Throw it down and kill it."

Monsieur the Viscount made no reply. His hands had moved towards his breast, against which he was holding his golden-eyed friend. There are times in life when the brute creation contrasts favourably with the lords thereof, and this was one of them. It was hard to part just now.

Antoine, who had been internally cursing his own folly in bringing such a companion into the cell, now interfered. "If you are going to stay here to be bitten or spit at, François, my friend," said he, "I am not. Thou art zealous, my comrade, but dull as an owl. The Republic is far-sighted in the wisdom beyond thy coarse ideas, and has more ways of taking their heads from these aristocrats than one. Dost thou not see?" And he tapped his forehead significantly, and looked at the prisoner; and so, between talking and pushing, got his sulky companion out of the cell, and locked the door after them.

"And so, my friend—my friend!" said Monsieur the Viscount, tenderly, "We are safe once more; but it will not be for long, my Crapaud. Something tells me that I cannot much longer be overlooked. A little while, and I shall be gone; and thou wilt have, perchance, another master, when I am summoned before mine."

Monsieur the Viscount's misgivings were just. François, on whose stupidity Antoine had relied, was (as is not uncommon with people stupid in other respects) just clever enough to be mischievous. Antoine's evident alarm, made him suspicious, and he began to talk about the too-elegant-looking young lawyer who was imprisoned "in secret," and permitted by the gaoler to keep venomous beasts. Antoine was examined and committed to one of his own cells, and Monsieur the Viscount was summoned before the revolutionary tribunal.

There was little need even for the scanty inquiry that in those days preceded sentence. In every line of his beautiful face, marred as it was by sickness and suffering—in the unconquerable dignity which dirt and raggedness were powerless to hide, the fatal nobility of his birth and breeding were betrayed. When he returned to the ante-room, he did not positively know his fate; but in his mind there was a moral certainty that left him no hope.

The room was filled with other prisoners awaiting trial; and, as he entered, his eyes wandered round it to see if there were any familiar faces. They fell upon two figures standing with their backs to him—a tall, fierce-looking man, who, despite his height and fierceness, had a restless, nervous despondency expressed in all his movements; and a young girl who leant on his arm as if for support, but whose steady quietude gave her more the air of a supporter. Without seeing their faces, and for no reasonable reason, Monsieur the Viscount decided with himself that they were the Baron and his daughter, and he begged the man who was conducting him for a moment's delay. The man consented. France was becoming sick of unmitigated carnage, and even the executioners sometimes indulged in pity by way of a change.

As Monsieur the Viscount approached the two they turned round, and he saw her face—a very fair and very resolute one, with ashen hair and large eyes. In common with almost all the faces in that room, it was blanched with suffering; and, it is fair to say, in common with many of them, it was pervaded by a lofty calm. Monsieur the Viscount never for an instant doubted his own conviction; he drew near and said in a low voice, "Mademoiselle de St. Claire!"

The Baron looked first fierce, and then alarmed. His daughter's face illumined; she turned her large eyes on the speaker, and said simply,

"Monsieur le Vicomte?"

The Baron apologized, commiserated, and sat down on a seat near, with a look of fretful despair; and his daughter and Monsieur the Viscount were left standing together. Monsieur the Viscount desired to say a great deal, and could say very little. The moments went by, and hardly a word had been spoken.

Valerie asked if he knew his fate.

"I have not heard it," he said, "but I am morally certain. There can be but one end in these days."

She sighed. "It is the same with us. And if you must suffer, Monsieur, I wish that we may suffer together. It would comfort my father—and me."

Her composure vexed him. Just, too, when he was sensible that the desire of life was making a few fierce struggles in his own breast.

"You seem to look forward to death with great cheerfulness, Mademoiselle."

The large eyes were raised to him with a look of surprise at the irritation of his tone.

"I think," she said gently, "that one does not look forward *to*, but *beyond* it." She stopped and hesitated, still watching his face, and then spoke hurriedly and diffidently:—

"Monsieur, it seems impertinent to make such suggestions to you, who have doubtless a full fund of consolation; but I remember, when a child, going to hear the preaching of a monk who was famous for his eloquence. He said that his text was from the Scriptures—it has been in my mind all to-day—'*There the wicked cease from troubling, and there the weary be at rest.*' The man is becoming impatient. Adieu! Monsieur. A thousand thanks and a thousand blessings."

She offered her cheek, on which there was not a ray of increased colour, and Monsieur the Viscount stooped and kissed it, with a thick mist gathering in his eyes, through which he could not see her face.

"Adieu! Valerie!"

"Adieu! Louis!"

So they met, and so they parted; and as Monsieur the Viscount went back to his prison, he flattered himself that the last link was broken for him in the chain of earthly interests.

When he reached the cell he was tired, and lay down, and in a few seconds a soft scrambling over the floor announced the return of Monsieur Crapaud from his hiding-place. With one wrinkled leg after another he clambered on to the stone, and Monsieur the Viscount started when he saw him.

"Friend Crapaud! I had actually forgotten thee. I fancied I had said adieu for the last time"; and he gave a choked sigh, which Monsieur Crapaud could not be expected to understand. In about five minutes, he sprang up suddenly. "Monsieur Crapaud, I have not long to live, and no time must be lost in making my will." Monsieur Crapaud was too wise to express any astonishment; and his master began to hunt for a tidy-looking stone (paper and cambric were both at an end). They were all rough and dirty; but necessity had made the Viscount inventive, and he took a couple and rubbed them together till he had polished both.

Then he pulled out the little pencil, and for the next half hour composed and wrote busily. When it was done he lay down, and read it to his friend. This was Monsieur the Viscount's last will and testament:—

To My Successor in this Cell

To you whom Providence has chosen to be the inheritor of my sorrows and my captivity, I desire to make another bequest. There is in this prison a toad. He was tamed by a man (peace to his memory!) who tenanted this cell before me. He has been my friend and companion for nearly two years of sad imprisonment. He has sat by my bedside, fed from my hand, and shared all my confidence. He is ugly, but he has beautiful eyes; he is silent, but he is attentive; he is a brute, but I wish the men of France were in this respect more his superiors! He is very faithful. May you never have a worse friend! He feeds upon insects, which I have been accustomed to procure for him. Be kind to him; he will repay it. Like other men, I bequeath what I would take with me if I could.

Fellow-sufferer, adieu! God comfort you as He has comforted me! The sorrows of this life are sharp but short; the joys of the next life are eternal. Think sometimes on him who commends his friend to your pity, and himself to your prayers.

This is the last will and testament of Louis Archambaud Jean-Marie Arnaud, Vicomte de B—.

Monsieur the Viscount's last will and testament was with difficulty squeezed into the surface of the larger of the stones. Then he hid it where the priest had hidden *his* bequest long ago, and then lay down to dream of Monsieur the Preceptor, and that they had met at last.

The next day was one of anxious suspense. In the evening, as usual, a list of those who were to be guillotined the next morning, was brought into the prison; and Monsieur the Viscount begged for a sight of it. It was brought to him. First on the list was Antoine! Halfway down was his own name, "Louis de B—," and a little lower his fascinated gaze fell upon names that stirred his heart with such a passion of regret as he had fancied it would never feel again, "Henri de St. Claire, Valerie de St. Claire."

Her eyes seemed to shine on him from the gathering twilight, and her calm voice to echo in his ears: "*It has been in my mind all to-day. There the wicked cease from troubling, and there the weary be at rest.*"

There! He buried his face and prayed.

He was disturbed by the unlocking of the door, and the new gaoler appeared with Antoine! The poor wretch seemed overpowered by terror. He had begged to be imprisoned for this last night with Monsieur the Viscount. It was only a matter of a few hours, as they were to die at daybreak, and his request was granted.

Antoine's entrance turned the current of Monsieur the Viscount's thoughts. No more selfish reflections now. He must comfort this poor creature, of whose death he was to be the unintentional cause. Antoine's first anxiety was that Monsieur the Viscount should bear witness that the gaoler had treated him kindly, and so earned the blessing and not the curse of Monsieur le Curé, whose powerful presence seemed to haunt him still. On this score he was soon set at rest, and then came the old, old story. He had been but a bad man. If his life were to come over again, he would do differently. Did Monsieur the Viscount think that there was any hope?

Would Monsieur the Viscount have recognized himself, could he, two years ago, have seen himself as he was now? Kneeling by that rough, uncultivated figure, and pleading with all the eloquence he could master to that rough uncultivated heart, the great Truths of Christianity—so great and few and simple in their application to our needs! The violet eyes had never appealed more tenderly, the soft voice had never been softer than now, as he strove to explain to this ignorant soul, the cardinal doctrines of Faith and Repentance, and Charity, with an earnestness that was perhaps more effectual than his preaching.

Monsieur the Viscount was quite as much astonished as flattered by the success of his instructions. The faith on which he had laid hold with such mortal struggles, seemed almost to "come natural" (as people say) to Antoine. With abundant tears he professed the deepest penitence for his past life, at the same time that he accepted the doctrine of the Atonement as a natural remedy, and never seemed to have a doubt in the Infinite Mercy that should cover his infinite guilt.

It was all so orthodox that even if he had doubted (which he did not) the sincerity of the gaoler's contrition and belief, Monsieur the Viscount could have done nothing but envy the easy nature of Antoine's convictions. He forgot the difference of their respective capabilities!

When the night was far advanced the men rose from their knees, and Monsieur the Viscount persuaded Antoine to lie down on his pallet, and when the gaoler's heavy breathing told that he was asleep, Monsieur the Viscount felt relieved to be alone once more—alone, except for Monsieur Crapaud, whose round fiery eyes were open as usual.

The simplicity with which he had been obliged to explain the truths of Divine Love to Antoine, was of signal service to Monsieur the Viscount himself. It left him no excuse for those intricacies of doubt, with which refined minds too often torture themselves; and as he paced feebly up and down the cell, all the long-withheld peace for which he had striven since his imprisonment seemed to flood into his soul. How blessed—how undeservedly blessed—was his fate! Who or what was he that after such short, such mitigated sufferings, the crown of victory should be so near? The way had seemed long to come, it was short to look back on, and now the golden gates were almost reached, the everlasting doors were open. A few more hours, and then—! And as Monsieur the Viscount buried his worn face in his hands, the tears that trickled from his fingers were literally tears of joy.

He groped his way to the stone, pushed some straw close to it, and lay down on the ground to rest, watched by Monsieur Crapaud's fiery eyes. And as he lay, faces seemed to him to rise out of the darkness, to take the form and features of the face of the priest, and to gaze at him with unutterable benediction. And in his mind, like some familiar piece of music, awoke the words that had been written on the fly-leaf of the little book; coming back, sleepily and dreamily, over and over again—

Souvenez-vous du Sauveur! Souvenez-vous du Sauveur!
(Remember the Saviour!)

In that remembrance he fell asleep.

Monsieur the Viscount's sleep for some hours was without a dream. Then it began to be disturbed by that uneasy consciousness of sleeping too long, which enables some people to awake at whatever hour they have resolved upon. At last it became intolerable, and wearied as he was, he awoke. It was broad daylight, and Antoine was snoring beside him. Surely the cart would come soon. The executions were generally at an early hour. But time went on, and no one came, and Antoine awoke. The hours of suspense passed heavily, but at last there were steps and a key rattled into the lock. The door opened, and the gaoler appeared with a jug of milk and a loaf. With a strange smile he set them down.

"A good appetite to you, citizens."

Antoine flew on him. "Comrade! We used to be friends. Tell me, what is it? Is the execution deferred?"

"The execution has taken place at last," said the other, significantly; "*Robespierre is dead!*" And he vanished.

Antoine uttered a shriek of joy. He wept, he laughed, he cut capers, and flinging himself at Monsieur the Viscount's feet, he kissed them rapturously. When he raised his eyes to Monsieur the Viscount's face, his transports moderated. The last shock had been too much; he seemed almost in a stupor. Antoine got him on the pallet, dragged the blanket over him, broke the bread into the milk, and played the nurse once more.

On that day thousands of prisoners in the city of Paris alone awoke from the shadow of death to the hope of life. The Reign of Terror was ended.

Chapter III

It was a year of Grace early in the present century.

We are again in the beautiful country of beautiful France. It is the château once more. It is the same, but changed. The unapproachable elegance, the inviolable security, have witnessed invasion. The right wing of the château is in ruins, with traces of fire upon the blackened walls; while here and there, a broken statue or a roofless temple are sad memorials of the Revolution. Within the restored part of the château, however, all looks well. Monsieur the Viscount has been fortunate, and if not so rich a man as his father, has yet regained enough of his property to live with comfort, and, as he thinks, luxury. The long rooms are little less elegant than in former days, and Madame the present Viscountess's boudoir is a model of taste. Not far from it is another room, to which it forms a singular contrast. This room belongs to Monsieur the Viscount. It is small, with one window. The floor and walls are bare, and it contains no furniture; but on the floor is a worn-out pallet, by which lies a stone, and on that a broken pitcher, and in a little frame against the wall is preserved a crumpled bit of paper like the fly-leaf of some little book, on which is a half-effaced inscription, which can be deciphered by Monsieur the Viscount if by no one else. Above the window is written in large letters, a date and the word "Remember." Monsieur the Viscount is not likely to forget, but he is afraid of himself and of prosperity lest it should spoil him.

It is evening, and Monsieur the Viscount is strolling along the terrace with Madame on his arm. He has only one to offer her, for where the other should be an empty sleeve is pinned to his breast, on which a bit of ribbon is stirred by the breeze. Monsieur the Viscount has not been idle since we saw him last; the faith that taught him to die, has taught him also how to live—an honourable, useful life.

It is evening, and the air comes up perfumed from a bed of violets by which Monsieur the Viscount is kneeling. Madame (who has a fair face and ashen hair) stands by him with her little hand on his shoulder, and her large eyes upon the violets.

"My friend! My friend! My friend!" It is Monsieur the Viscount's voice, and at the sound of it, there is a rustle among the violets that sends the perfume high into the air. Then from the parted leaves come forth first a dirty wrinkled leg, then a dirty wrinkled head with gleaming eyes, and Monsieur Crapaud crawls with self-satisfied dignity on to Monsieur the Viscount's outstretched hand.

So they stay laughing and chatting, and then Monsieur the Viscount bids his friend good-night, and holds him towards Madame that she may do the same. But Madame (who did not enjoy Monsieur Crapaud's society in prison) cannot be induced to do more than scratch his head delicately with the tip of her white finger. But she respects him greatly, at a distance, she says. Then they go back along the terrace, and are met by a man-servant in Monsieur the Viscount's livery. Is it possible that this is Antoine, with his shock head covered with powder?

Yes; that grating voice, which no mental change avails to subdue, is his, and he announces that Monsieur le Curé has arrived. It is the old Curé of the village (who has survived the troubles of the Revolution), and many are the evenings he spends at the château, and many the times in which the closing acts of a noble life are recounted to him, the life of his old friend whom he hopes ere long to see—of Monsieur the Preceptor. He is kindly welcomed by Monsieur and by Madame, and they pass on together into the château. And when Monsieur the Viscount's steps have ceased to echo from the terrace, Monsieur Crapaud buries himself once more among the violets.

◆   ◆   ◆

Monsieur the Viscount is dead, and Madame sleeps also at his side; and their possessions have descended to their son.

Not the least valued among them is a case with a glass front and sides, in which seated upon a stone is the body of a toad stuffed with exquisite skill, from whose head gleam eyes of genuine topaz. Above it in letters of gold is a date, and this inscription:—

Monsieur the Viscount's Friend
Adieu!

CHAPTER 2

The Imagination as Wizard: "Christmas Crackers"

In a letter written from Fredericton, New Brunswick, Canada, to her mother, Margaret Gatty, and dated "Sexagesima [January 31], 1869," Juliana Ewing indicated that she was "sending . . . 2 fairy stories—for yr editorial consideration."[1] That is, she was sending them for the purpose of being published in *Aunt Judy's Magazine* of which her mother was editor. More than likely, one of those stories was "Christmas Crackers," which appeared serially in the last issue of the magazine for 1869 and the first issue of 1870, and carried the subtitle of "A Fantasia," which is a work of the fancy where the author is free to trespass even into the often forbidden areas of the grotesque and bizarre. She pulled up the idea of the story from the depths of her "fertile imagination,"[2] and she wrote it as a paean to that marvelous faculty. "Christmas Crackers" is unique among her writings because it is the only one in which she wrote about the remarkable function of the imagination and in which one of the characters in the story is its personification. The story is a tour de force of originality that has heretofore gone unnoticed as such.

As if to remind her mother that she was well equipped to compose such a fantasia, she wrote in her letter:

> In old days when I used to tell stories to the others [her siblings] —I used to have to produce them [stories] in considerable numbers & without much preparation, & as that argues a *certain* amount of imagination—I have determined to try if I can write a few fairy tales of the genuine "uninstructive" type.[3]

"A *certain* amount of imagination" is a grinning understatement.[4] Throughout her lifetime, she was blessed with a swelling abundance of that gift for invention that her sister has called "the prolific power of her imagination."[5] It was so strong and enduring that it outlived her physical ability to manifest it in her writings. Her sister remembers that "Even when she was very ill, and unable to use her hands at all, the sight of a lot of good German woodcuts, which were sent to me at Bath, suggested so many fresh ideas to her brain, that she only longed to be able to seize her pen and write tales to the pictures."[6] There came a time in her career as an author when aspiring writers would sometimes correspond with her and ask her to suggest to them fruitful subjects they could use. Her reaction to these inquiries was impatient surprise that they did not have enough imagination to find their own subjects. Her sister writes: "Julie had often said how strange it seemed to her, when people who had a ready pen for *writing* consulted her as to what they should *write about*! She suffered so much from over-abundance of ideas which she had not the physical strength to put on paper."[7] Those galloping ideas emerging from her brain had been created there by "her powers of invention."[8] Though arrogance was foreign to her nature, she possessed an unshakable and constant belief in herself as a writer mainly because she was so keenly aware that she was endowed with an exceptional imagination.

That creative power within her was also responsible for the pleasure she took in sketching with a high degree of self-confidence. Horatia Eden writes: "My sister's artistic as well as literary powers were so strong that through all her life the two ever ran side by side, each aiding and developing the other, so that it is difficult to speak of them apart."[9] When with money earned from her writings, she took her elder brother to Holland and Antwerp, she "filled her sketch-book with pictures."[10] Her brother remembers one occasion when she completely lost herself in her art, her imagination absorbing her:

> It was in Rotterdam ... that I left her with her camp-stool and water-colours for a moment in the street, to find her, on my return, with a huge crowd round her, and before—a baker's man holding back a blue veil that would blow before her eyes—and she sketching down an avenue of spectators, to whom she kept

motioning with her brush to stand aside. Perfectly unconscious
she was of *how* she looked, and I had great difficulty in getting
her to pack up and move on.[11]

In his perceptive treatment of Ewing and her writings, U. C.
Knoepflmacher points out that she was "ever the stylist concerned with
the craft of fiction,"[12] a truth that should be stressed in any appraisal of
her and her writings, for it is that—her consistent conscious artistry—
that empowers her work to soar from the tree tops of good, instructive
children's literature to the mountain tops of challenging adult fiction.
As the prototypical conscious artist, she was always aware that it is the
author's imagination that awakens the writer to a promising subject to
write about and then plays a predominant role in all other aspects of the
process of composition. It was not only the inspirer in her view but very
much the creator as well, telling the writer what to write but also telling
him or her how to write it.

When in his autobiography, Rudyard Kipling praised Ewing's work,
and especially the novel *Six to Sixteen*, he did so because he found that
"here was a history of real people and real things."[13] If Ewing could have
read this comment of Kipling's, she would not have disagreed with his
assessment of her novel but would have found it highly flattering and
would have been pleased inasmuch as it was, in her view, indirect praise
of her imagination, for she considered a great realistic story just as much
a product of the imagination as is a great fairy tale. Nothing was more
important to her than what she knew to be her own most distinctive gift:
her ability to create. Although she did not write the following statement,
she could have, for it expresses the function she herself attributed to
the imagination in the creation of art whether in literature, music, or
painting: "One supreme fact which I have discovered is that it is not
willpower but fantasy—imagination—that creates. Imagination is the
creative force. Imagination creates reality."[14]

Ewing's tribute to the imagination, her short story "Christmas
Crackers," is one of her finest achievements yet one of the least appreciated
of her works. A reviewer for the London *Times Literary Supplement*
praised it highly in a review of 1911 but only in general terms:

> *Christmas Crackers* . . . is a thing as perfect in its kind as can
> be desired, a sketch of a few pages in which an air of unstudied
> musing over a pinch of the slenderest material conceals the
> exquisite care to which every touch is inserted and every word
> made to give its full effect . . . It is difficult in praising this little
> tale not to seem to overweigh it. Yet the more closely it is read the
> more faultless will its art appear; the light and just slightly fantastic
> characterization, the wide-awake comfort and warmth in which
> it opens, the sudden deft infusion of something enigmatic and
> mysterious, the old imperceptible lapse into a world of dreams
> young and old, the visions set free by the crackling fire that yet
> blends and mingles with them, waking with a final touch of pure
> pathos into the stainless sparkle of a Christmas morning.[15]

As eloquently laudatory as this review is, it fails to explain what the
story is about, the writer apparently content to suggest that it deals with
"something enigmatic and mysterious" and that the author of the work
indulges in a "just slightly fantastic characterization," apparently referring
to the tutor.

The central character in "Christmas Crackers" is the tutor, about whom
Ewing discloses little but hints much. He is unquestionably a magician
of sorts, but with powers beyond the usual type. Clearly, he is neither
a saint nor a villain of the kind found in many fairy tales for children.
He possesses something of both and is therefore largely inscrutable by
authorial intention. He has apparently lived for some time in the house
where the action of the story takes place, and he has done the family no
harm but has served to tutor successfully the daughter of the family (the
girl whose face is "like a summer's day") and her younger twin brothers,
Jim and Tom. At the same time, he has puzzled and fascinated them with
his magic powers, creating mechanical games that enthrall them. In fact,
the daughter calls him "Godpapa Grosselmayer, after that delightful old
fellow in Hoffman's tale of the Nut Cracker."[16]

The most valuable information about the tutor is furnished by this
young lady as she responds to the comment of the young man who is
courting her (the "visitor" as he is called in the story) that the tutor is "a
strange fellow": "'He is strange,' said the young lady . . . 'but I am very fond

of him. He has been with us so long he is like one of the family; though we know as little of his history as we did on the day that he came'" (p. 167). When the visitor further remarks that the tutor "looks clever," the young lady answers: "He is clever . . . wonderfully clever; so clever and so odd that sometimes I fancy he is hardly 'canny.' There is something almost supernatural about his acuteness and his ingenuity, but they are so kindly used; I wonder he has not brought out any playthings for us tonight" (p. 167).

With these comments, Ewing comes closer than at any other point in the narrative to explaining who or what the tutor is. Certainly, the most puzzling comment that the young lady makes about him is that he is "so odd that sometimes I fancy he is hardly 'canny.'" The word *canny* was in Ewing's time a frequently used term in Scotland and northern England meaning "acute." What the speaker seems to be saying, then, is that the word *canny* is hardly adequate to describe the acuteness of the tutor. Indeed, he seems to her often to be supernatural in his acuteness and ingenuity.

It is evident, then, that this magician or wizard, who is also a tutor, is no ordinary practitioner of legerdemain. His past is a mystery—as is the source of the imagination—for no one in the family that has engaged him as a tutor has any information about where he came from or what he did previously. What they do know is that "he has been all over the world, and he produces Indian puzzles, Japanese flower-buds that bloom in hot water, and German toys with complicated machinery, which," adds the young lady, his student, "I suspect of manufacturing himself" (pp. 167–8). Just previously she had commented: "I wonder he has not brought out any playthings for us tonight" (p. 167).

This should be an adequate clue that the Christmas crackers, which the tutor distributes from his deep pockets, are of his own making. They are the "playthings" the daughter in the family refers to, and they play a key role in the story, for the personification of the imagination, the tutor—aptly named since it is the primary tutor in our lives, especially of those who indulge in the writing of imaginative literature—has through his wizardry made the crackers so that their sound opens human beings up to the workings of the imagination. The cracking sound made when one person pulls from one end of the cracker and another person pulls from the other makes the pullers vulnerable to its magic. The smoke from the white powder, which is again a product of the tutor's wizardry, proves to be another ingredient of the imaginative experience, for it determines what form a person's vision will take depending upon that individual's personality traits, his or her hopes and fears.

The tutor has seen to it that each person present this Christmas Eve in this traditional home sitting in a big room with a roaring fire in the fireplace will undergo an imaginative experience, produced by the tutor, and each in keeping with his or her own deepest hopes, fears, and desires. Through his "playthings," the crackers, the white powder producing mild smoke with the most pleasing of odors, and the yule log, the wizard brings on for each a hypnotic vision, nine in all, the story describing one after the other, the final one experienced by "the master of the house" (p. 192) but not described in the detail that accompanies the others. With a touch of humor that reverberates through the story the two dogs present—belonging to the twin boys—also have their imaginative visions, their dreams "testified to" by their behavior during the vision: "low growls and whines" (p. 192).

The visions or dreams experienced by the group illustrate not only what may be in the hearts and minds of those present but also the wide variety of imaginary experiences the wizard is capable of creating. The imagination is sometimes nobly creative as in the case of the parson, who is to preach a sermon the next morning on the coming of Christ, a subject that has been heard so many times by his congregation that he fears it has lost its force. He wants and needs desperately a new way of approaching the old, old story of the birth of Jesus. When he pulls one of the Christmas crackers with the grandmother and smells the aroma of the powder coming from the burning yule log in the fireplace, he suddenly is carried away by the imagination to the time of the Magi watching for a bright and unusual star. He is among them, one of them watching for the star of Bethlehem. When he sees it, he is overwhelmed with the experience, inexpressibly moved, and the next day he will preach a sermon on what it was like to see that star, to be one of the Magi, a sermon so movingly effective that the grandmother tells him that his sermon was the most creative and powerful Christmas sermon she had ever heard him preach: "In all the thirty-five years we have been privileged to hear you, sir," she told the rector next day after the service, "I never heard such a Christmas sermon before" (p. 193). It was new; it was inventive; it was the product of the creative imagination working in the area of religious faith as it is capable of working elsewhere.

The grandmother was as equally inspired as the parson and filled with new hope as a result of what the imagination revealed to her on that Christmas Eve. It took her back in time to her honeymoon as she took off her bonnet and shawl and looking in the mirror, glanced "with pardonable pride at the fair face" reflected there. The imagination is not bound by time, and in the next few moments, the grandmother's life had passed, and she heard the tolling church bells announcing her funeral. In her dream, the beautiful bride was now suddenly an aged woman that lay dead on the bed, and as the grandmother looked at the face of the corpse, she realized that it was her own. The magic of the creative imagination worked further, however. Within a few seconds, on that aged, deeply wrinkled face on the bed emerged "a beauty not doomed to wither," and she realized that this was the face and body that God had promised and which she would have for eternity. As in the case of the parson, the imagination had provided a spiritual experience to the grandmother to be remembered for a lifetime.

It is clear, however, that in Ewing's concept of the imagination its function is not confined to doing God's work. In fact, Ewing takes some pains to indicate what is sometimes a servant of God is at other times a child of Satan. Early in the story, the character who is its personification is described as "grotesque-looking at any time" (p. 161). He talks to the fire as if it is related to him, and the yule log "flared and crackled in return, till the tutor's face shone like his own" (p. 161). His eyes change color frequently, and when he is excited or amused, "his eyes shone like a cat's" (p. 163); they glow in the firelight: "He certainly was an alarming object . . . like a picture of Bogy himself" (p. 164).

The tutor as Ewing characterizes him is not the devil, but he is certainly devilish, as is the imagination at times. His torment of the little boy, Macready Jones (known as MacGreedy to his cousins because of his selfish tendencies), is just one step away from sadistic, secretly making ugly faces at the little boy and doing his best to terrify him. He is highly successful at this pastime performed for his own amusement. The boy's terror is caused by the imagination's convincing him that what he sees is actually a monster, nothing less than "Bogy himself." To children awake in a dark room or having to walk past a cemetery, the dark side of the imagination is frequently in evidence.

The widow, Mrs. Jones, mother of Macready, fares no better with the imagination than does her young son. When it acts upon her, she sees horrible forms, and "the tutor's face kept appearing and vanishing with horrible grimaces through the mist" (p. 190). After this terrifying prelude, it creates for her a scenario in which she is married to Blue Beard, famous in folklore for his having married several wives and for killing all of them.[17] As the widow's dream-like state fades, she is pleading for her life, but Blue Beard is in the act of killing her, too: "As he waved his scimitar over her head, he seemed unaccountably to assume the form and features of the tutor" (p. 190).

Though capable of involving one in illusory dramas that can terrify and at the same time appear to be real-life situations, the imagination can also function as an excellent tutor, especially for the young, for it is indispensable for the maximum development of creativity and the intellect. Except for MacGreedy, that paradigm of selfishness (the greatest of sins for Juliana Ewing), the young people in "Christmas Crackers" profit greatly in their upbringing from the tutor. He feeds their hunger to create, and he shows them sights they never see in books. The twin boys are perfectly comfortable in his presence, hanging "over the tutor's chair" (p. 169) and later "reposing lazily at the tutor's feet" (p. 174). Their older sister has over the years learned to respect the tutor's shrewdness and inventiveness. She comments to the visitor that "his acuteness and ingenuity" have been "kindly used" for as long as he has been their tutor, and she admits that she is "very fond of him" (p. 167).

Acting with benevolence, the imagination sees to it that these three young people undergo in their visions the fulfillment of their dearest wishes. Jim has his heart set on becoming a soldier, and the imagination accommodates him, placing him in a realistic battle situation. The noise of the Christmas cracker that Jim is pulling with his brother Tom becomes for him the sound of gunfire in combat of which he is about to be a part:

"The firing has begun," he murmured involuntarily; "steady, steady!" These last words were to his horse, who seemed to be moving under him, not from fear, but from impatience. What had been the red and gold paper of the cracker was now the scarlet and gold lace on his own cavalry uniform . . . Presently the horse erects his head . . . It is the trumpet! Fan farrâ! Fan farrâ! The brazen voice speaks—the horses move—the plumes wave—the helmets shine . . . They ride, to Death or Glory. Fan farrâ! Fan farrâ! Fan farrâ! (p. 175)

In this little inner drama, a mere boy suddenly envisioned himself as a heroic cavalry soldier taking part in an important conflict where the result will be either "Death or Glory." But the character in the story is not the only one obviously indebted to the imagination. The author's artistic ability to switch abruptly from the traditional, ordinary world in which the boy exists to the imaginary world where he is a kind of heroic figure in a dangerous situation of war and making that dramatic contrast believable as a glimpse into the character's inner world suggests that she herself was under the magic spell of the imagination.

The imaginative experience of young Tom is similar to that of his twin brother Jim, except that it involves an episode aboard a ship. Whereas the sound of the Christmas cracker being pulled at both ends is to Jim the sound of gunfire, the beginning of a battle, to Tom, who unlike his brother wishes to be a sailor, it is "The noise of a heavy sea beating against the ship's side in a gale" (p. 175). The storm subsides in this imaginative episode that takes Tom where he so yearns to be, on the sea, and he finds himself "keeping the midnight watch on deck, gazing upon the liquid green of the waves, which, heaving and seething after the storm, were lit with phosphoric light, and as the ship held steadily on her course, poured past at the rate of twelve knots an hour in a silvery stream" (pp. 175-6).

The sister of the twin boys and her guest, the "visitor," each has a vision that works to bring them closer to each other and to assure them that marriage is in their future. In the visitor's imaginative experience, he sees himself with her in the most romantic of natural settings at night. A brook "rippled near with a soothing monotony" (p. 177), and in the distance they hear "a nightingale singing to his mate . . . The song was as plaintive as old memories, and as full of tenderness as the eyes of the young girl were full of tears" (p. 178). The visions of the young lady and the visitor foretell that he will be her husband and that they will soon embark on what will be a lifetime together. This is in sharp contrast to the grandmother's end-of-life imaginary experience where she sees herself in death. But both her vision and that of the elderly parson contain dramatic spiritual messages that transcend earthly existence and serve what was an important purpose for the author: namely, to connect the workings of the imagination to divine providence.

"Christmas Crackers," however, is not a story of unrelieved seriousness, for the wizard has a sense of humor that delights sometimes in performing his magic in certain ways that tend to make these mortals reveal what fools they are. For example, after pulling a Christmas cracker with the widow, Miss Letitia falls under the spell of the imagination and acts uncharacteristically, placing a paper hat that comes from inside the cracker on top of her head and comically bowing "gracefully hither and thither" (p. 189). Under imagination's influence—the tutor "had thrown some more powder on the coals," and the smoke reaches her—she takes on new and rather unorthodox tastes as to how one color "goes with" another, and she sanctions combinations that would disgust her ordinarily. "To the tutor" this performance "seemed to afford the most extreme amusement and he fairly shook with delight, his shadow dancing like a maniac beside him" (p. 189). Although what the imagination (that is, the tutor) does that causes young Macready to act as he does borders on cruelty, it is difficult to resist finding those actions humorous in themselves.

One of Juliana Ewing's most impressive achievements in "Christmas Crackers" is her success in convincingly characterizing the various people of the story. Using few words, she was able to delineate them both as individuals and as types. Building on that accomplishment, she proceeded to characterize the imagination itself as a wizard of almost inconceivable ability to create images and situations and to project them on the inward screen of human beings with results that range from terror to spiritual inspiration. The tutor emerges from "Christmas Crackers" not as God but sometimes serving God, not as the devil but sometimes serving the devil.

Few (if any) readers of *The New Yorker* magazine in 1939 realized that the brilliant technique employed by James Thurber in his short story, "The Secret Life of Walter Mitty," the highly original device of revealing what is going on in the character's day dreams that make him the hero that he wishes to be, was not original with Thurber. No doubt unknown to him, the technique of switching suddenly from the real world to an imagined world and then back again had been used in a short story sixty-nine years earlier by a woman who published mainly in a magazine for children. Thurber's story and Juliana Ewing's "Christmas Crackers" are radically different in many ways, but the way in which the imagination is used is markedly similar in the two works. One of the stories is a masterpiece of gentle humor; the other is simply a masterpiece.

Christmas Crackers

A Fantasia

It was Christmas-eve in an old-fashioned country-house, where Christmas was being kept with old-fashioned form and custom. It was getting late. The candles swaggered in their sockets, and the yule log glowed steadily like a red-hot coal.

"The fire has reached his heart," said the tutor: he is warm all through. How red he is! He shines with heat and hospitality like some warm-hearted old gentleman when a convivial evening is pretty far advanced. To-morrow he will be as cold and grey as the morning after a festival, when the glasses are being washed up, and the host is calculating his expenses. Yes! You know it is so;" and the tutor nodded to the yule log as he spoke; and the log flared and crackled in return, till the tutor's face shone like his own. He had no other means of reply.

The tutor was grotesque-looking at any time. He was lank and meagre, with a long body and limbs, and high shoulders. His face was smooth-shaven, and his skin like old parchment stretched over high cheek-bones and lantern jaws; but in their hollow sockets his eyes gleamed with the changeful lustre of two precious gems. In the ruddy firelight they were like rubies, and when he drew back into the shade they glared green like the eyes of a cat. It must not be inferred from the tutor's presence this evening that there were no Christmas holidays in this house. They had begun some days before; and if the tutor had had a home to go to, it is to be presumed that he would have gone.

As the candles got lower, and the log flared less often, weird lights and shades, such as haunt the twilight, crept about the room. The tutor's shadow, longer, lanker, and more grotesque than himself mopped and mowed upon the wall beside him. The snapdragon burnt blue, and as the raisin-hunters stirred the flaming spirit, the ghastly light made the tutor look so hideous that the widow's little boy was on the eve of howling, and spilled the raisins he had just secured. (He did not like putting his fingers into the flames, but he hovered near the more adventurous school-boys and collected the raisins that were scattered on the table by the hasty *grabs* of braver hands.

The widow was a relative of the house. She had married a Mr. Jones, and having been during his life his devoted slave, had on his death transferred her allegiance to his son. The late Mr. Jones was a small man with a strong temper, and large appetite, and a taste for drawing-room theatricals. So Mrs. Jones had called her son Macready; "for," she said, "his poor papa would have made a fortune on the stage, and I wish to commemorate his talents. Besides, Macready sounds better than Jones than a commoner Christian name would do."

But his cousins called him MacGreedy.

"The apples of the enchanted garden were guarded by dragons. Many knights went after them. One wished for the apples, but he did not like to fight the dragons."

It was the tutor who spoke from the dark corner by the fire-place. His eyes shone like a cat's, and MacGreedy felt like a half-scared mouse, and made up his mind to cry. He put his right fist into one eye, and had just taken it out, and was about to put his left fist into the other, when he saw that the tutor was no longer looking at him. So he made up his mind to go on with the raisins, for one can have a peevish cry at any time, but plums are not scattered broadcast every day. Several times he had tried to pocket them, but just at the moment the tutor was sure to look at him, and in his fright he dropped the raisins, and never could find them again. So this time he resolved to eat them then and there. He had just put one into his mouth when the tutor leaned forward, and his eyes, glowing in the firelight, met MacGreedy's, who had not even the presence of mind to shut his mouth, but remained spellbound, with a raisin in his cheek.

Flicker, flack! The school-boys stirred up snapdragon again, and with the blue light upon his features the tutor made so horrible a grimace that MacGreedy swallowed the raisin with a start. He had bolted it whole, and it might have been a bread pill for any enjoyment he had of the flavour. But the tutor laughed aloud. He certainly was an alarming object, pulling those grimaces in the blue brandy glare; and unpleasantly like a picture of Bogy himself with horns and a tail, in a juvenile volume upstairs. True, there were no horns to speak of among the tutor's grizzled curls, and his coat seemed to fit as well as most people's on his long back, so that unless he put his tail in his pocket, it is difficult to see how he could have had one. But then (as Miss Letitia said) "With dress one can do anything and hide anything," and on dress Miss Letitia's opinion was final.

Miss Letitia was a cousin. She was dark, high-coloured, glossy-haired, stout, and showy. She was as neat as a new pin, and had a will of her own. Her hair was firmly fixed by bandoline, her garibaldis by an arrangement which failed when applied to those of the widow, and her opinions by the simple process of looking at everything from one point of view. Her *forte* was dress and general ornamentation; not that Miss Letitia was extravagant—far from it. If one may use the expression, she utilized for ornament a hundred bits and scraps that most people would have wasted. But, like other artists, she saw everything from the medium of her own art. She looked at birds with an eye to hats, and at flowers with reference to evening parties. At picture exhibitions and concerts she carried away jacket patterns and bonnets in her head, as other people make mental notes of an aërial effect or a bit of fine instrumentation. An enthusiastic horticulturist once sent Miss Letitia cut specimen of a new flower. It was a lovely spray from a lately-imported shrub. A botanist would have pressed it—an artist must have taken its portrait—a poet might have written a sonnet in praise of its beauty. Miss Letitia twisted a piece of wire round its stem, and fastened it on to her black lace bonnet. It came on the day of a review, when Miss Letitia had to appear in a carriage, and it was quite a success. As she said to the widow, "It was so natural that no one could doubt its being Parisian."

"What a strange fellow that tutor is!" said the visitor. He spoke to the daughter of the house, a girl with a face like a summer's day, and hair like a ripe corn-field rippling in the sun. He was a fine young man, and had a youth's taste for the sports and amusements of his age. But lately he had changed. He seemed to himself to be living in a higher, nobler atmosphere than hitherto. He had discovered that he was poetical—he might prove to be a genius. He certainly was eloquent; he could talk for hours, and did so—to the young lady with the sunshiny face. They spoke on the highest subjects, and what a listener she was! So intelligent and appreciative, and with such an exquisite *pose* of the head—it must inspire a block of wood merely to see such a creature in a listening attitude. As to our young friend, he poured forth volumes; he was really clever, and for her he became eloquent. To-night he spoke of Christmas, of time-honoured custom and old association; and what he said would have made a Christmas article for a magazine of the first class. He poured scorn on the cold nature that could not, and the affectation that would not, appreciate the domestic festivities of this sacred season. What, he asked, could be more delightful, more perfect than such a gathering as this, of the family circle round the Christmas hearth? He spoke with feeling, and it may be said with disinterested feeling, for he had not joined his family circle himself this Christmas, and there was a vacant place by the hearth of his own home.

"He is strange," said the young lady (she spoke of the tutor in answer to the above remark); "but I am very fond of him. He has been with us so long he is like one of the family; though we know as little of his history as we did on the day that he came."

"He looks clever," said the visitor. (Perhaps that is the least one can say for a fellow-creature who shows a great deal of bare skull, and is not otherwise good-looking.)

"He is clever," she answered, "wonderfully clever; so clever and so odd that sometimes I fancy he is hardly 'canny.' There is something almost supernatural about his acuteness and his ingenuity, but they are so kindly used; I wonder he has not brought out any playthings for us tonight."

"Playthings?" inquired the young man.

"Yes; on birthdays or festivals like this he generally brings out of those huge pockets of his. He has been all over the world, and he produces Indian puzzles, Japanese flower-buds that bloom in hot water, and German toys with complicated machinery, which I suspect him of manufacturing himself. I call him Godpapa Drosselmeyer, after that delightful old fellow in Hoffman's tale of the Nut Cracker."

"What's that about crackers?" inquired the tutor, sharply, his eyes changing colour like a fine opal.

"I am talking of *Nussnacker und Mausekönig*," laughed the young lady. "Crackers do not belong to Christmas; fireworks come on the 5th of November."

"Tut, tut!" said the tutor; "I always tell your ladyship that you are still a tom-boy at heart, as when I first came, and you climbed trees and pelted myself and my young students with horse-chestnuts. You think of crackers to explode at the heels of timorous old gentlemen in a November fog; but I mean bonbon crackers, coloured crackers, dainty crackers—crackers for young people with mottoes of sentiment" (here the tutor shrugged his high shoulders an inch or two higher, and turned the palms of his hands outwards with a glance indescribably comical)—"crackers with paper prodigies, crackers with sweetmeats—*such* sweetmeats!" He smacked his lips with a grotesque contortion, and looked at Master MacGreedy, who choked himself with his last raisin, and forthwith burst into tears.

The widow tried in vain to soothe him with caresses, but he only stamped and howled the more. But Miss Letitia gave him some smart smacks on the shoulders to cure his choking fit, and as she kept up the treatment with vigour, the young gentleman was obliged to stop and assure her that the raisin had "gone the right way" at last. "If he were my child," Miss Letitia had been known to observe, with that confidence which characterizes the theories of those who are not parents, "I would, etc., etc., etc.;" in fact, Miss Letitia thought she would have made a very different boy of him—as, indeed, I believe she would.

"Are crackers all that you have for us, sir?" asked one of the two school-boys, as they hung over the tutor's chair. They were twins, grand boys, with broad, good-humoured faces, and curly wigs, as like as two puppy dogs of the same breed. They were only known apart by their intimate friends, and were always together, romping, laughing, snarling, squabbling, huffing and helping each other against the world. Each of them owned a wiry terrier, and in their relations to each other the two dogs (who were marvelously alike) closely followed the example of their masters.

"Do you not care for crackers, Jim?" asked the tutor.

"Not much, sir. They do for girls: but, as you know, I care for nothing but military matters. Do you remember that beautiful toy of yours—'The Besieged City'? Ah! I liked that. Look out, Tom! You're shoving my arm. Can't you stand straight, man?"

"R-r-r-r—r-r, snap!"

Tom's dog was resenting contact with Jim's dog on the hearthrug. There was a hustle among the four, and then they subsided.

"The Besieged City was all very well for you, Jim," said Tom, who meant to be a sailor; "but please to remember that it admitted of no attack from the sea; and what was there for me to do? Ah, sir! You are so clever, I often think you could help me to make a swing with ladders instead of single ropes, so that I could run up and down the rigging whilst it was in full go."

"That would be something like your fir-tree prank, Tom," said his sister. "Can you believe," she added, turning to the visitor, "that Tom lopped the branches of a tall young fir-tree all the way up, leaving little bits for foothold, and then climbed up it one day in an awful storm of wind, and clung on at the top, rocking backwards and forwards? And when Papa sent word for him to come down, he said parental authority was superseded at sea by the rules of the service. It was a dreadful storm, and the tree snapped very soon after he got safely to the ground."

"Storm!" sneered Tom, "a capful of wind. Well, it did blow half a gale at the last. But oh! It was glorious!"

"Let us see what we can make of the crackers," said the tutor—and he pulled some out of his pocket. They were put in a dish upon the table, for the company to choose from; and the terriers jumped and snapped, and tumbled over each other, for they thought that the plate contained eatables. Animated by the same idea, but with quieter steps, Master MacGreedy also approached the table.

"The dogs are noisy," said the tutor, "too noisy. We must have quiet—peace and quiet." His lean hand was once more in his pocket, and he pulled out a box, from which he took some powder, which he scattered on the burning log. A slight smoke now rose from the hot embers, and floated into the room. Was the powder one of those strange compounds that act upon the brain? Was it a magician's powder? Who knows? With it came a sweet, subtle fragrance. It was strange—everyone fancied that he had smelt it before, and all were absorbed in wondering what it was, and where they had met with it. Even the dogs sat on their haunches with their noses up, sniffing in a speculative manner.

"It's not lavender," said the grandmother, slowly, "and it's not rosemary. There is something of tansy in it (and a very fine tonic flavour too, my dears, though it's *not* in fashion now). Depend upon it, it's a potpourri, and from an excellent recipe, sir"—and the old lady bowed courteously towards the tutor. "My mother made the best potpourri in the county, and it was very much like this. Not quite, perhaps, but much the same, much the same."

The grandmother was a fine old gentlewoman "of the old school," as the phrase is. She was very stately and gracious in her manners, daintily neat in her person, and much attached to the old parson of the parish, who now sat near her chair. All her life she had been very proud of her fine stock of fair linen, both household and personal; and for many years past she had kept her own graveclothes ready in a drawer. They were bleached as white as snow, and lay amongst bags of dried lavender and potpourri. Many times had it seemed likely that they would be needed, for the old lady had had severe illnesses of late, when the good parson sat by her bedside, and read to her of the coming of the Bridegroom, and of that "fine linen clean and white," which is "the righteousness of the saints." It was of that drawer, with its lavender and potpourri bags, that the scented smoke had reminded her.

"It has rather an overpowering odour," said the old parson; "it is suggestive of incense. I am sure I once smelt something like it in the Church of the Nativity at Bethlehem. It is very delicious."

The Parson's long residence in his parish had been marked by one great holiday. With the savings of many years he had performed a pilgrimage to the Holy Land; and it was rather a joke against him that he illustrated a large variety of subjects by reference to his favourite topic, the holiday of his life.

"It smells of gunpowder," said Jim, decidedly, "and something else. I can't tell what."

"Something one smells in a seaport town," said Tom.

"Can't be very delicious, then," Jim retorted.

"It's not *quite* the same," piped the widow; "but it reminds me very much of an old bottle of attar of roses that was given to me when I was at school, with a copy of verses, by a young gentleman who was brother to one of the pupils. I remember Mr. Jones was quite annoyed when he found it in an old box, where I am sure I had not touched it for ten years or more; and I never spoke to him, but once, on Examination Day (the young gentleman, I mean). And it's like—yes it's certainly like a hair wash Mr. Jones used to use. I've forgotten what it was called, but I know it cost fifteen shillings a bottle; and Macready threw one over a few weeks before his dear papa's death, and annoyed him extremely."

Whilst the company were thus engaged, Master MacGreedy took advantage of the general abstraction to secure half-a-dozen crackers to his own share; he retired to a corner with them, where he meant to pick them quietly to pieces by himself. He wanted the gay paper, and the motto, and the sweetmeats; but he did not like the report of the cracker. And then what he did want, he wanted all to himself.

"Give us a cracker," said Master Jim, dreamily.

The dogs, after a few dissatisfied snorts, had dropped from their sitting posture, and were lying close together on the rug, dreaming and uttering short commenting barks and whines at intervals. The twins were now reposing lazily at the tutor's feet, and did not feel disposed to exert themselves even so far as to fetch their own bonbons.

"There's one," said the tutor, taking a fresh cracker from his pocket. One end of it was of red and gold paper, the other of transparent green stuff with silver lines. The boys pulled it.

◆　　◆　　◆

The report was louder than Jim had expected.

"The firing has begun," he murmured, involuntarily; "steady, steady!" These last words to his horse, who seemed to be moving under him, not from fear, but from impatience. What had been the red and gold paper of the cracker was now the scarlet and gold lace of his own cavalry uniform. He knocked a speck from his sleeve, and scanned the distant ridge, from which a thin line of smoke floated solemnly away, with keen, impatient eyes. Were they to stand inactive all the day?

Presently the horse erects his head. His eyes sparkle—he pricks his sensitive ears—his nostrils quiver with a strange delight. It is the trumpet! Fan farrâ! Fan farrâ! The brazen voice speaks—the horses move—the plumes wave—the helmets shine. On a summer's day they ride slowly, gracefully, calmly down a slope, to Death or Glory. Fan ferrâ! Fan ferrâ! Fan ferrâ!

◆　　◆　　◆

Of all this Master Tom knew nothing. The report of the cracker seemed to him only an echo in the brain of a sound that had been in his ears for thirty-six weary hours. The noise of a heavy sea beating against the ship's side in a gale. It was over now, and he was keeping the midnight watch on deck, gazing upon the liquid green of the waves, which, heaving and seething after storm, were lit with phosphoric light, and as the ship held steadily on her course, poured past at the rate of twelve knots an hour in a silvery stream. Faster than any ship can sail his thoughts travelled home; and as old times came back to him, he hardly knew whether what he looked at was the phosphor-lighted sea, or green gelatine paper barred with silver. And did the tutor speak? Or was it the voice of some sea-monster sounding in his ears?

"The spirits of the storm have gone below to make their report. The treasure gained from sunk vessels has been reckoned, and the sea is illuminated in honour of the spoil."

◆　　◆　　◆

The visitor now took a cracker and held it to the young lady. Her end was of white paper with a raised pattern; his of a dark-blue gelatine with gold stars. It snapped, the bonbon dropped between them, and the young man got the motto. It was a very bald one—

> My heart is thine.
> Wilt thou be mine?

He was ashamed to show it to her. What could be more meagre? One could write a hundred better couplets "standing on one leg," as the saying is. He was trying to improvise just one for the occasion, when he became aware that the blue sky over his head was dark with the shades of night, and lighted with stars. A brook rippled near with a soothing monotony. The evening wind sighed through the trees, and wafted the fragrance of the sweet bay-leaved willow towards him, and blew a stray lock of hair against his face. Yes! *She* also was there, walking beside him, under the scented willow-bushes. Where, why, and whither he did not ask to know. She was with him—with him; and he seemed to tread on the summer air.

He had no doubt as to the nature of his own feelings for her, and here was such an opportunity for declaring them as might never occur again. Surely now, if ever, he would be eloquent! Thoughts of poetry clothed in words of fire must spring unbidden to his lips at such a moment. And yet somehow he could not find a single word to say. He beat his brains, but not an idea would come forth. Only that idiotic cracker motto, which haunted him with its meagre couplet:

> My heart is thine.
> Wilt thou be mine?

Meanwhile they wandered on. The precious time was passing. He must at least make a beginning.

"What a fine night it is!" he observed. But, oh dear! That was a thousand times balder and more meagre than the cracker motto; and not another word could he find to say. At this moment the awkward silence was broken by a voice from a neighbouring copse. It was a nightingale singing to its mate. There was no lack of eloquence, and of melodious eloquence, there. The song was as plaintive as old memories, and as full of tenderness as the eyes of the young girl were full of tears. They were standing still now, and with her graceful head bent she was listening to the bird. He stooped his head near hers, and spoke with a simple natural outburst almost involuntary.

"Do you ever think of old times? Do you remember the old house, and the fun we used to have? And the tutor whom you pelted with horse-chestnuts when you were a little girl? And those cracker bonbons, and the motto *we* drew—

> My heart is thine.
> Wilt thou be mine?

She smiled, and lifted her eyes ("blue as the sky, and bright as the stars," he thought) to his, and answered "Yes."

Then the bonbon motto was avenged, and there was silence. Eloquent, perfect, complete, beautiful silence! Only the wind sighed through the fragrant willows, the stream rippled, the stars shone, and in the neighbouring copse the nightingale sang, and sang, and sang.

◆   ◆   ◆

When the white end of the cracker came into the young lady's hand, she was full of admiration for the fine raised pattern. As she held it between her fingers it suddenly struck her that she had discovered what the tutor's fragrant smoke smelt like. It was like the scent of orange-flowers, and had certainly a soporific effect upon the senses. She felt very sleepy, and as she stroked the shiny surface of the cracker she found herself thinking it was very soft for paper, and then rousing herself with a start, and wondering at her own folly in speaking thus of the white silk in which she was dressed, and of which she was holding up the skirt between her finger and thumb, as if she were dancing a minuet.

"It's Grandmamma's egg-shell brocade!" she cried. "Oh, Grandmamma! Have you given it to me? That lovely old thing! But I thought it was the family wedding-dress, and that I was not to have it till I was a bride."

"And so you are, my dear. And a fairer bride the sun never shone on," sobbed the old lady, who was kissing and blessing her, and wishing her, in the word of the old formula—

> Health to wear it,
> Strength to tear it,
> And money to buy another.

"There is no hope for the last two things, you know," said the young girl; "for I am sure that the flag that braved a thousand years was not half so strong as your brocade; and as to buying another, there are none to be bought in these degenerate days."

The old lady's reply was probably very gracious, for she liked to be complimented on the virtues of old things in general, and for her egg-shell brocade in particular. But of what she said her granddaughter heard nothing. With the strange irregularity of dreams, she found herself, she knew not how, in the old church. It was true. She was a bride, standing there with old friends and old associations thick around her, on the threshold of a new life. The sun shone through the stained glass of the windows, and illuminated the brocade, whose old-fashioned stiffness so became her childish beauty, and flung a thousand new tints over her sunny hair, and drew so powerful a fragrance from the orange-blossom with which it was twined, that it was almost overpowering. Yes! It was too sweet—too strong. She certainly would not be able to bear it much longer without losing her senses. And the service was going on. A question had been asked of her, and she must reply. She made a strong effort, and said, "Yes," simply and very earnestly, for it was what she meant. But she had no sooner said it than she became uneasily conscious that she had not used the right words. Someone laughed. It was the tutor, and his voice jarred and disturbed the dream, as a stone troubles the surface of still water. The vision trembled, and then broke, and the young lady found herself still sitting by the table and fingering the cracker paper, whilst the tutor chuckled and rubbed his hands by the fire, and his shadow scrambled on the wall like an ape upon a tree. But her "Yes" had passed into the young man's dream without disturbing it, and he dreamt on.

◆   ◆   ◆

It was a cracker like the preceding one that the grandmother and the parson pulled together. The old lady had insisted upon it. The good rector had shown a tendency to low spirits this evening, and a wish to withdraw early. But the old lady did not approve of people "shirking" (as boys say) either their duties or their pleasures; and to keep a "merry Christmas" in a family circle that had been spared to meet in health and happiness, seemed to her to be both the one and the other.

It was his sermon for the next day which weighed on the parson's mind. Not that he was behindhand with that part of his duties. He was far too methodical in his habits for that, and it had been written before the bustle of Christmas week began. But after preaching Christmas sermons from the same pulpit for thirty-five years, he felt keenly how difficult it is to awaken due interest in subjects that are so familiar, and to give new force to lessons so often repeated. So he wanted a quiet hour in his own study before he went to rest, with the sermon that did not satisfy him, and the subject that should be so heart-stirring and ever-new,—the story of Bethlehem.

He consented, however, to pull one cracker with the grandmother, though he feared the noise might startle her nerves, and said so.

"Nerves were not invented in my young days," said the old lady, firmly; and she took her part in the ensuing explosion without so much as a wink.

As the cracker snapped, it seemed to the parson as if the fragrant smoke from the yule log were growing denser in the room. Through the mist from time to time the face of the tutor loomed large, and then disappeared. At last the clouds rolled away, and the parson breathed clear air. Clear, yes, and how clear! The brilliant freshness, these intense lights and shadows, this mildness and purity in the night air—

"It is not England," he muttered. "It is the East. I have felt no air like this since I breathed the air of Palestine."

Over his head, through immeasurable distances, the dark blue space was lighted by the great multitude of the stars, whose glittering ranks have in that atmosphere a distinctness and a glory unseen with us. Perhaps no scene of beauty in the visible creation has proved a more hackneyed theme for the poet and the philosopher than a starry night. But not all the superabundance of simile and moral illustration with which the subject has been loaded can rob the beholder of the freshness of its grandeur or the force of its teaching; that noblest and most majestic vision of the handiwork of God on which the eye of man is here permitted to rest.

As the parson gazed he became conscious that he was not alone. Other eyes besides his were watching the skies to-night. Dark, profound, patient, Eastern eyes, used from the cradle to the grave to watch and wait. The eyes of star-gazers and dream-interpreters; men who believed the fate of empires to be written in shining characters on the face of heaven, as, the "Mene, Mene" was written in fire on the walls of the Babylonian palace. The old parson was one of the many men of real learning and wide reading who pursue their studies in the quiet country parishes of England, and it was with the keen interest of intelligence that he watched the group of figures that lay near him.

"Is this a vision of the past?" he asked himself. "There can be no doubt as to these men. They are star-gazers, magi, and, from their dress and bearing, men of high rank; perhaps 'teachers of a higher wisdom' in one of the purest philosophies of the old heathen world. When one thinks," he pursued, "of the intense interest, the eager excitement which the student of history finds in the narrative of the past as unfolded in dusty records written by the hand of man, one may realize how absorbing must have been that science which professed to unveil the future, and to display to the eyes of the wise the fate of dynasties written with the finger of God amid the stars."

The dark-robed figures were so still that they might almost have been carved in stone. The air seemed to grow purer and purer; the stars shone brighter and brighter; suspended in ether the planets seemed to hang like lamps. Now a shooting meteor passed athwart the sky, and vanished behind the hill. But not for this did the watchers move; in silence they watched on—till, on a sudden, how and whence the parson knew not, across the shining ranks of that immeasurable host, whose names and number are known to God alone, there passed in slow but obvious motion one brilliant solitary star—a star of such surpassing brightness that he involuntarily joined in the wild cry of joy and greeting with which the Men of the East now prostrated themselves with their faces to the earth.

He could not understand the language in which, with noisy clamour and gesticulation, they broke their former profound and patient silence, and greeted the portent for which they had watched. But he knew now that these were the Wise Men of the Epiphany, and that this was the Star of Bethlehem. In his ears rang the energetic simplicity of the Gospel narrative, "When they saw the Star, they rejoiced with exceeding great joy."

With exceeding great joy! Ah! Happy Magi, who (more blest than Balaam the son of Beor) were faithful to the dim light vouchsafed to you; the Gentile Church may well be proud of your memory. Ye travelled long and far to bring royal offerings to the King of the Jews, with a faith not found in Israel. Ye saw Him whom prophets and kings had desired to see, and were glad. Wise men indeed, and wise with the highest wisdom, in that ye suffered yourselves to be taught of God.

Then the parson prayed that if this were indeed a dream he might dream on; might pass, if only in a vision, over the hill, following the footsteps of the Magi, whilst the Star went before them, till he should see it rest above that city, which, little indeed among the thousands of Judah, was yet the birthplace of the Lord's Christ.

"Ah!" he almost sobbed, "let me follow! On my knees let me follow into the house and see the Holy Child. In the eyes of how many babies I have seen mind and thought far beyond their powers of communication, every mother knows. But if at times, with a sort of awe, one sees the immortal soul shining through the prison-bars of helpless infancy, what, oh! What must it be to behold the God-head veiled in flesh through the face of a little child!"

The parson stretched out his arms, but even with the passion of his words the vision began to break. He dared not move for fear it should utterly fade, and as he lay still and silent, the wise men roused their followers, and, led by the Star, the train passed solemnly over the distant hills.

Then the clear night became clouded with a fragrant vapour, and with a sigh the parson awoke.

◆　　◆　　◆

When the cracker snapped and the white end was left in the grandmother's hand, she was astonished to perceive (as she thought) that the white lace veil which she had worn over her wedding bonnet was still in her possession, and that she was turning it over in her fingers. "I fancied I gave it to Jemima when her first baby was born," she muttered dreamily. It was darned and yellow, but it carried her back all the same, and recalled happy hours with wonderful vividness. She remembered the post-chaise and the postillion. "He was such a pert little fellow, and how we laughed at him! He must be either dead or a very shaky old man by now," said the old lady. She seemed to smell the scent of meadow-sweet that was so powerful in a lane through which they drove; and how clearly she could see the clean little country inn where they spent their honeymoon! She seemed to be there now, taking off her bonnet and shawl, in the quaint clean chamber, with the heavy oak rafters, and the jasmine coming in at the window, and glancing with pardonable pride at the fair face reflected in the mirror. But as she laid her things on the patchwork coverlet, it seemed to her that the lace veil became fine white linen, and was folded about a figure that lay on the bed; and when she looked round the room again everything was draped in white—white blinds hung before the windows, and even the old oak chest and the press were covered with clean white cloths, after the decent custom of the country; whilst from the church tower without the passing bell tolled slowly. She had not seen the face of the corpse, and a strange anxiety came over her to count the strokes of the bell, which tell if it is a man, woman, or child who has passed away. One, two, three, four, five, six, seven! No more. It was a woman, and when she looked at the face of the dead she saw her own. But even as she looked the fair linen of the grave-clothes became the buoyant drapery of another figure, in whose face she found a strange recognition of the lineaments of the dead with all the loveliness of the bride. But ah! More, much more! On that face was a beauty not doomed to wither. Before those happy eyes lay a future unshadowed by the imperfections of earthy prospects, and the folds of that robe as no fuller on earth can white them. The window curtain parted, the jasmine flowers bowed their heads, the spirit passed from the chamber of death, and the old lady's dream was ended.

◆ ◆ ◆

Miss Letitia had shared a cracker with the widow. The widow squeaked when the cracker went off, and then insisted upon giving up the smart paper and everything to Miss Letitia. She had always given up everything to Mr. Jones; she did so now to Master MacGreedy, and was quite unaccustomed to keep anything for her own share. She did not give this explanation herself, but so it was.

The cracker that thus fell into the hands of Miss Letitia was one of those new-fashioned ones that have a paper pattern of some article of dress wrapped up in them instead of a bonbon. This one was a paper bonnet made in the latest *mode*—of green tissue-paper; and Miss Letitia stuck it on the top of her chignon with an air that the widow envied from the bottom of her heart. She had not the gift of "carrying off" her clothes. But to the tutor, on the contrary, it seemed to afford the most extreme amusement; and as Miss Letitia bowed gracefully hither and thither in the energy of her conversation with the widow, the green paper fluttering with each emphasis, he fairly shook with delight, his shadow dancing like a maniac beside him. He had scattered some more powder on the coals, and it may have been that the smoke got into her eyes, and confused her ideas of colour, but Miss Letitia was struck with a fervid and otherwise unaccountable admiration for the paper ends of the cracker, which were most unusually ugly. One was of a sallowish salmon-colour, and transparent; the other was of brick-red paper with a fringe. As Miss Letitia turned them over, she saw, to her unspeakable delight, that there were several yards of each material, and her peculiar genius instantly seized upon the fact that in the present rage for double skirts there might be enough of the two kinds to combine into a fashionable dress.

It had never struck her before that a dirty salmon went well with brick-red. "They blend so becomingly, my dear," she murmured; "and I think the under-skirt will sit well; it is so stiff."

The widow did not reply. The fumes of the tutor's compound made her sleepy, and though she nodded to Miss Letitia's observations, it was less from appreciation of their force, than from inability to hold up her head. She was dreaming uneasy, horrible dreams like nightmares in which from time to time there mingled expressions of doubt and dissatisfaction which fell from Miss Letitia's lips. "Just half-a-yard short—no gores—false hem," (and the melancholy reflection that) "flounces take so much stuff." Then the tutor's face kept appearing and vanishing with horrible grimaces through the mist. At last the widow fell fairly asleep, and dreamed that she was married to the Blue Beard of nursery annals, and that on his return from his memorable journey he had caught her in the act of displaying the mysterious cupboard to Miss Letitia. As he waved his scimitar over her head, he seemed unaccountably to assume the form and features of the tutor. In her agitation the poor woman could think of no plea against his severity, except that the cupboard was already crammed with the corpses of his previous wives, and there was no room for her. She was pleading this argument when Miss Letitia's voice broke in upon her dream with decisive accent:

"There's enough for two bodies."

The widow shrieked and awoke.

"High and low," explained Miss Letitia. "My dear, what *are* you screaming about?"

"I am very sorry indeed," said the widow; "I beg your pardon, I'm sure, a thousand times. But since Mr. Jones's death I have been so nervous, and I had such a horrible dream. And, oh dear! oh dear!" she added, "what is the matter with my precious child? Macready, love, come to your mamma, my pretty lamb."

"Ugh! Ugh!" There were groans from the corner where Master MacGreedy sat on his crackers as if they were eggs, and he hatching them. He had only touched one, as yet, of the stock he had secured. He had picked it to pieces, had avoided the snap, and had found a large comfit like an egg with a rough egg shell inside. Every one knows that the goodies in crackers are not of a very superior quality. There is a large amount of white lead in the outside thinly disguised by a shabby flavour of sugar. But that outside once disposed of, there lies an almond at the core. Now an almond is a very delicious thing in itself, and doubly nice when it takes the taste of white paint and chalk out of one's mouth. But in spite of all the white lead and sugar and chalk through which he had sucked his way, MacGreedy could not come to the almond. A dozen times had he been on the point of spitting out the delusive sweetmeat; but just as he thought of it he was sure to feel a bit of hard rough edge, and thinking he had gained the kernel at last, he held valiantly on. It only proved to be a rough bit of sugar, however, and still the interminable coating melted copiously in his mouth; and still the clean, fragrant almond evaded his hopes. At last with a groan he spat the seemingly undiminished bonbon on the floor, and turned as white and trembling as an arrowroot blanc-mange.

In obedience to the widow's entreaties the tutor opened a window, and tried to carry MacGreedy to the air; but that young gentleman utterly refused to allow the tutor to approach him, and was borne howling to bed by his mamma.

With the fresh air the fumes of the fragrant smoke dispersed, and the company aroused themselves.

"Rather oppressive, eh?" said the master of the house, who had had his dream too, with which we have no concern.

The dogs had had theirs also, and had testified to the same in their sleep by low growls and whines. Now they shook themselves, and rubbed against each other, growling in a warlike manner through their teeth, and wagging peaceably with their little stumpy tails.

The twins shook themselves, and fell to squabbling as to whether they had been to sleep or no; and, if either, which of them had given way to that weakness.

Miss Letitia took the paper bonnet from her head with a nervous laugh, and after looking regretfully at the cracker papers put them in her pocket.

The parson went home through the frosty night. In the village street he heard a boy's voice singing two lines of the Christian hymn—

Trace we the Babe Who hath redeemed our loss
From the poor Manger to the bitter Cross

—and his eyes filled with tears.

The old lady went to bed and slept in peace.

"In all the thirty-five years we have been privileged to hear you, sir," she told the rector next day after service, "I never heard such a Christmas sermon before."

The visitor carefully preserved the blue paper and the cracker motto. He came down early next morning to find the white half to put with them. He did not find it, for the young lady had taken it the night before.

The tutor had been in the room before him, wandering round the scene of the evening's festivities.

The yule log lay black and cold upon the hearth, and the tutor nodded to it. "I told you how it would be," he said; "but never mind, you have had your day, and a merry one too." In the corner lay the heap of crackers which Master MacGreedy had been too ill to remember when he retired. The tutor pocketed them with a grim smile.

As to the comfit, it was eaten by one of the dogs, who had come down earliest of all. He swallowed it whole, so whether it contained an almond or not remains a mystery to the present time.

CHAPTER 3

Too Much of a Good Thing: "Madam Liberality"

Almost from the time that Ewing's challenging story "Madam Liberality" appeared in *Aunt Judy's Magazine* (December 1873), readers were prone to connect the titular character with the author herself.[1] Those who knew something of her history were aware that certain details in the story, such as that involving the heroine's painful bout with a quinsy, seem to parallel episodes in Ewing's childhood. And since Juliana had once been referred to by a friend as being "Like little body with a mighty heart," and since she used that very quotation from Act 2 of Shakespeare's *King Henry V* as the story's epigraph, it has seemed that she was, indeed, the Madam Liberality of the story.

Once the connection was made in print, it became customary to assume that the work is autobiographical, especially since Juliana's sister, Horatia K. F. Eden, stated that such is the case. In her book about her sister, she wrote: "Certainly in her story of 'Madam Liberality' Mrs. Ewing drew a picture of her own character that can never be surpassed."[2] This statement from her sister seems to leave little doubt that in creating the character of Madam Liberality, Ewing had herself in mind. Marghanita Laski states that in dealing with the conflict within the character of Madam Liberality between generosity and economy, Ewing "is describing her own conflict in this score."[3]

In the main, however, critics and biographers have qualified their position somewhat by arguing that Ewing was not aware of the extent that Madam Liberality is a self-portrait. The most insistent of those convinced that Juliana Ewing and Madam Liberality are one and certainly the person most likely to know what she is talking about, Ewing's sister,

Horatia Eden, writes that even though it is clear that "Madam Liberality bears a wonderfully strong likeness to my sister," at the same time, "she [Juliana] did this quite unintentionally, I know."[4] Gillian Avery comments in her monograph that in the character of Madam Liberality, Ewing "had unconsciously drawn herself."[5]

Christabel Maxwell, however, cautioned about too readily identifying Madam Liberality with Ewing. She observes that writers at the time of and of the rather genteel background of Juliana Ewing avoided writing about themselves as a matter of principle and decorum, and she is sure that Ewing did likewise:

> Brought up in those days when "nice feeling" demanded proper humility when speaking of oneself, it always struck me as strange that Madam Liberality was stated by our elders and betters to refer to Mrs. Ewing herself. To write autobiographically under such a commendatory title seemed to me to be in very questionable taste. Now I realise that this was by no means her intention, and any likeness to the author can be said to be purely coincidental.[6]

Nevertheless, it seems unwise to overlook the fact that there are definite resemblances between Ewing and Madam Liberality; and Christabel Maxwell, though making an excellent point, may go too far when she claims that "any likeness" of Madam Liberality to Juliana Ewing "can be said to be purely coincidental."[7] While the resemblance between author and character is accompanied by extensive differences, the similarities should not be ignored or casually designated as coincidental. At the same time, Maxwell is undoubtedly correct that Ewing was not likely to create a character in her fiction that is an *overt* autobiographical duplicate of herself. But she could, and I believe did, create a character who was a version of herself as she feared she might become given her own strong belief in the virtue of unselfishness or liberality.

As an initial step in developing this theory, it is necessary to analyze in some detail what the narrator of the story, presumably Ewing herself, thinks of the protagonist, Madam Liberality. Does the story as a whole praise Madam Liberality? Is it a sort of tribute to her or to whomever she may represent? Is it a sympathetic portrayal?

It may be contrary to how many readers of "Madam Liberality" think of the protagonist, and it probably goes against the way the few informed critics and biographers who have written about the story interpret it, but it is nevertheless important to state here that "Madam Liberality" is not a tribute to the author. It is a character study of an imaginary person who in some ways resembles the author; it is a probing into the way that character's mind works. Contrary to how "Madam Liberality" has usually been interpreted, it is a rather sad story about a pathetic character, not an inspiring story about an admirable heroine who embodies the spirit of hope. The reason that it is misread is that its camouflage of sympathy is so cleverly articulated that it skillfully disguises what is under it as a sugar coating covers a bitter pill. The opening pages of the story illustrate the technique Ewing employs first to create sympathy for Madam Liberality because of her unending generosity, even when a child, and then to question her motivation for being unselfish. The story opens with what seems to be praise of the person who has been able to acquire such "a commendatory title,"[8] as has the protagonist of this story even in her childhood:

> It [Madam Liberality] was not her real name: it was given to her by her brothers and sister. People with very marked qualities of character do sometimes get such distinctive titles, to rectify the indefiniteness of those they inherit and those they receive in baptism. The ruling peculiarity of a character is apt to show itself early in life, and it showed itself in Madam Liberality when she was a little child.[9]

The authorial duplicity that runs through the story is in evidence here in the very first paragraph. Ewing seems to be saying that it was a compliment to Madam Liberality that she began to be called by that title from an early age, the reason being that she exhibited from that time an unusual degree of liberality, that is, generosity, and, of course, generosity, or unselfishness, is an unquestionable virtue. Such "distinctive titles," Ewing continues, are awarded when a "ruling peculiarity of a character" reveals itself, which often is in early life. That is to say, in this particular person, liberality was not merely an aspect of her personality but was the dominant aspect. Indeed, she was *ruled* by it.

When the opening paragraph is read carefully, especially when reread after one has finished the story, the sugar coating of praise begins to wear away and something not quite so sweet begins to show itself: namely, the all-important underlying message or theme of the story. It is an old truth. Socrates expressed it as "Know thyself." Aristotle expressed it as "Nothing in excess," the Golden Mean. In *As You Like It*, Shakespeare has Rosaline express the same idea as "Too much of a good thing." More modern philosophers of the practical have occasionally added to the phrase: "Too much of a good thing is not a good thing." However it is articulated, the idea is at the very heart of "Madam Liberality." It is about a woman who is fanatical about giving—too much of a good thing—and how this excess takes over her life.

It is clear that even in her later years when self-knowledge should add substantially to one's collective wisdom, Madam Liberality does not "know herself" in the Socratic sense and never has. Since childhood, her obsession with giving to members of her family, of being generous, has left her without a strong sense of who she is as a person. Generosity is a prized virtue when exercised in moderation, but when carried to the extreme to which she carries it, it becomes destructive to personal identity. She becomes self-less in the sense of having no strong core of self. She lives totally in the lives of others and for the satisfaction she derives from giving to them. The story never reveals her real name, never refers to her by any name other than that applied to her by others, by her brothers and sister to whom she has given everything, even her personal identity. She is known by her obsession; that has become her only identity: Madam Liberality: "And they called her Madam Liberality, so Madam Liberality she shall remain" (p. 260). She does, indeed, *remain* Madam Liberality, for her obsession with giving is lifelong.

When Ewing writes early in the story that "Madam Liberality kept her plums for other people" (p. 258), she is referring to more than the fruits found in plum cakes, which Madam Liberality tediously and meticulously picked out and saved so that she could have a kind of tea party and serve them to her siblings. Later in the story her godmother gives her a beautiful pink dress, but she immediately gives it to her sister, Darling. To

put it simply, she lives to give. But for what reason? What is her motive
for such liberality? Quite early in the story, Ewing indicates that all may
not be well in terms of her motivation:

> I have doubted whether Madam Liberality's besetting virtue
> were a virtue at all. Was it unselfishness or a love of approbation,
> benevolence or fussiness, the gift of sympathy or the lust of
> power? Or was it something else? She was a very sickly child,
> with much pain to bear, and many pleasures to forgo. Was it, as
> doctors say, "an effort of nature," to make her live outside herself
> and be happy in the happiness of others? (p. 259)

When Ewing writes, "I have doubted whether Madam Literality's
besetting virtue were a virtue at all," it is likely that she is writing about
herself and questioning the motive for her own gift-giving tendency,
a proclivity which she obviously enjoyed, probably overly enjoyed as
she suspected when composing "Madam Liberality." Marghanita Laski
observes that Ewing's "generosity was a decisive factor in her nature."
As an example, she "devoted her first literary earnings to generous gifts
for other people."[10] She had a well-earned reputation for generosity. In
creating "Madam Liberality," she engaged in some serious soul searching
as to what was behind her drive to give, why it was so important to her,
and what it could do to her.

In the case of her fictional character, it is not as if she belonged to
an affluent family and had so much herself that she could easily afford
to give gifts freely to others. Ewing dwells frequently on the fact that
although Madam Liberality comes from a genteel background with rich
relations, her immediate family is quite poor: "It has been hinted that
there was a reason for the scarceness of the plums in the plum-cake.
Madam Liberality's father was dead, and her mother was very poor, and
had several children. It was not an easy matter with her to find bread
for the family, putting currants and raisins out of the question" (p. 260).

In such a situation, Madam Liberality's obsession with giving demands
that she scrimp and save with great skill and determination so that she
can practice her liberality. It is this quality in her, her severe "economy,"
that motivates her brother Tom to say to her while he is still quite young:

"You're the most meanest and the *generoustest* person I ever knew" (p. 275). By "meanest," he is referring to her habit of saving every cent that comes her way so that she may buy or make something for her siblings. When Tom accuses her of miserly proclivities, she weeps because "it was the touch of truth that made Madam Liberality cry. To the end of their lives Tom and she were alike and yet different in this manner. Madam Liberality saved, and pinched, and planned, and then gave away, and Tom gave away without the pinching and saving" (pp. 275–6). Long before Tom expressed his opinion of his sister's extreme economy, "Madam Liberality was pinching and plotting, and saving bits of coloured paper and ends of ribbon, with a thriftiness which seemed to justify Tom's view of her character" (p. 276).

Her "character" is that which is in question in the story. It is tempting to view her as a long suffering but eternally hopeful, self-abnegating saint who never really thinks of herself but spends her life thinking of and plotting what she can do for others, what she can give them that will make them happy, for it is only their praise of her for her gifts that keeps her going. Her early interests and endeavors are centered on two things: "birthday presents and Christmas boxes. They were the chief cares and triumphs of Madam Liberality's childhood" (p. 277).

The sustained and ingenious characterization that makes up "Madam Liberality" is in the final analysis not the portrait of an ideally unselfish person, though she has no doubt been viewed that way repeatedly. What underlies the often sympathetic tone of the narrative is a fatalism that creates more pathos than inspiration. By far the most persistent idea that runs through the story and, indeed, accounts for its structure—its division into two parts, the first dealing with Madam Liberality's childhood and the second with her adult life, later years and demise—is that of the unchanging nature of what rules her existence. That "ruling peculiarity," as Ewing calls it in the first paragraph of the story, begins ruling when she is in early childhood and rules her until she dies.

As the story reaches its conclusion, Ewing indulges in alternate descriptions of her later life. In one scenario, she inherits a great deal of money and is affluent until her death. In the alternate ending, she does not inherit wealth but remains in relative poverty. The point Ewing wishes to make in positing these alternative destinies is that no matter what happens to Madam Liberality, no matter what her environment, no matter how much money she has or how little, she will not change; she cannot change. She will always be Madam Liberality, which does not mean that she will remain the wonderfully hopeful and unselfish person she has always been but that the obsession with giving that has ruled her will continue to do so regardless of her circumstances.

Her life is riddled with disappointments. They are brought on by her imagination, which is a servant to the two dominant tendencies in her thinking: her unshakable dedication to hope and her unquenchable desire to give. Her ever-active imagination creates plans, sometimes rather elaborate plans, for giving—how she will gather the money or the material for gifts to family members especially during the Christmas season. Once her plans are laid out for giving, her imagination then creates for her lovely pictures of the praise she will receive and how happy she will be as a result of the approbation. Then comes the disappointment. At one time, she is able to gather together enough money to finance the elaborate plans she has for Christmas. Her mother gives the children a kind of reward when they have a tooth pulled: sixpence for a tooth without roots and a shilling for a tooth with roots. What Madam Liberality is willing to go through to obtain her shilling is indicative of the power of her obsession. She allows an assistant to dig out the roots of a tooth that have been left in her gums when the tooth was pulled during the same visit to the office of the old doctor. It is excruciatingly painful, but she even promises that she will sit perfectly still during the procedure. With almost superhuman control, she does sit still, collects the shilling from her mother but then loses it. When her mother takes care of that problem, another one follows. Christmas is coming, and she has imagined how her siblings will love what she has planned, but she becomes so ill with a quinsy that she cannot speak and has to write on a slate. She is confined to her bed through fever and pain. In Ewing's descriptions of these harrowing disappointments in the life of Madam Liberality, there is always a subtle indication in Ewing's treatment of them that the person to blame for all these terrible disappointments is Madam Liberality herself. For example, at one point, the narrator comments: "It is true that she was constantly planning; and if one builds castles, one must expect a few loose stones about one's ears now and then" (p. 268).

She is pathetic rather than heroic, and her troubles can be traced to her obsession with giving from which no disappointments can alienate her; no sickness can quiet the exciting plans created by her imagination.

To describe Madam Liberality's outlook on life, Ewing uses a term that exemplifies perfectly the authorial duality of the entire narrative. She is described as possessing "obdurate hopefulness" (p. 284). Hopefulness, of course, is a good thing. In this quotation, it represents that level of the story that seems to give us a warm feeling. To meet a character in fiction who seems to have a good deal of ill luck, as does Madam Liberality, but who never loses her hope, her optimism, her belief that the cloud has a silver lining—*that* is a character to be admired, even loved, for her persistent hope. But the other word in this two-word description represents the strong undercurrent of fatalism in the work. To be obdurate is to be unchanging, stubborn. Whatever happens, Madam Liberality will never be anything but—as it turns out—foolishly hopeful. Despite constant setbacks, she always hopes that the means will come to her to be able to give and give liberally. That is not reality but what is called in the story Madam Liberality's "visions" or "fancy," terms for her imagination. Ewing describes them as being brought on by the character's strong and unchanging desire to give. That is, the wish is so all-consuming that it creates in the imagination a fulfilling vision of how the wish will become a reality. Sometimes she even believes it has become a reality when it has not. When blunt reality forces itself into her life and destroys her plans, Madam Liberality is severely disappointed. But, as Ewing writes: "Madam Liberality was accustomed to disappointment" (p. 268). She puts it behind her and starts planning again.

It is inconceivable that in the character of Madam Liberality Ewing painted a flattering portrait of herself. What she did create is an imaginative version of what she thought she might have become or could become if her pleasure in giving to others dominated her life. In creating Madam Liberality, she revealed a remarkable insight into the obsessed human mind.[11] More than that, she proved that unlike the unwanted version of herself, she knew that the unexamined life is not worth living and that she could and would keep her own admirable liberality within the golden mean. By doing so, she thus retained her identity as Juliana

Ewing, the writer, and never lost her identity by becoming Madam Liberality, the giver.

"Madam Liberality" is Ewing's recognition that she had come to realize what causes the desire to give to others to transmute from the primary virtue, unselfishness, to the primary vice, selfishness. It is the addicting power of approbation, which acts as the catalyst in the transmutation. Madam Liberality is what she is because of her unquenchable hunger for the praise and gratitude she receives from others when she exercises her liberality. The act of giving has the power to make another person happy, and in addition to her craving for praise, she lusts for this power, which she experiences over and over. Thus, the questions that Ewing raises early in the story are more than questions: they are answers. The lines quoted earlier deserve to be quoted again: "I have doubted whether Madam Liberality's besetting virtue were a virtue at all. Was it unselfishness or a love of approbation, benevolence or fussiness, the gift of sympathy or the lust of power?" (p. 259).

In certain stories that were published after "Madam Liberality," Ewing continued to hold high the banner of unselfishness as the fountainhead of all virtues, but the characters in these stories who exemplify this admirable trait practice it in a different manner from Madam Liberality. The poisonous catalyst of praise is not an ingredient because the unselfish character has refused to allow it to be included. In "Ladders to Heaven," a short story published three years after "Madam Liberality," the protagonist, a monk who has charge of the monastery garden, discovers that some of the flowers that he plants there bring him praise and a degree of notoriety, which in turn feeds his pride and gives him a sense of worldly power. He examines himself, as Madam Liberality fails to do, and concludes that the flowers that would bring him approbation, for example, those called Ladders to Heaven (Lilies of the Valley), he will plant in another place outside the monastery, a place by the river. He will in a sense, then, give them to strangers who pass that way and can view and enjoy them without his receiving credit for planting and caring for them. They are, therefore, his ladders to heaven, inasmuch as he will not have incurred the sin of pride that would have resulted from his having received praise and fame for growing them had he used the monastery garden.

At some point in her life, Ewing read a book on religious orders and was apparently struck by the description of one group, Fratelli della Misericordia, which seemed to illustrate perfectly her idea of the nobility of giving without receiving credit for it, indeed, by giving without those who receive even knowing the identity of the givers. She doubtlessly thought that their insistence on secrecy was a way of preventing approbation from turning the unselfishness of the men of this unusual group into a form of selfishness. In 1877, she published "Brothers of Pity," a story in which this group plays an important role in inspiring the narrator, a young boy, to imitate their form of giving. The boy encounters the book on religious orders while he is playing in the study of his godfather, to whom he asks about an illustration in the volume: "The picture I'm looking at has two men dressed in black, with their faces covered all but their eyes, and they are carrying another man with something blue over him."[12] The boy's godfather identifies the group as the Fratelli della Misericordia, explains what they are doing, and why they have their faces covered:

> They belong to a body of men . . . who bind themselves to be ready in their turn to do certain offices of mercy, pity, and compassion to the sick, the dying, and the dead. The brotherhood is six hundred years old, and still exists. The men who belong to it receive no pay, and they equally reject the reward of public praise, for they work with covered faces, and are not known even to each other. Rich men and poor men, noble men and working men, men of letters and the ignorant, all belong to it, and each takes his turn when it comes round to nurse the sick, carry the dying to hospital, and bury the dead.[13]

In both "Ladders to Heaven" and "Brothers of Pity," the act of anonymous giving is portrayed as contagious. Long after Brother Benedict of the former story dies, his form of giving is carried on by a young boy to whom the idea of secret unselfishness strongly appeals. The same situation prevails in "Brothers of Pity." The boy is curious about the picture he sees in a book on religious orders and then hears his godfather's explanation of how the members of the Fratelli della Misericordia go about the work of its members giving their time and efforts without ever revealing their identities. This secret benevolencce appeals dramatically to the boy, who manages to have a mask made for him and then begins his secret acts of burying dead animals, an act of giving that reflects his unselfishness inasmuch as no one knows about it.

Ewing's final treatment of secret unselfishness is her late work, *Mary's Meadow*. A book by Alphonse Karr, *A Tour Round My Garden* (1855), plays a significant role in *Mary's Meadow*. In brief, Karr's book becomes a guidebook in teaching the children of the story the importance and nobility of unselfish giving in the context of gardening. From the opening words of the novel, it is clear that self-denial will be a principal theme, for that is how the story opens—upon Mary's recounting of how she and her siblings have been constantly reminded by their mother to exercise unselfishness, not for any personal reward but simply because it is the right thing to do.

These later writings, "Ladders to Heaven," "Brothers of Pity," and *Mary's Meadow,* all portray characters who avoid the pathetic path through life taken by Madam Liberality. Unlike Madam Liberality, who lives for the praise and power generated by her gifts to others, the protagonists of these later stories are drawn by something in their character, their nature, to a different kind of liberality: that which does not evoke praise and produce a sense of power, those tempting rewards that make Madam Liberality what she is, a sad, obsessed soul, the slave of motivations that she does not even realize are motivations.

Madam Liberality

Part I

"Like little body with a mighty heart."

King Henry V, Act 2

It was not her real name: it was given to her by her brothers and sister. People with very marked qualities of character do sometimes get such distinctive titles, to rectify the indefiniteness of those they inherit and those they receive in baptism. The ruling peculiarity of a character is apt to show itself early in life, and it showed itself in Madam Liberality when she was a little child.

Plum-cakes were not plentiful in her home when Madam Liberality was young, and such as there were, were of the "wholesome" kind—plenty of bread-stuff, and the currants and raisins at a respectful distance from each other. But few as the plums were, she seldom ate them. She picked them out very carefully, and put them into a box, which was hidden under her pinafore.

When we grown-up people were children, and plum-cake and plum-pudding tasted very much nicer than they do now, we also picked out the plums. Some of us ate them at once, and had then to toil slowly through the cake or pudding, and some valiantly dispatched the plainer portion of the feast at the beginning, and kept the plums to sweeten the end. Sooner or later we ate them ourselves, but Madam Liberality kept her plums for other people.

When the vulgar meal was over—that commonplace refreshment ordained and superintendent by the elders of the household—Madam Liberality would withdraw into a corner, from which she issued notes of invitation to all the dolls. They were "fancy written" on curl papers and folded into cocked hats.

Then began the real feast. The dolls came, and the children with them. Madam Liberality had no toy tea-sets or dinner-sets, but there were acorn-cups filled to the brim, and the water tasted deliciously, though it came out of the ewer in the night nursery, and had not even been filtered. And before every doll was a flat oyster-shell covered with a round oyster-shell, a complete set of complete pairs, which had been collected by degrees, like old family plate. And when the upper shell was raised, on every dish lay a plum. It was then that Madam Liberality got her sweetness out of the cake.

She was in her glory at the head of the inverted tea-chest; and if the raisins would not go round, the empty oyster-shell was hers, and nothing offended her more than to have this noticed. That was her spirit, then and always. She could "do without" anything, if the wherewithal to be hospitable was left to her.

When one's brain is no stronger than mine is, one gets very much confused in disentangling motives and nice points of character. I have doubted whether Madam Liberality's besetting virtue were a virtue at all. Was it unselfishness or a love of approbation, benevolence or fussiness, the gift of sympathy or the lust of power? Or was it something else? She was a very sickly child, with much pain to bear, and many pleasures to forgo. Was it, as doctors say, "an effort of nature," to make her live outside herself and be happy in the happiness of others?

Equal doubt may hang over the conduct of her brothers and sister toward her. Did they more love her, or find her useful? Was their gratitude—as gratitude has been defined to be—"a keen sense of favors to come"? They certainly got used to her services, and to begging and borrowing the few things that were her "very own," without fear of refusal. But if they rather took her benevolence for granted, and thought that she "liked lending her things," and that it was her way of enjoying possessions, they may have been right; for next to one's own soul, one's own family is perhaps the best judge of one's temper and disposition.

And they called her Madam Liberality, so Madam Liberality she shall remain.

It has been hinted that there was a reason for the scarceness of the plums in the plum-cake. Madam Liberality's father was dead, and her mother was very poor, and had several children. It was not an easy matter with her to find bread for the family, putting currants and raisins out of the question.

Though poor, they were, however, gentle-folk, and had, for that matter, rich relations. Very rich relations, indeed! Madam Liberality's mother's first cousin had fifteen thousand a year. His servants did not spend ten thousand. (As to what he spent himself, it was comparatively trifling.) The rest of the money accumulated. Not that it was being got together to do something with by and by. He had no intention of ever spending more than he spent at present. Indeed, with a lump of coal taken off here, and a needless candle blown out there, he rather hoped in the future to spend less.

His wife was Madam Liberality's godmother. She was a good-hearted woman, and took real pleasure in being kind to people, in the way she thought best for them. Sometimes it was a graceful and appropriate way, and very often it was not. The most acceptable act of kindness she ever did to her god-daughter was when the child was recovering from an illness, and she asked her to visit her at the seaside.

Madam Liberality had never seen the sea, and the thought of it proved a better stimulus than the port wine which the doctor ordered so easily, and her mother got with such difficulty.

When new clothes were bought, or old ones refurbished, Madam Liberality, as a rule, went to the wall. Not because her mother was ever guilty of favouritism, but because such occasions afforded an opportunity of displaying generosity towards her younger sister.

But this time it was otherwise; for whatever could be spared towards "summer things" for the two little girls was spent upon Madam Liberality's outfit for the seaside. There was a new dress, and a jacket "as good as new," for it was cut out of "mother's" cloth cloak and made up, with the best bindings and buttons in the shop, by the village tailor. And he was bribed, in a secret visit, and with much coaxing from the little girls, to make real pockets instead of braided shams. The *second-best* frock was compounded of two which had hitherto been *very bests*—Madam Liberality's own, eked out by "Darling's" into a more fashionable fullness, and with a cape to match.

There was a sense of solid property to be derived from being able to take in at a glance the stock of well-mended under-garments, half of which were generally at the wash. Besides, they had been added to, and all the stockings were darned, and only one pair in the legs where it would show, below short petticoat mark.

Then there was a bonnet newly turned and trimmed, and a pair and a half of new boots, for surely boots are at least half new when they have been (as the village cobbler described it in his bill) "souled and healed."

Poor little Madam Liberality! When she saw the things that covered her bed in their abundance, it seemed to her an outfit for a princess. And yet when her godmother asked Podmore, the lady's-maid, "How is the child off for clothes?" Podmore unhesitatingly replied, "She've nothing fit to be seen, ma'am," which shows how differently the same things appear in different circumstances.

Podmore was a good friend to Madam Liberality. She had that open-handed spirit which one acquires quite naturally in a house where everything goes on on a large scale, at somebody else's expense. Now Madam Liberality's godmother, from the very largeness of her possessions, was obliged to leave the care of them to others, in such matters as food, dress, the gardens, the stables, etc. So, like many other people in a similar case, she amused herself and exercised her economical instincts by troublesome little thriftinessees, by making cheap presents, dear bargains, and so forth. She was by nature a managing woman; and when those very grand people, the butler, the housekeeper, the head-gardener, and the lady's-maid had divided her household duties among them, there was nothing left for her to be clever about, except such little matters as joining the fag-ends of the bronze sealing-wax sticks which lay in the silver inkstand on the malachite writing-table, and being good-natured at the cheapest rate at which her friends could be benefited.

Madam Liberality's best neckerchief had been very pretty when it was new, and would have been pretty as well as clean still if the washerwoman had not used rather too hot an iron on it, so that the blue in the check pattern was somewhat faded. And yet it had felt very smart as Madam Liberality drove in the carrier's cart to meet the coach at the outset of her journey. But when she sat against the rich blue leather of her godmother's coach as they drove up and down the esplanade, it was like looking at fairy jewels by daylight when they turn into faded leaves.

"Is that your best neckerchief, child?" said the old lady.

"Yes, ma'am," blushed Madam Liberality.

So when they got home her godmother went to her odds-and-ends drawer.

Podmore never interfered with this drawer. She was content to be despotic among the dresses, and left the old lady to faddle to her heart's content with bits of old lace and ribbon which she herself would not have condescended to wear.

The old lady fumbled them over. There were a good many half-yards of ribbon with very large patterns, but nothing really fit for Madam Liberality's little neck but a small Indian scarf of many-coloured silk. It was old, and Podmore would never have allowed her mistress to drive on the esplanade in anything so small and youthful-looking; but the colours were quite bright, and there was no doubt but that Madam Liberality might be provided for by a cheaper neck-ribbon. So the old lady shut the drawer, and toddled down the corridor that led to Podmore's room.

She had a good general idea that Podmore's perquisites were large, but perquisites seem to be a condition of valuable servants in large establishments, and then anything which could be recovered from what had already passed into Podmore's room must be a kind of economy. So she resolved that Podmore should "find something" for Madam Liberality's neck.

"I never noticed it, ma'am, till I brought your shawl to the carriage," said Podmore. If I had seen it before, the young lady shouldn't have come with you so. I'll see to it, ma'am."

"Thank you, Podmore."

"Can you spare me to go into the town this afternoon, ma'am?" added the lady's-maid. I want some things at Huckaback and Woolsey's."

Huckaback and Woolsey were the linendrapers where Madam Liberality's godmother "had an account." It was one of the things on a large scale over the details of which she had no control.

"You'll be back in time to dress me?"

"Oh dear, yes, ma'am. And having settled the old lady's shawl on her shoulders, and drawn out her cap-lappets, Podmore returned to her work.

It was a work of kindness. The old lady might deal shabbily with her faded ribbons and her relations, but the butler, the housekeeper, and the lady's-maid did their best to keep up the credit of the family.

It was well known that Madam Liberality was a cousin, and Podmore resolved that she should have a proper frock to go down to dessert in.

So she had been very busy making a little slip out of a few yards of blue silk which had been over and above one of the old lady's dresses, and now she betook herself to the draper's to get spotted muslin to cover it and ribbons to trim it with.

And whilst Madam Liberality's godmother was still feeling a few twinges about the Indian scarf, Podmore ordered a pink neckerchief shot with white, and with pink and white fringes, to be included in the parcel.

But it was not in this way alone that Podmore was a good friend to Madam Liberality.

She took her out walking, and let her play on the beach, and even bring home dirty weeds and shells. Indeed, Podmore herself was not above collecting cowries in a pill-box for her little nephews.

When Mrs. Podmore met acquaintances on the beach, Madam Liberality played alone, and these were her happiest moments. She played amongst the rotting, weed-grown stakes of an old pier, and "fancied" rooms among them—suites of rooms, in which she would lodge her brothers and sister if they came to visit her, and where—with cockle-shells for teacups, and lava for vegetables, and fucus-pods for fish—they should find themselves as much enchanted as Beauty in the palace of the Beast.

Again and again she "fancied" Darling into her shore-palace, the delights of which should only be marred by the growls which she herself would utter from time to time from behind the stakes, in the character of a sea-beast, and which should but enhance the moment when she would rush out and throw her arms round Darling's neck and reveal herself as Madam Liberality.

"Darling" was the pet name of Madam Liberality's sister—her only sister, on whom she lavished the intensest affection of a heart which was always a large one in proportion to her little body. It seemed so strange to play at any game of fancies without Darling, that Madam Liberality could hardly realize it.

She might be preparing by herself a larger treat than usual for the others; but it was incredible that no one would come after all, and that Darling would never see the palace on the beach, and the state rooms, and the limpets, and the sea-weed, and the salt-water soup, and the real fish (a small dab discarded from a herring-net) which Madam Liberality had got for her.

Her mind was filled with day-dreams of Darling's coming, and of how she would display to her all the wonders of the seashore, which would reflect almost as much credit upon her as if she had invented razor-shells and crabs. She thought so much about it that she began quite to expect it.

Was it not natural that her godmother should see that she must be lonely, and ask Darling to come and be with her? Perhaps the old lady had already done so, and the visit was to be a surprise. Madam Liberality could quite imagine doing a nice thing like this herself, and she hoped it so strongly that she almost came to believe in it.

Every day she waited hopefully, first for the post, and then for the time when the coach came in, the hour at which she herself had arrived; but the coach brought no Darling, and the post brought no letter to say that she was coming, and Madam Liberality's hopes were disappointed.

Madam Liberality was accustomed to disappointment.

From her earliest years it had been a family joke that poor Madam Liberality was always in ill-luck's way.

It is true that she was constantly planning; and if one builds castles, one must expect a few loose stones about one's ears now and then. But, besides this, her little hopes were constantly being frustrated by fate.

If the pigs or the hens got into the garden, Madam Liberality's bed was sure to be laid waste before any one came to the rescue. When a picnic or a tea party was in store, if Madam Liberality did not catch cold, so as to hinder her from going, she was pretty sure to have a quinsy from fatigue or wet feet afterwards. When she had a treat she paid for the pleasurable excitement by a headache, just as when she ate sweet things they gave her toothache.

But if her luck was less than other people's, her courage and good spirits were more than common. She could think with pleasure about the treat when she had forgotten the headache. One side of her little face would look fairly cheerful when the other was obliterated by a flannel bag of hot chamomile flowers, and the whole was redolent of every horrible domestic remedy for toothache, from oil of cloves and creosote to a baked onion in the ear. No sufferings abated her energy for fresh exploits, or quenched the hope that cold, and damp, and fatigue would not hurt her "this time."

In the intervals of wringing out hot flannels for her own quinsy, she would amuse herself by devising a desert island expedition on a larger and possibly a damper scale than hitherto, against the time when she should be out again.

It is a very old simile, but Madam Liberality really was like a cork rising on the top of the very wave of ill-luck that had swallowed up her hopes. Her little white face and undaunted spirit bobbed up after each mischance or malady as ready and hopeful as ever.

Though her day-dream about Darling and the shore palace was constantly disappointed, this did not hinder her from indulging new hopes and fancies in another place to which she went with Podmore; a place which was filled with wonders of a different kind from the treasures of the palace on the shore.

It was called the Bazaar. It would be a very long business to say what was in it. But amongst other things there were foreign cage-birds, and musical-boxes, and camp-stools, and baskets, and polished pebbles, and paper patterns, and a little ladies' and children's millinery, and a good deal of mock jewelry, and some very bad soaps and scents, and some very good children's toys.

It was Madam Liberality's godmother who first took her to the bazaar. A titled lady of her acquaintance had heard that wire flower-baskets of a certain shape could be bought in the bazaar cheaper (by two-pence-halfpenny each) than in London; and after writing to her friend to ascertain the truth of the statement, she wrote again to authorize her to purchase three on her behalf. So Madam Liberality's godmother ordered out the blue carriage and pair, and drove with her little cousin to the bazaar.

And as they came out, followed by a bearded man, bowing very low, and carrying the wire baskets, Madam Liberality's godmother stopped near the toy-stall to button her glove. And when she had buttoned it (which took a long time, because her hands were stout, and Podmore generally did it with a hook), she said to Madam Liberality, "Now, child, I want to tell you that if you are very good whilst you are with me, and

Podmore gives me a good report of you, I will bring you here before you go home, and buy you a present."

Madam Liberality's heart danced with delight. She wished her godmother would stand by the toy-stall for an hour, that she might see what she most hoped the present would be. But the footman tucked them into the carriage, and the bearded man bowed himself back into the bazaar, and they drove home. Then Madam Liberality's godmother directed the butler to dispatch the wire baskets to her ladyship, which he did by coach. And her ladyship's butler paid the carriage, and tipped the man who brought the parcel from the coach-office, and charged these items in his account. And her ladyship wrote a long letter of thanks to Madam Liberality's godmother for her kindness in saving her unnecessary expense.

The old lady did not go to the bazaar again for some time, but Madam Liberality went there with Podmore. She looked at the toys and wondered which of them might one day be her very own. The white china tea-service with the green rim, big enough to make real tea in, was too good to be hoped for, but there were tin tea-sets where the lids would come off, and wooden ones where they were stuck on; and there were all manner of toys that would be invaluable for all kinds of nursery games and fancies.

They helped a "fancy" of Madam Liberality even then. She used to stand by the toy-stall and fancy that she was as rich as her godmother, and was going to give Christmas-boxes to her brothers and sister, and her amusement was to choose, though she could not buy them.

Out of this came a deep mortification. She had been playing at this fancy one afternoon, and having rather confused herself by changing her mind about the toys, she went through her final list in an undertone, to get it clearly into her head. The shopman was serving a lady, and Madam Liberality thought that he could not hear her as she murmured, "The china tea-set, the box of beasts, the doll's furniture for Darling," etc., etc. But the shopman's hearing was very acute, and he darted forward, crying, "The china tea-set, did you say, miss?"

The blood rushed up to poor Madam Liberality's face till it seemed to choke her, and the lady, whom the shopman had been serving, said kindly, "I think the little girl said the box of beasts."

Madam Liberality hoped it was a dream, but having pinched herself, she found that it was not.

Her mother had often said to her, "When you can't think what to say, tell the truth." It was not a very easy rule, but Madam Liberality went by it.

"I don't want anything, thank you," said she; "at least, I mean I have no money to buy anything with: I was only counting the things I should like to get if I had.

And then, as the floor of the bazaar would *not* open and swallow her up, she ran away, with her red face and her empty pocket, to shelter herself with Podmore at the mock-jewellery stall, and she did not go to the bazaar any more.

Once again disappointment was in store for Madam Liberality. The end of her visit came, and her godmother's promise seemed to be forgotten. But the night before her departure, the old lady came into her room and said:

"I couldn't take you with me to-day, child, but I didn't forget my promise. Podmore says you've been very good, and so I've brought you a present. A very *useful* one, I hope," added the old lady, in a tone as if she were congratulating herself upon her good sense. "And tell Catherine—that's your mother, child—with my love, always to have you dressed for the evening. I like to see children come in to dessert, when they have good manners—which I must say you have; besides, it keeps the nurses up to their work."

And then she drew out from its paper a little frock of pink *mousseline-de-laine*, very prettily tacked together by the young woman at the millinery-stall, and very cheap for its gay appearance.

Down came all Madam Liberality's visions in connection with the toy-stall; but she consoled herself that night with picturing Darling's delight when she gave her (as she meant to give her) the pink dress.

She had another source of comfort and anticipation—*the scallop-shells*.

But this requires to be explained. The greatest prize which Madam Liberality had gained from her wanderings by the seashore was a complete scallop-shell. When washed the double shell was as clean and as pretty as any china muffin-dish with a round top; and now her ambition was to get four more, and thus to have a service for doll's feast which should far surpass the oyster-shells. She was talking about this to Podmore one day when they were picking cowries together, and Podmore cried, "Why, this little girl would get you them, miss, I'll be bound!"

She was a bare-footed little girl, who sold pebbles and seaweed, and salt water for sponging with, and she had undertaken to get the scallop-shells and had run off to pick seaweed out of the newly landed net before Madam Liberality could say "Thank you."

She heard no more of the shells, however, until the day before she went away, when the butler met her as she came indoors, and told her that the little girl was waiting. And it was not till Madam Liberality saw the scallop-shells lying clean and pink in a cotton handkerchief that she remembered that she had no money to pay for them.

Here was another occasion for painful truth telling! But to make humiliating confession before the butler seemed almost beyond even Madam Liberality's moral courage. He went back to his pantry, however, and she pulled off her pretty pink neckerchief and said:

"I am *very* sorry, little girl, but I've got no money of my own; but if you would like this instead—" And the little girl seemed quite pleased with her bargain, and ran hastily off, as if afraid that the young lady would change her mind.

And this was how Madam Liberality got her scallop-shells.

It may seem strange that Madam Liberality should ever have been accused of meanness, and yet her eldest brother did once shake his head at her and say: "You're the most meanest and the *generoustest* person I ever knew!" And Madam Liberality wept over the accusation, although her brother was then too young to form either his words or his opinion correctly.

But it was the touch of truth in it which made Madam Liberality cry. To the end of their lives Tom and she were alike and yet different in this matter. Madam Liberality saved, and pinched, and planned, and then gave away, and Tom gave away without the pinching and saving. This sounds much handsomer, and it was poor Tom's misfortune that he always believed it to be so; though he gave away what did not belong to him, and fell back for the supply of his own pretty numerous wants upon other people, not forgetting Madam Liberality.

Painful experience convinced Madam Liberality in the end that his way was a wrong one, but she had her doubts many times in her life whether there were not something unhandsome in her own decided talent for economy. Not that economy was always pleasant to her. When people are very poor for their position in life, they can only keep out of debt by stinting on many occasions when stinting is very painful to a liberal spirit. And it requires a sterner virtue than good-nature to hold fast the truth that it is nobler to be shabby and honest than to do things handsomely in debt.

But long before Tom had a bill even for bull's-eyes and Gibraltar Rock, Madam Liberality was pinching and plotting, and saving bits of coloured paper and ends of ribbon, with a thriftiness which seemed to justify Tom's view of her character.

The object of these savings was twofold: birthday presents and Christmas-boxes. They were the chief cares and triumphs of Madam Liberality's childhood. It was with the next birthday or the approaching Christmas in view that she saved her pence instead of spending them, but she so seldom had any money that she chiefly relied on her own ingenuity. Year by year it became more difficult to make anything which would "do for a boy"; but it was easy to please Darling, and "Mother's" unabated appreciation of pincushions, and of needle-books made out of old cards, was most satisfactory.

To break the mystery in which it always pleased Madam Liberality to shroud her small preparations, was to give her dire offence. As a rule, the others respected this caprice, and would even feign a little more surprise than they felt, upon occasion. But if during their preparations she had given umbrage to one of the boys, her retreat was soon invaded with cries of—"Ah! I see you, making birthday presents out of nothing and a quarter of a yard of ribbon!" Or—"There you are! At it again, with two old visiting cards and a ha'porth of flannel!" And only Darling's tenderest kisses could appease Madam Liberality's wrath and dry her tears.

She had never made a grander project for Christmas, or had greater difficulty carrying it out, than in the winter which followed her visit to the seaside. It was in the house of her cousin that she had first heard of Christmas-trees, and to surprise the others with a Christmas-tree she was quite resolved. But as the time drew near, poor Madam Liberality was almost in despair about her presents, and this was doubly provoking, because a nice little fir tree had been promised her. There was no blinking the fact that "Mother" had been provided with pincushions to repletion. And most of these made the needles rusty, from being stuffed with damp pig-meal, when the pigs and the pincushions were both being fattened for Christmas.

Madam Liberality sat with her little pale face on her hand and her slate before her, making her calculations. She wondered what emery-powder cost. Supposing it to be very cheap, and that she could get a quarter of a pound for "next to nothing," how useful a present might be made for "Mother" in the shape of an emery pincushion, to counteract the evil effects of the pig-meal ones! It would be a novelty even to Darling, especially if hers were made by gluing a tiny bag of emery into the mouth of a "boiled fowl cowry." Madam Liberality had seen such a pincushion in Podmore's work-basket. She had a shell of the kind, and the village carpenter would always let her put a stick into his glue-pot if she went to the shop.

But then, if emery were only a penny a pound, Madam Liberality had not a farthing to buy a quarter of a pound with. As she thought of this her brow contracted, partly with vexation, and partly because of a jumping pain in a big tooth, which, either from much illness or many medicines, or both, was now but the wreck of what a tooth should be. But as the toothache grew worse, a new hope dawned upon Madam Liberality. Perhaps one of her troubles would mend the other!

Being very tender-hearted over children's sufferings, it was her mother's custom to bribe rather than coerce when teeth had to be taken out. The fixed scale of reward was sixpence for a tooth without fangs, and a shilling for one with them. If pain were any evidence, this tooth certainly had fangs. But one does not have a tooth taken out if one can avoid it, and Madam Liberality bore bad nights and painful days till they could be endured no longer; and then, because she knew it distressed her mother to be present, she went alone to the doctor's house to ask him to take out her tooth.

The doctor was a very kind old man, and he did his best, so we will not say anything about his antique instruments, or the number of times he tied a pocket-handkerchief round an awful-looking claw, and put both into Madam Liberality's mouth without effect.

At last he said he had got the tooth out, and he wrapped it in paper, and gave it to Madam Liberality, who, having thought it was her head he had extracted from its socket, was relieved to get away.

As she ran home she began to plan how to lay out her shilling for the best, and when she was nearly there she opened the bit of paper to look at her enemy, and it had no fangs!

"I'm *sure* it was more than a sixpenny one," she sobbed; "I believe he has left them in."

It involved more than the loss of half the funds she had reckoned upon. Perhaps this dreadful pain would go on even on Christmas Day. Her first thought was to carry her tears to her mother; her second that, if she could only be brave enough to have the fangs taken out, she might spare mother all distress about it till it was over, when she would certainly like her sufferings to be known and sympathized with. She knew well that courage does not come with waiting, and making a desperate rally of stout-heartedness, she ran back to the doctor.

He had gone out, but his assistant was in. He looked at Madam Liberality's mouth, and said that the fangs were certainly left in and would be much better out.

"Would it hurt *very* much?" asked Madam Liberality, trembling.

The assistant blinked the question of "hurting."

"I think I could do it," said he, "if you could sit still. Not if you were jumping about."

"I will sit still," said Madam Liberality.

"The boy shall hold your head," said the assistant.

But Madam Liberality rebelled; she could screw up her sensitive nerves to endure the pain, but not to be coerced by "the boy."

"I give you my word of honour I will sit still," said she, with plaintive earnestness.

And the assistant (who had just remembered that the boy was out with the gig) said, "Very well, miss."

We need not dwell upon the next few seconds. The assistant kept his word, and Madam Liberality kept hers. She sat still, and went on sitting still after the operation was over till the assistant became alarmed, and revived her by pouring some choking stuff down her throat. After which she staggered to her feet and put out her hand and thanked him.

He was a strong, rough, good-natured young man, and little Madam Liberality's pale face and politeness touched him.

"You're the bravest little lady I ever knew," he said kindly; "and you keep your word like a queen. There's some stuff to put to the place, and there's sixpence, miss, if you'll take it, to buy lollipops with. You'll be able to eat them now."

After which he gave her an old pill-box to carry the fragments of her tooth in, and it was labelled "three to be taken at bed-time."

Madam Liberality staggered home, very giddy, but very happy. Moralists say a great deal about pain treading so closely on the heels of pleasure in this life, but they are not always wise or grateful enough to speak of the pleasure which springs out of pain. And yet there is a bliss which comes just when pain has ceased, whose rapture rivals even the high happiness of unbroken health; and there is a keen relish about small pleasures hardly earned, in which the full measure of those who can afford anything they want is sometimes lacking.

Relief is certainly one of the most delicious sensations which poor humanity can enjoy! Madam Liberality enjoyed it to the full, and she had more happiness yet in her cup. I fear praise was very pleasant to her, and the assistant had praised her, not undeservedly, and she knew that further praise was in store from the dearest source of approbation—from her mother. Ah! How pleased she would be! And so would Darling, who always cried when Madam Liberality was in great pain.

And this was only the beginning of pleasures. The sixpence would amply provide "goodies" for the Christmas-tree, and much might be done with the forthcoming shilling. And if her conduct on the present occasion would not support a request for a few ends of candles from the drawing-room candle-sticks, what profit would there be in being a heroine?

When her mother gave her two shillings instead of one, Madame Liberality felt in honour bound to say that she had already been rewarded with sixpence; but her mother only said:

"You quite deserved it, I'm sure," and she found herself in possession of no less than half-a-crown.

And now it is sad to relate that misfortune again overtook Madam Liberality. All the next day she longed to go into the village to buy sweetmeats, but it snowed and rained, and was bitterly cold, and she could not.

Just about dusk the weather slightly cleared up, and she picked her way through the melting snow to the shop. Her purchases were most satisfactory. How the boys would enjoy them! Madam Liberality enjoyed them already, though her face was still sore, and the pain had spread to her throat; and though her ideas seemed unusually brilliant, and her body pleasantly languid, which, added to a peculiar chill trembling of the knees—generally forewarned her of a coming quinsy. But warnings were thrown away upon Madam Liberality's obdurate hopefulness.

Just now she could think of nothing but the coming Christmas-tree. She hid the sweetmeats, and put her hand into her pocket for the two shillings, the exact outlay of which, in the neighbouring town, by means of the carrier, she had already arranged. But—the two shillings were gone! How she had lost them Madam Liberality had no idea.

She trudged through the dirty snow once more to the shop, and the counter was examined, and old Goody looked under the flour scales and in the big chinks of the stone floor. But the shillings were not there, and Madam Liberality kept her eyes on the pavement as she ran home, with as little result. Moreover, it was nearly dark.

It snowed heavily all night, and Madam Liberality slept very little from pain and anxiety; but this did not deter her from going out with the first daylight in the morning to rake among the snow near the door, although her throat was sore beyond concealment, her jaws stiff, and the pleasant languor and quick-wittedness had given way to restless fever.

Her conscience did prick her a little for the anxiety she was bringing upon her mother (her own sufferings she never forecast); but she could not give up her Christmas-tree without a struggle, and she hoped by a few familiar remedies to drive back the threatened illness.

Meanwhile, if the shillings were not found before eleven o'clock it would be too late to send to the town shop by the carrier. But they were not found, and the old hooded cart rumbled away without them.

It was Christmas Eve. The boys were bustling about with holly. Darling was perched on a very high chair in the kitchen, picking raisins in the most honourable manner, without eating one, and Madam Liberality ought to have been the happiest of all.

Even now she dried her tears, and made the best of her ill-luck. The sweetmeats were very good; and it was yet in her power to please the others, though by a sacrifice from which she had shrunk. She could divide her scallop-shells among them. It was economy—economy of resources—which made her hesitate. Separated—they would please the boys once, and then be lost. Kept together in her own possession—they would be a constant source of triumph for herself, and for treats for her brothers and sister.

Meanwhile, she would gargle her throat with salt and water. As she crept up-stairs with this purpose, she met her mother.

Madam Liberality had not looked in the looking-glass lately, so she did not understand her mother's exclamation of distress when they met. Her face was perfectly white, except where dark marks lay under her eyes, and her small lips formed between them the rigid line of pain. It was impossible to hold out any longer, and Madam Liberality broke down and poured forth all her woes.

"I'll put my feet in hot water, and do anything you like, mother dear," said she, "if only you will let me try and have a tree, and keep it secret from the others. I do so want to surprise them."

"If you will go to your room, my darling, and do as I tell you, I'll keep your secret, and help you with your tree," said her mother. "Don't cry, my child, don't cry; it's so bad for your throat. I think I can find you some beads to make a necklace for Darling, and three pencils for the boys, and some paper which you can cut up into drawing-books for them."

A little hope went a long way for Madam Liberality, and she began to take heart. At the same time she felt her illness more keenly now there was no need for concealing it. She sat over the fire and inhaled steam from an old teapot, and threaded beads, and hoped she would be allowed to go to church next day, and to preside at her Christmas-tree afterwards.

In the afternoon her throat grew rapidly worse. She had begged—almost impatiently—that Darling would not leave the Christmas preparations to sit with her, and as talking was bad for her, and as she had secret preparations to make on her own account, her mother had supported her wish to be left alone.

But when it grew dusk, and the drawing-books were finished, Madam Liberality felt lonely. She put a shawl round her head, and went to the window. There was not much to be seen. The fields were deeply buried in snow, and looked like great white feather beds, shaken up unequally against the hedges. The road was covered so deeply that she could hardly have traced it, if she had not known where it was. How dark the old church tower looked amid so much whiteness!

And the snow-flakes fell like sugar-plums among the black trees. One could almost hear the keen wind rustling through the bending sedges by the pond, where the ice looked quite "safe" now. Madam Liberality hoped she would be able to get out before this fine frost was over. She knew of an old plank which would make an admirable sledge, and she had a plan for the grandest of winter games all ready in her head. It was to be called Arctic Discovery—and she was to be the chief discoverer.

As she fancied herself—starving but scientific, chilled to the bone, yet undaunted—discovering a north-west passage at the upper end of the goose pond, the clock struck three from the old church tower. Madam Liberality heard it with a pang. At three o'clock—if he had had her shillings—she would have been expecting the return of the carrier, with the presents for her Christmas-tree.

Even as she thought about it, the old hooded waggon came lumbering down among the snow-drifts in the lane. There was a bunch of mistletoe at the head, and the old carrier went before the horse, and the dog went before the carrier. And they were all three up to their knees in snow, and all three had their noses down, as much as to say, "Such is life; but we must struggle on."

Poor Madam Liberality! The sight of the waggon and the mistletoe overwhelmed her. It only made matters worse to see the waggon come towards the house. She rather wondered what the carrier was bringing; but whatever it was, it was not the toys.

She went back to her seat by the fire, and cried bitterly; and, as she cried, the ball in her throat seemed to grow larger, till she could hardly breathe. She was glad when the door opened, and her mother's kind face looked in.

"Is Darling here?" she asked.

"No, mother," said Madam Liberality huskily.

"Then you may bring it in," said her mother to someone outside, and the servant appeared, carrying a wooden box, which she put down before Madam Liberality, and then withdrew. "Now don't speak," said her mother, "it is bad for you, and your eyes have asked fifty questions already, my child. Where did the box come from? The carrier brought it. Who is it for? It's for you. Who sent it? That I don't know. What is inside? I thought you would like to be the first to see. My idea is that perhaps your godmother has sent you a Christmas-box, and I thought that there may be things in it which would help you with your Christmas-tree, so I have not told anyone about it."

To the end of her life Madam Liberality never forgot that Christmas-box. It did not come from her godmother, and the name of the giver she never knew. The first thing in it was a card, on which was written—"A Christmas-box from an unknown friend;" and the second thing in it was the set of china tea-things with the green rim; and the third thing was a box of doll's furniture.

"Oh, Mother!" cried Madam Liberality, "they're the very things I was counting over in the bazaar, when the shopman heard me."

"Did anybody else hear you?" asked her mother.

"There was a lady, who said, 'I think the little girl said the box of beasts.' And, oh! Mother, Mother! Here *is* the box of beasts! They're not common beasts, you know—not wooden ones, painted; they're rough, something like hair. And feel the old elephant's ears, they're quite leathery, and the lion has real long hair for his mane and the tip of his tail. They are such thorough beasts. Oh, how the boys will like them! Tom shall have the darling brown bear. I do think he is the very best beast of all; his mouth is a little open, you know, and you can see his tongue, and it's red. And, Mother! The sheep are curly! And oh, what a dog! With real hair. I think I *must* keep the dog. And I shall make him a paper collar, and print 'Faithful' on it, and let him always stand on the drawers by our bed, and he'll be Darling's and my watch-dog."

Happiness is sometimes very wholesome, but it does not cure a quinsy off hand. Darling cried that night when the big pillow was brought out, which Madam Liberality always slept against in her quinsies, to keep her from choking. She did not know of that consolatory Christmas-box in the cupboard.

On Christmas Day Madam Liberality was speechless. The quinsy had progressed very rapidly.

"It generally breaks the day I have to write on my slate," Madam Liberality wrote, looking up at her mother with piteous eyes.

She was conscious that she had been greatly to blame for what she was suffering, and was anxious to "behave well about it" as an atonement. She begged—on her slate—that no one would stay away from church on her account, but her mother would not leave her.

"And now the others are gone," said Mother, "since you won't let the Christmas-tree be put off, I propose that we have it up, and I dress it under your orders, whilst the others are out, and then it can be moved into the little book-room, all ready for tonight."

Madam Liberality nodded like a china Mandarin.

"But you are in sad pain, I fear?" said her mother.

"One can't have everything," wrote Madam Liberality on her slate. Many illnesses had made her a very philosophical little woman; and, indeed, if the quinsy broke and she were at ease, the combination of good things would be more than anyone could reasonably expect, even at Christmas.

Every beast was labelled, and hung up by her orders. The box of furniture was addressed to herself and Darling, as a joint possession, and the sweetmeats were tied in bags of muslin. The tree looked charming. The very angel at the top seemed proud of it.

"I'll leave the tea-things up-stairs," said Mother.

But Madam Liberality shook her head vigorously. She had been making up her mind, as she sat steaming over the old teapot; and now she wrote on her slate, "Put a white cloth round the tub, and put out the tea-things like a tea-party, and put a ticket in the slop-basin—*For Darling. With very*, VERY *Best Love*. Make the last 'very' very big."

Madam Liberality's mother nodded, but she was printing a ticket; much too large a ticket, however, to go into the green and white slop-basin. When it was done she hung it on the tree, under the angel. The inscription was—*from Madam Liberality*.

When supper was over, she came up to Madam Liberality's room, and said:

"Now, my dear, if you like to change your mind and put off the tree till you are better, I will say nothing about it."

But Madam Liberality shook her head more vehemently than before, and her mother smiled and went away.

Madam Liberality strained her ears. The book-room door opened—she knew the voice of the handle—there was a rush and a noise, but it died away into the room. The tears broke down Madam Liberality's cheeks. It was hard not to be there now. Then there was a patter up the stairs, and flying steps along the landing, and Madam Liberality's door was opened by Darling. She was dressed in the pink dress, and her cheeks were pinker still, and her eyes full of tears. And she threw herself at Madam Liberality's feet, crying: "Oh, *how* good, how *very* good you are!"

At this moment a roar came up from below, and Madam Liberality wrote:

"What is it?" and then dropped the slate to clutch the arms of her chair, for the pain was becoming almost intolerable. Before Darling could open the door her mother came in, and Darling repeated the question: "What is it?"

But at this moment the reply came from below, in Tom's loudest tones. It rang through the house, and up into the bedroom.

"Three cheers for Madam Liberality! Hip, hip, hooray!"

The extremes of pleasure and of pain seemed to meet in Madam Liberality's little head. But overwhelming gratification got the upper hand, and, forgetting even her quinsy, she tried to speak, and after a brief struggle she said, with tolerable distinctness,

"Tell Tom I am very much obliged to him."

But what they did tell Tom was that the quinsy had broken, on which he gave three cheers more.

Part II

Madam Liberality grew up into much the same sort of person that she was when a child. She always had been what is termed old-fashioned, and the older she grew the better her old-fashionedness became her, so that at last her friends would say to her, "Ah, if we all wore as well as you do, my dear! You've hardly changed at all since we remember you in short petticoats." So far as she did change, the change was for the better. (It is

to be hoped we do improve a little as we get older!) She was still liberal
and economical. She still planned and hoped indefatigably. She was still
tender-hearted in the sense in which Gray speaks:

> To each his sufferings, all are men
> condemned alike to groan,
> The tender for another's pain,
> The unfeeling for his own.

She still had a good deal of ill-health and ill-luck, and a good deal of
pleasure in spite of both. She was still happy in the happiness of others,
and pleased by their praise. But she was less headstrong and opinionated
in her plans, and less fretful when they failed. It is possible, after one has
cut one's wisdom-teeth, to cure one's self even of a good deal of vanity, and
to learn to play the second fiddle very gracefully; and Madam Liberality
did not resist the lessons of life.

God teaches us wisdom in divers ways. Why He suffers some people to
have so many troubles and so little of what we call pleasure in this world
we cannot in this world know. The heaviest blows often fall on the weakest
shoulders, and how these endure and bear up under them is another of
the things which God knows better than we.

I will not pretend to decide whether grown-up people's troubles are
harder to bear than children's troubles, but they are of a graver kind. It is
very bitter when the boys melt the nose of one's dearest doll against the
stove, and living pets with kind eyes and friendly paws grow aged and
die; but the death of friends is a more serious and lasting sorrow, if it is
not more real.

Madam Liberality shed fewer tears after she grew up than she had
done before, but she had some heartaches which did not heal.

The thing that did most to cure her of being too managing for the good
of other people was Darling's marriage. If ever Madam Liberality had felt
proud of self-sacrifice and success, it was about this. But when Darling
was fairly gone, and "Faithful"—very grey with dust and years—kept
watch over only one sister in "the girls' room," he might have seen Madam
Liberality's nightly tears if his eyes had been made of anything more
sensitive than yellow paint.

Desolate as she was, Madam Liberality would have hugged her grief if she could have had her old consolation, and been happy in the happiness of another. Darling never said she was not happy. It was what she left out, not what she put into the long letters she sent from India that cut Madam Liberality to the heart.

Darling's husband read all her letters, and he did not like the home ones to be too tender—as if Darling's mother and sister pitied her. And he read Darling's letters before they went away by the mail.

From this it came about that the sisters' letters were very commonplace on the surface. And though Madam Liberality cried when Darling wrote, "Have swallows built in the summer-house this year? Have you put my old doll's chest of drawers back in its place since the room was papered? What colour is the paper?"—the Major only said that stuff like that was hardly worth the postage to England. And when Madam Liberality wrote, "The clump of daffodils in your old bed was enormous this spring. I have not touched it since you left. I made Mother's birthday wreath out of flowers in your bed and mine. Jemima broke the slop-basin of the green and white tea-set to-day. It was the last piece left. I am trying to forgive her,"—the Major made no harsher remark than, "A storm in a slop-basin! Your sister is not a brilliant letter-writer, certainly."

The source for another heartache for Madam Liberality was poor Tom. He was as liberal and hospitable as ever in his own way. He invited his friends to stay with his mother, and when they and Tom had gone, Madam Liberality and her mother lived without meat to get the housekeeping book straight again. Their great difficulty in the matter was the uncertain nature of Tom's requirements. And when he did write for money he always wrote in such urgent need that there was no refusing him if by the art of "doing without" his wants could be supplied.

But Tom had a kindly heart; he sent his sister a gold locket, and wrote on the box, "For the best and the most generous of sisters."

Madam Liberality liked praise and she dearly liked praise from Tom; but on this occasion it failed to soothe her. She said curtly, "I suppose it's not paid for. If we can't afford much, we can afford to live at our own expense, and not on the knavery or the forbearance of tradesmen." With which she threw the locket into a box of odds and ends, and turned the key with some temper.

Years passed, and Madam Liberality was alone. Her mother was dead, and Tom—poor Tom!—had been found drowned. Darling was still in India, and the two living boys were in the colonies, farming.

It seemed to be an aggravation of the calamity of Tom's death that he died, as he had lived, in debt. But, as regards Madam Liberality, it was not an unmixed evil. It is one of our bitterest pangs when we survive those we love that with death the opportunity has passed for being kind to them, though we love them more than ever. By what earthly effort could Madam Liberality's mother now be pleased, whom so little had pleased heretofore?

But for poor Tom it was still possible to plan, to economize, to be liberal—and by these means to pay his debts, and save the fair name of which he had been as reckless as of everything else which he possessed.

Madam Liberality had had many a hard struggle to get Tom a birthday present, but she had never pinched and planned and saved on his behalf as she did now. There is a limit, however, to the strictest economies. It would have taken a longer time to finish her labour of love but for "the other boys." They were good, kind fellows, and having had to earn daily bread where larks do not fall ready cooked into the mouth, they knew more of the realities of life than poor Tom had ever learned. They were prosperous now, and often sent a few pounds to Madam Liberality "to buy a present with."

"And none of your old 'Liberality' tricks, mind!" George wrote on one occasion. "Fit yourself thoroughly out in the latest fashions, and do us credit!"

But all went to Tom's tailor.

She felt hardly justified in diverting George's money from his purpose; but she had never told the boys of Tom's debts. There was something of her old love of doing things without help in this, and more of her special love for Tom.

It was not from the boys alone that help came to her. Madam Liberality's godmother died, and left her fifty pounds. In one lump she had now got enough to finish her work.

The acknowledgments of these last payments came on Tom's birthday. More and more courteous had grown the tradesmen's letters, and Madam

Liberality felt a foolish pleasure in seeing how respectfully they all spoke now of "Your lamented brother, Madam!"

The jeweller's bill was the last; and when Madam Liberality tied up the bundle, she got out Tom's locket and put a bit of his hair into it, and tied it round her throat, sobbing as she did so, "Oh, Tom, if you *could* have lived and been happy in a small way! Your debts are paid now, my poor boy. I wonder if you know. Oh, Tom, Tom!

It was her greatest triumph—to have saved Tom's fair name in the place where he had lived so foolishly and died so sadly.

But the triumphs of childhood cast fewer shadows. There was no one now to say, "Three cheers for Madam Liberality!"

It was a very cold winter, but Madam Liberality and Jemima, the maid-of-all-work, were warmer than they had been for several previous winters, because they kept better fires. Time heals our sorrows in spite of us, and Madam Liberality was a very cheerful little body now, and as busy as ever about her Christmas-boxes. Those for her nephews and nieces were already dispatched. "The boys" were married; Madam Liberality was godmother to several children she had never seen; but the Benjamin of his aunt's heart was Darling's only child—Tom—though she had not seen even him.

Madam Liberality was still in the thick of her plans, which were chiefly to benefit the old people and the well-behaved children of the village. All the Christmas-boxes were to be "surprises," and Jemima was in every secret but the one which most concerned her.

Madam Liberality had even some plans for her own benefit. George had talked of coming home in the summer, and she began to think of saving up for a new carpet for the drawing-room. Then the last time she went to the town she saw some curtains of a most artistic pattern, and particularly cheap. So much good taste for so little money was rare in provincial shops. By and by she might do without something which would balance the cost of the curtains. And she had another ambition—to provide Jemima with black dresses and white muslin aprons for afternoon wear in addition to her wages, that the outward aspect of that good soul might be more in accordance than hitherto with her intrinsic excellence.

She was pondering this when Jemima burst in in her cooking apron, followed up the passage by the steam of Christmas cakes, and carrying a letter.

"It's a big one, Miss," said she. "Perhaps it's a Christmas-box, Miss." And beaming with geniality and kitchen warmth, Jemima returned to her labours.

Madam Liberality made up her mind about the dresses and aprons; then she opened her letter.

It announced the death of her cousin, her godmother's husband. It announced also that, in spite of the closest search for a will, which he was supposed to have made, this could not be found.

Possibly he had destroyed it, intending to make another. As it was, he had died intestate, and succession not being limited to heirs male, and Madam Liberality being the eldest child of his nearest relative—the old childish feeling of its being a dream came over her.

She pinched herself, however, to no purpose. There lay the letter, and after a second reading Madam Liberality picked up the thread of the narrative and arrived at the result—she had inherited fifteen thousand a year.

The first rational idea which came to her was that there was no difficulty now about getting the curtains; and the second was that their chief merit was a merit no more. What is the good of a thing being cheap when one has fifteen thousand a year?

Madam Liberality poked the fire extravagantly, and sat down to think.

The curtains naturally led her to household questions, and those to that invaluable person, Jemima. That Jemima's wages should be doubled, trebled, quadrupled, was a thing of course. What post she was to fill in the new circumstances was another matter. Remembering Podmore, and recalling the fatigue of dressing herself after her pretty numerous illnesses, Madam Liberality felt that a lady's-maid would be a comfort to be most thankful for. But she could not fancy Jemima in that capacity, or as a housekeeper, or even as head house-maid or cook. She had lived for years with Jemima herself, but she could not fit her into a suitable place in the servants' hall.

However, with fifteen thousand a year, Madam Liberality could buy, if needed, a field, and build a house, and put Jemima into it with a servant to wait upon her. The really important question was about her new domestics. Sixteen servants are a heavy responsibility.

Madam Liberality had very high ideas of the parental duties involved in being the head of a household. She had suffered—more than Jemima—over Jemima's lack of scruple as to telling lies for good purposes. Now a footman is a young man who has, no doubt, his own peculiar temptations. What check could Madam Liberality keep upon him? Possibly she might—under the strong pressure of moral responsibility—give good general advice to the footman; but the idea of the butler troubled her.

When one has lived alone in a little house for many years one gets timid. She put a case to herself. Say that she knew the butler to be in the habit of stealing the wine, and suspected the gardener of making a good income by the best of the wall fruit, would she have the moral courage to be as firm with the important personages as if she had caught one of the school-children picking and stealing in the orchard? And if not, would not family prayers be a mockery?

Madam Liberality sighed. Poor dear Tom! He had had his faults certainly; but how well he would have managed a butler!

This touched the weak point of her good fortune to the core. It had come too late to heap luxuries about dear "Mother"; too late to open careers for the boys; too late to give mad frolics and girlish gaieties to light hearts, such as she and Darling had once had. Ah, if they could have enjoyed it together years ago!

There remained, however, Madam Liberality's old consolation: one can be happy in the happiness of others. There were nephews and nieces to be provided for, and a world so full of poor and struggling folk that fifteen thousand a year would only go a little way. It was, perhaps, useful that there had been so many articles lately in the papers about begging letters, and impostors, and the evil effects of the indiscriminate charity of elderly ladies; but the remembrance of them made Madam Liberality's head ache, and troubled her dreams that night.

It was well that the next day was Sunday. Face to face with those greater interests common to the rich and the poor, the living and the dead, Madam Liberality grew calmer under her new cares and prospects. It did not need that brief pause by her mother's grave to remind her how little money can do for us; and the sight of other people wholesomely recalled how much it can effect. Near the church porch she was passed by the wife of a retired chandler, who dressed in very fine silks, and who was accustomed to eye Madam Liberality's old clothes as she bowed to her more obviously than is consistent with good breeding. The little lady nodded very kindly in return. With fifteen thousand a year one can afford to be *quite* at ease in an old shawl.

The next day was Christmas Eve. Madam Liberality caught herself thinking that if the legacy had been smaller—say fifty pounds a year—she would at once have treated herself to certain little embellishments of the old house, for which she had long been ambitious. But it would be absurd to buy two or three yards of rosebud chintz, and tire herself by making covers to two very old sofa-cushions, when the point to be decided was in which of three grandly furnished mansions she would first take up her abode. She ordered a liberal supper, however, which confirmed Jemima in her secret opinion that the big letter had brought good news.

When, therefore, another letter of similar appearance arrived, Jemima snatched up the waiter and burst breathlessly in upon Madam Liberality, leaving the door open behind her, though it was bitterly cold and the snow fell fast.

And when Madam Liberality opened this letter she learned that her cousin's will had been found, and that (as seems to be natural) he had left his money where it would be associated with more money and kept well together. His heir was a cousin also, but in the next degree—an old bachelor, who was already wealthy; and he had left Madam Liberality five pounds to buy a mourning ring.

It had been said that Madam Liberality was used to disappointment, but some minutes passed before she quite realized the downfall of her latest visions. Then the old sofa-cushions resumed their importance, and she flattened the fire into a more economical shape, and set vigorously to work to decorate the house with the Christmas evergreens. She had just finished and gone up-stairs to wash her hands when the church clock struck three.

It was an old house, and the window of the bedroom went down to the floor, and had a deep window-seat. Madam Liberality sat down in it and looked out. She expected some linsey-woolsey by the carrier, to make Christmas petticoats, and she was glad to see the hooded waggon ploughing its way through the snow. The goose-pond was firmly frozen, and everything looked as it had looked years ago, except that the carrier's young son went before the waggon and a young dog went before him. They passed slowly out of sight, but Madam Liberality sat on. She gazed dreamily at the old church, and the trees, and the pond, and thought of the past; of her mother, and of poor Tom, and of Darling, and she thought till she fancied that she heard Darling's voice in the passage below. She got up to go down to Jemima, but as she did so she heard a footstep on the stairs, and it was not Jemima's tread. It was too light for the step of any man or woman.

Then the door opened, and on the threshold of Madam Liberality's room stood a little boy dressed in black, with his little hat pushed back from the loveliest of baby faces set in long flaxen hair. The carnation colour of his cheeks was deepened by the frost, and his bright eyes were brighter from mingled daring and doubt and curiosity, as he looked leisurely round the room and said in a slow, high-pitched, and very distinct tone,

"Where are you, Aunt Liberality?"

But, lovely as he was, Madam Liberality ran past him, for another figure was in the doorway now, also in black, and with a widow's cap; and Madam Liberality and Darling fell sobbing into each other's arms.

"This is better than fifteen thousand a year," said Madam Liberality.

◆   ◆   ◆

It is not necessary to say much more. The Major had been killed by a fall from horseback, and Darling came back to live at her old home. She had a little pension, and the sisters were not parted again.

It would be idle to dwell on Madam Liberality's devotion to her nephew, or the princely manner in which he accepted her services. That his pleasure was the object of a new series of plans, and presents, and surprises, will be readily understood. The curtains were bought, but the new carpet had to be deferred in consequence of an extravagant outlay on mechanical toys. When the working of these brought a deeper tint into his cheeks, and a brighter light into his eyes, Madam Liberality was quite happy; and when he broke them one after another, his infatuated aunt believed this to be a precocious development of manly energies.

The longest lived, if not the favourite, toys with him were the old set of scallop-shells, with which he never wearied of making feasts, to which Madam Liberality was never weary of being invited. He had more plums than had ever sweetened her childhood, and when they sat together on two footstools by the sofa, and Tom announced the contents of the dishes in his shrillest voice and lifted the covers, Madam Liberality would say in a tone of apology,

"It's very odd, Darling, and I'm sure at my time of life it's disgraceful, but I cannot feel old!"

We could hardly take leave of Madam Liberality in pleasanter circumstances. Why should we ask whether, for the rest of her life, she was rich or poor, when we may feel so certain that she was contented? No doubt she had many another hope and disappointment to keep life from stagnating.

As a matter of fact she outlived the bachelor cousin, and if he died intestate she must have been rich after all. Perhaps she was. Perhaps she never suffered again from insufficient food or warmth. Perhaps the illnesses of her later years were alleviated by skill and comforts such as hitherto she had never known. Perhaps Darling and she enjoyed a sort of second spring in their old age, and went ever year to the Continent, and grew wonderful flowers in the greenhouse, and sent Tom to Eton, and provided for their nephews and nieces, and built churches to their mother's memory, and never had to withhold the liberal hand from helping because it was empty; and so passed by a time of wealth to the hour of death.

Or perhaps the cousin took good care to bequeath his money where there was more money for it to stick to. And Madam Liberality pinched out her little presents as heretofore, and kept herself warm with a hot bottle when she could not afford a fire, and was too thankful to have Darling with her when she was ill to want anything else. And perhaps Darling and she prepared Tom for school, and (like many another widow's son) he did them credit. And perhaps they were quite happy with a few common pot-plants in the sunny window, and kept their mother's memory green by flowers about her grave, and so passed by a life of small cares and small pleasures to where "Divided households re-unite."

Of one thing we may be quite certain. Rich or poor, she was always MADAM LIBERALITY.

CHAPTER 4

Portrait of a Moral
Phenomenon: *Jackanapes*

When Ewing's story *Jackanapes* first appeared in the October 1879 issue of *Aunt Judy's Magazine*, it was an immediate hit—to a surprising extent among adult readers, some of whom were so impressed that they urged others to read this forceful, unusual work. This story of an idyllic English village, Goose Green, and a singular young orphan named Theodore, but called by everyone in the village by the odd name "Jackanapes," possesses so much that is appealing and, indeed, profound that after appearing in book form, it became the most popular of all Ewing's works. In a letter at Christmas 1883, she wrote to the Reverend Edward Thring, Headmaster of Uppingham, that *Jackanapes* was "selling at the rate of 500 a day, 19,000 have been ordered already, and the printers can't get them out fast enough." Trying to keep intact her modesty but unable to hide her pleasure, she continues: "This of course . . . may fairly be called a success," and she admits that *Jackanapes* is the "favorite child of my brain."[1] The book was "A late-Victorian best-seller" as *The Victorian Web: Literature, History & Culture in the Age of Victoria* has observed.[2] Horatia K. F. Eden points out in her book that it was this work, *Jackanapes*, that "made Julie's [Ewing's] name famous."[3] It is the work with which Ewing's name has become most frequently associated. Eden argues that the story deserves such popularity, "for it contains her highest teaching" and it is "her best piece of literary art."[4]

Such praise for *Jackanapes* has become commonplace, but perhaps the most impressive assessment contemporary with its publication in book form was that of the master of the art of fiction, Henry James, upon whom *Jackanapes* seems to have had a powerful and lasting effect both aesthetically and emotionally. Frances Mary Peard, a friend and the author of more than forty books herself, was nothing less than awed by the extraordinary magnetism of *Jackanapes* and strongly urged James to read it. He did, and his response was remarkable. In a letter to her of 24 December 1884, he awarded *Jackanapes* the rare—certainly for him—designation of "a genuine masterpiece." He found in it a wonderful "mixture of nature and art" and the work as a whole "touching beyond anything I have read in a long time." He goes on to praise "the lightness and grace of touch, without effort or mannerism," which "place the thing quite apart." What seemed to have impressed James most about *Jackanapes* was an indescribable but moving quality of the young hero of the story. "I defy anyone," he boldly stated, "to read it without an access of the melting mood."[5] James had no patience with cheap sentimentality created by second-rate writers who expect readers to cry on cue. He clearly did not consider Ewing to be an author of that ilk nor *Jackanapes* to be a story of that sort but something so genuinely touching and artistically accomplished as to deserve to be considered "a masterpiece."

Reviews in magazines with a literary bent in Great Britain as well as in America were similarly positive. For example, the reviewer for the American periodical *Every Other Saturday* wrote that *Jackanapes* "is an exquisite bit of finished work—a Meissonier, in its way."[6] Ewing must have been extremely pleased to read that "the favourite child of her brain" was described as "exquisite" and compared favorably with the highly acclaimed paintings of the French artist Ernest Meissonier (1815–91), especially since the art critic she admired most, John Ruskin, had analyzed closely Meissonier's work and praised it for its precise detailing and economy— nothing wasted. She would have felt pleasantly rewarded because she worked diligently on stylistic economy while writing *Jackanapes*—the reason she was compared with Meissonier. She painstakingly chose words that bore the most fruit, and she made sparse use of any other kind. She knew that Meissonier's work proved that a large canvas is not essential in producing a work of art that evokes a large impact.

Although Christabel Maxwell's overall assessment of Ewing's style is not entirely complimentary, she is undoubtedly correct that "Mrs Ewing . . . clipped, condensed and pruned her style." In Maxwell's opinion, "she was the complete miniaturist."[7] Jennifer Litster has gone so far as to conclude that Ewing "valued brevity above all else."[8]

Ewing considered "condensation," as she called it, to be the central practice of wise and efficient rewriting. For her, it consisted of the fine art of revision by deletion followed by a heightening of cohesiveness achieved through what might be termed the "remembrance" technique, frequently recalling subtly what has been written earlier so that the past and the present in the story are ingeniously merged into the moment of reading. Her self-discipline was the ally rather than the enemy of her imagination so that she could rather easily delete passages that she had admired at the time of writing them. Her ability to know which word to use and then in the process of creating to know how to condense the narrative—knowing what to retain and what to omit—amounted to that kind of intuitive judgment that marks the best writers. In her thinking, a work that is too long dulls the imagination of the reader and puts it to sleep, whereas a work creatively condensed stimulates the imagination, awakens it, which is an aesthetic coup, for the imagination of the reader is often a better author than the author. She explained this theory in a letter of 21 February 1880 to her husband in which she pointed out a serious flaw—as she took it to be—in the work of Elizabeth Barrett Browning:

> Reading away at Mrs. Browning lately has very much confirmed my notion that the fault of her things is lack of condensation. They are almost without exception too long. *I doubt if one should ever leave less than fifty per cent, of a situation, to one's readers' own imagination,* if one aims at the highest class of readers [italics mine]. That swan song to Camoens from his dying lady would have been very perfect in FIVE verses. As it is, one gets tired even of the exquisite refrain "Sweetest eyes were ever seen" (an expression he had used about her eyes in a song, and which haunts her).[9]

In one respect, diligent and efficient condenser as she was, Ewing was a printer's nightmare, for she confessed to her mother in a letter of 3 February 1868 that most of her compressing took place after she received the proof. About her story "Reka Dom," she wrote:

I mean to compress it very much. I will keep the river part, though that is really the shadow of some of my best writing, I think, in the *Dutch* tale describing that scene at Topsham . . . But the sight of proof will help me more than anything . . . In print it comes freshly on me, and I can criticize it more fairly.[10]

Jackanapes is the example *par excellence* of Ewing's technique of condensation. It covers the life of Jackanapes from his birth to his death as a young officer of cavalry in the British Army. Many authors would be convinced that there is material here for a novel of 300 pages and thus would proceed laboriously and repetitively to use all of those 300 pages and, by doing so, lead readers into a realm of tedium provoking sleep. Instead, *Jackanapes* is a tight, artistically stunning story of fifty pages.

Yet, fifty pages is all the condensing Juliana Ewing needed. With accounts of events that reveal the rare qualities of Jackanapes in childhood and boyhood, including the time when he rides the Gipsy red horse Lollo with extraordinary expertise for one so young and hangs on as he rides a mechanical horse, the most challenging ride at the annual fair, and with the presentation of brief events that point convincingly to what kind of person he is—with these and other such glimpses into the first ten or twelve years of Jackanapes's life, it comes as no surprise that as a young cavalry officer he is greatly admired and respected by his fellow soldiers, that he retains his boyhood friendship with Tony Johnson, who loves him without reservation, that he has a profound influence on those, like his grandfather, the Old General, and later the major, his commanding officer, who are sensitive enough to realize what an extraordinary person he is, unlike anyone else they have ever known in their long and varied experiences. Nor is it a surprise that given all these insights into the character of this young man, who in some ways seems too good for this world, too unprepared for its darkness, too innocently direct and honest for its self-absorbed falseness, and too brave and noble to understand its cowardice, that he would without a moment's hesitation go through the hell of close combat with the enemy to rescue a friend, decidedly inferior to himself but nevertheless beloved, at the cost of his own life.

What holds the story together, the ingenious unifying feature that prevents disjointedness, is the Grey Goose, very much an indispensable character in the work, occupying a prominent place in the first few pages and referred to humorously (but with serious intent) as a person who lives in Jackanapes's village of Goose Green. The personified Grey Goose is linked with Jackanapes's great aunt: "The Grey Goose and the big Miss Jessamine were the only elderly persons who kept their ages secret."[11] Like other residents of the village, "the Grey Goose also avoided dates, but this was partly because her brain, though intelligent, was not mathematical, and computation was beyond her" (p. 10). The Grey Goose is thus in evidence through much of the early chapters, and the mention of her at the beginning of the second part of the story furnishes a needed transition to the later period: "Twenty and odd years later the Grey Goose was still alive, and in full possession of her faculties, such as they were. She lived slowly and carefully, and she lived long" (p. 42).

Personified as one of the "residents" of Goose Green, she also functions as representative of them, and they in turn represent a certain segment of humankind, those who live "slowly and carefully" and thus "live long." The Grey Goose philosophy of life is to avoid danger at all cost. In contrast, Jackanapes has no hesitancy in mounting that horse in a ride on the giddy-go-round that is so perilous that only the bravest risk it. Jackanapes's conduct while on the frightening ride tellingly portrays what kind of boy he is. On the ride, he

> stuck to him [the horse on the ride] as a horseman should. During the first round he waved his hat ... At the second, he looked a little pale, but sat upright, though somewhat unnecessarily rigid; at the third round he shut his eyes. During the fourth his hat fell off, and he clasped the horse's neck. By the fifth he had laid his yellow head against the ... [horse's] mane and so clung anyhow till the hobby-horses stopped, when the proprietor assisted him to alight, and he sat down rather suddenly and said he had enjoyed it very much. (p. 29)

Immediately following this description of Jackanapes's disregard of possible bodily harm and physical sickness and in stark opposition to it is another description, this one of how the Grey Goose reacts to the threat of bodily harm and physical sickness: Jackanapes hastens into the danger; the Grey Goose hastens away from it:

> The Grey Goose always ran away at the first approach of the caravans and never came back to the Green till there was nothing left of the Fair but foot-marks and oyster-shells. Running away was her pet principle; the only system, she maintained, by which you can live long and easily, and lose nothing. If you run away when you see danger, you can come back when all is safe. Run quickly, return slowly, hold your head high, and gabble as loud as you can, and you'll preserve the respect of the Goose Green to a peaceful old age. Why should you struggle and get hurt, if you can lower your head and swerve, and not lose a feather? Why in the world should any one spoil the pleasure of life, or risk his skin, if he can help it? (pp. 29–30)

The Grey Goose philosophy of life, suggests Ewing, is that of the multitude and thus in stark contrast to that of the hero of the story. He is unique among them because everything about him suggests the opposite of their slowness and carefulness. As Jackanapes and Lollo speed madly over the village green, it is as though they are rushing through time without thought of danger to an early death. Lollo is described by the horse's Gipsy owner as "a racer," and that word fits Jackanapes perfectly as Ewing skillfully sets him apart from the world in which he lives, so different that he is, in a sense, an alien in the wrong place.

It was strictly Ewing's own concept of such a boy—different, even unique, racing through life to an early death—that served as the idea around which she constructed *Jackanapes*. It has sometimes been assumed, however, that she got the notion from a drawing that the illustrator who was to work with her on a new book, Randolph Caldecott, sent to her. Ewing herself is largely responsible for this misconception, for in a letter to her husband she wrote: "I have done my little story [*Jackanapes*] *to Caldecott's picture*, and I have a strong notion it will please you [italics mine]."[12] The truth is that she had in her mind the image of a handsome, yellow-haired boy riding a fast red pony with wild abandon through a village green scattering behind him the slow geese and the slow residents of the village—an image that encapsulates the story of *Jackanapes*—before she ever received the drawing from her illustrator. In fact, she *instructed* him as to what was to be in that very drawing. In her letter to him of 4 August 1879, she requested the following: "If the coloured sketch would be easily concocted out of a laddie with an aureole of warm yellow hair on a red-haired pony, full tilt among the geese over a village green (the geese to include pretty frightened members of my sex!)."[13] Thus, she did not create Jackanapes from Caldecott's picture; Caldecott created his picture from her concept of Jackanapes.

What Ewing wished to underscore forcefully regarding her young hero, then, was the brevity of his life and the speed with which he lives it out. Consequently, she skillfully associates him with speed at every turn. He wants Lollo because the horse is extremely fast, and he rides the horse through the green as he rides through life—fast. Some twenty years of his life whirl by so fast in the story that there is time for the author to mention only a few happenings during that period. Since the motif of speed is central to the story, Ewing had no hesitation in utilizing her key practice of condensation so that she could suggest the speed of time by passing with breakneck speed through the brief life of Jackanapes. Furthermore, such a gap, she believed, can satisfactorily be filled in by the imagination of a perceptive reader. To quote again one of her most telling remarks about the importance of condensing: "I doubt if one should ever leave less than fifty per cent, of a situation, to one's readers' own imagination if one aims at the highest class of readers." There seems little doubt that with *Jackanapes*, she aimed at "the highest class of readers."

When he becomes a cavalry officer, which also takes place fast, he acquires another horse as fast as Lollo and with the same name. Ewing includes numerous minor details such as this, sometimes so subtle that one may not realize that they are part of the motif of speed. For example, the real name of the story's young hero is "Theodore," but that fact is mentioned only on a single page because the name does not fit him, and everyone, even the old General, his grandfather, calls him by the name that seems meant for him, "Jackanapes," which ironically is a slightly longer word than "Theodore," but which by most speakers is pronounced more rapidly. "Theodore" is too slow a name for the fast Jackanapes, and so that is what he is called. The doctor who delivers him gives him that name at his birth, predicting that he will be a fast moving, active child.[14]

Significantly, Jackanapes is called by that one name always and no mention is ever made of his last name. On the other hand, Ewing is careful to give the full name of his best friend, Tony Johnson, and to refer to him that way often. This difference (what might be termed a "fast" name as opposed to a "slower" one in pronunciation) works toward underscoring the extreme contrast between the two characters. Indeed, the sole function of Tony Johnson is as a character foil to Jackanapes, who is fast in every way while his inept friend Tony Johnson is slow. Because of that, Tony Johnson is placed in the story's scheme with the Grey Goose and all those residents of Goose Green, who live quietly and slowly and live to a ripe old age whereas the one who is truly different from all others, the unique Jackanapes, is the one who dies at the story's end as Tony Johnson lives on.

Condensing by omission, points out Marghanita Laski, can be a risky procedure, and she finds Ewing guilty of the literary unforgivable sin of leaving out so much of what occurred in the life of Jackanapes in those missing twenty years that his characterization in the story is not convincing and the work badly flawed:

> The story [*Jackanapes*], too, oddly lacks continuity. We see the honest brave child that Jackanapes was and it is reasonable to suppose that he will grow up into the kind of man who gives his life for his friend. But we are not shown any of the stages by which his character develops. Here, at one moment is a nice mischievous little boy; here, twenty years later, is a gallant young soldier, dying as he hears a prayer; but there is no real thread of causation between the two. It is a moral tale that we have here rather than a real story.[15]

The major flaw in Laski's analysis is that it presupposes that *Jackanapes* is a maturation or coming-of-age story when it is not. She makes this error because Jackanapes is first described as a little boy and then toward the end as a young man. Such an argument ignores the numerous details in the story that make it clear that Jackanapes does not change, does not mature. It is extremely important in grasping what kind of story this is to understand that he remains always the same Jackanapes. This point is underscored in the passage describing Miss Jessamine's attitude toward his name: "She had always most fully intended that he should be called Theodore when he had outgrown the ridiculous appropriateness of his nickname. *The fact was that he had not outgrown it*" (p. 33, italics mine). So he is Jackanapes until the end, even when he has become an officer in the cavalry.

Ironically, the final sentence of Laski's statement, intended no doubt as perceptive fault-finding, is accidental brilliance: "It is a moral tale that we have here rather than a real story." In truth, *Jackanapes* is not a "real story" nor is it intended to be if by "real" is implied realistic or what is usually expected in a story by way of structure and character development. *Jackanapes* is, indeed, a "moral tale," and that is precisely what Ewing meant it to be. It is a moral tale inasmuch as it deals with an extraordinary person who is nothing less than a moral phenomenon.

This character type, the moral phenomenon, is rare in literature and usually is depicted as a young male whose innate and all-pervading innocence is so pronounced that he stands in stark contrast to those with whom he is thrown. The best-known character of this sort is probably Herman Melville's Billy Budd, the "Handsome Sailor" of the novel *Billy Budd, Sailor*. He is incapable of deception, that quality so entrenched in his nature that Melville describes him as incapable even of speaking ironically. Although he is radically different from his companions aboard his ship, or perhaps *because* he is so different from them, a picture of physical perfection, athletic ability of a striking degree, heedless of danger, a stranger to fear, and above all a lover of situations involving the sensation of participating in elating motion—because he is all of these things, he is a magnet to his fellow sailors. His good nature and his healthy attitude toward life win them over, but Satan's stand-in, the master-at-arms aboard the ship, hates the innocence in Billy Budd and because of that, he schemes for him to be hanged on a trumped-up charge of mutiny. Significantly, Melville describes Billy Budd as Adam before the Fall, one who is an alien in a fallen world and cannot exist for long in it. He is pre-lapsarian man in a post-lapsarian world.[16]

The plots of *Billy Budd, Sailor* and *Jackanapes* are quite different, but the central characters are cut from the same cloth. Jackanapes enjoys nothing more than the sensation of riding a fast horse at a "wild gallop" (p. 31). He even delights in the challenging ride on the giddy-go-round at the annual fair. Billy Budd is similarly fond of riding a yardarm as if it were a fast horse: "There he was, astride the weather yardarm, foot in the Flemish horse as stirrup, both hands tugging at the earing as a bridle, in very much the same attitude of young Alexander curbing the fiery Bucephalus. A superb figure, tossed up as by the horns of Taurus against the thunderous sky, cheerily hallowing to the strenuous file along the spar."[17] The mention of Bucephalus in both works is a strange coincidence as is their equal love of racing along in the wind, the one on a fast horse, the other aloft on a ship hurrying through the water as if on a horse, one blowing his trumpet in pure joy of the experience, the other shouting at the top of his lungs with the same joy, to the observers below.

In appearance, Billy Budd and Jackanapes might be twins. Both strikingly handsome, unusually athletic and powerful. What Melville writes about Billy Budd describes exactly Jackanapes: he is marked by "good looks, cheery health, and frank enjoyment of young life."[18] Both are blessed with a striking feature that is emphasized by both authors: a beautiful, full head of yellow (not light or blond, but conspicuously yellow) hair—and striking blue eyes—another in a string of strange coincidences. On his ship, Billy Budd is a great favorite among fellow crew members as is Jackanapes among the other soldiers in his unit. "From the first," Billy Budd captures the attention of his commanding officer, Captain Vere, who is drawn to him.[19] In a like manner, Jackanapes becomes the favorite of the major, his commanding officer, who is similarly drawn to him. The dying words of Billy Budd reflect his goodness, his unselfishness, and his pristine innocence: "God bless Captain Vere."[20] It is Captain Vere who brings on the death of Billy Budd. On his deathbed, Jackanapes asks the major to bless Tony Johnson by being patient with his weaknesses and considerate of him. It is Tony Johnson who indirectly is responsible for Jackanapes's death since he is fatally wounded while saving the life of Tony Johnson. There are more of these parallels, but the most obvious one is simply how much Jackanapes and Billy Budd resemble each other in the authorial concepts of what they are, the creative imagination's version of a pre-lapsarian man. And the profound and forceful thematic conclusion is basically the same in both works: the world is such that a person as that delineated in the two works cannot exist for long, for that which makes him so honorable and honest, so courageous, so loving, so direct and genuine, so obedient to the essential precepts of decency, cannot withstand the inexorable forces that take a thousand different forms in a world alien to their very nature.

With so much in common between two fictional characters who represent a type perhaps never dealt with in the same manner as these two in these two works, it is inevitable that the question arises as to the probability that one is based on the other, that one author was strongly influenced by the other. Evidence is not forthcoming that offers absolute proof of influence in this instance. Of course, Herman Melville's reputation overshadows Ewing's. He was her senior by twenty-two years, and much of his work was available during her lifetime so that she could have read some of it before she composed *Jackanapes* in 1879. But she could not have read *Billy Budd*, for it was not published until 1924, long after her death in 1885. Melville did not begin writing *Billy Budd* until 1886, a year after Ewing's death.[21] On the other hand, *Jackanapes* appeared first in magazine form in 1879 and as a book in 1883, adequate time for the widely reading Melville to have seen a review of it and through curiosity to have read it, although it is not listed in accounts of books he owned.[22]

One measure of an author's importance is the impact and influence his or her writings have had on other authors, especially those of universally acclaimed greatness. Rudyard Kipling read Juliana Ewing's *Jackanapes* and mentioned it in one of his own short stories (see Introduction). Henry James read *Jackanapes* and declared it "a genuine masterpiece." Is it, therefore, too much to suggest that Herman Melville's idea for the all but unique character at the center of *Billy Budd*, the product of his old age and considered a masterpiece second only to *Moby-Dick*, came to him through the all but unique character in Ewing's *Jackanapes*?

Jackanapes

Chapter I

Last noon beheld them full of lusty life,
Last eve in Beauty's circle proudly gay,
The midnight brought the signal-sound of strife,
The morn the marshalling in arms—the day
Battle's magnificently stern array!
The thunder-clouds close o'er it, which when rent
The earth is covered thick with other clay,
Which her own clay shall cover, heaped and pent,
Rider and horse—friend, foe,—in one red burial blent.

Their praise is hymn'd by loftier harps than mine:
Yet one I would select from that proud throng.
—to thee, to thousands, of whom each
And one as all a ghastly gap did make
In his own kind and kindred, whom to teach
Forgetfulness were mercy for their sake;
The Archangel's trump, not glory's, must awake
Those whom they thirst for.

Byron

Two Donkeys and the Geese lived on the Green, and all other residents of any social standing lived in houses round it. The houses had no names. Everybody's address was, "The Green" but the Postman and the people of the place knew where each family lived. As to the rest of the world, what has one to do with the rest of the world, when he is safe at home on his own Goose Green? Moreover, if a stranger did come on any lawful business, he might ask his way at the shop.

Most of the inhabitants were long-lived, early deaths (like that of the little Miss Jessamine) being exceptional; and most of the old people were proud of their age, especially the sexton, who would be ninety-nine come Martinmas, and whose father remembered a man who had carried arrows, as a boy, for the battle of Flodden Field. The Grey Goose and the big Miss Jessamine were the only elderly persons who kept their ages secret. Indeed, Miss Jessamine never mentioned any one's age, or recalled the exact year in which anything had happened. She said that she had been taught that it was bad manners to do so "in a mixed assembly."

The Grey Goose also avoided dates, but this was partly because her brain, though intelligent, was not mathematical. And computation was beyond her. She never got further than "last Michaelmas," "the Michaelmas before that," and "the Michaelmas before the Michaelmas before that." After this her head, which was small, became confused, and she said, "Ga, ga!" and changed the subject.

But she remembered the little Miss Jessamine, the Miss Jessamine with the "conspicuous" hair. Her aunt, the big Miss Jessamine, said it was her only fault. The hair was clean, was abundant, was glossy, but do what you would with it it never looked quite like other people's. And at church, after Saturday night's wash, it shone like the best brass fender after a Spring cleaning. In short, it was conspicuous, which does not become a young woman—especially in church.

These were worrying times altogether, and the Green was used for strange purposes. A political meeting was held on it with the village Cobbler in the chair, and a speaker that came by stage coach from the town, where they had wrecked the baker's shops, and discussed the price of bread. He came a second time, by stage, but the people had heard something about him in the meanwhile, and they did not keep him on the Green. They took him to the pond and tried to make him swim, which he could not do, and the whole affair was very disturbing to all quiet and peaceable fowls. After which another man came, and preached sermons on the Green, and a great many people went to hear him; for those were "trying times," and folk ran hither and thither for comfort. And then what did they do but drill the ploughboys on the Green, to get them ready to fight the French, and teach them the goose-step! However, that came to an end at last, for Bony was sent to St Helena, and the ploughboys were sent back to the plough.

Everybody lived in fear of Bony in those days, especially the naughty children, who were kept in order during the day by threats of, "Bony shall have you," and who had nightmares about him in the dark. They thought he was an Ogre in a cocked hat. The Grey Goose thought he was a Fox, and that all the men of England were going out in red coats to hunt him. It was no use to argue the point, for she had a very small head, and when one idea got into it there was no room for another.

Besides, the Grey Goose never saw Bony, nor did the children, which rather spoilt the terror of him, so that the Black Captain became more effective as a Bogy with hardened offenders. The Grey Goose remembered *his* coming to the place perfectly. What he came for she did not pretend to know. It was all part and parcel of the war and bad times. He was called the Black Captain, partly because of himself, and partly because of his wonderful black mare. Strange stories were afloat of how far and how fast that mare could go, when her master's hand was on her mane and he whispered in her ear. Indeed, some people thought we might reckon ourselves very lucky if we were not out of the frying-pan into the fire, and had not got a certain well-known Gentleman of the Road to protect us against the French. But that, of course, made him none the less useful to the Johnsons' Nurse, when the little Miss Johnsons were naughty.

"You leave off crying this minnit, Miss Jane, or I'll give you right away to that horrid wicked officer. Jemima! Just look out o' the windy, if you please, and see if the Black Cap'n's a-coming with his horse to carry away Miss Jane."

And there, sure enough, the Black Captain strode by, with his sword clattering as if it did not know whose head to cut off first. But he did not call for Miss Jane that time. He went on to the Green, where he came so suddenly upon the eldest Master Johnson, sitting in a puddle on purpose, in his new nankeen skeleton suit, that the young gentleman thought judgment had overtaken him at last, and abandoned himself to the howlings of despair. His howls were redoubled when he was clutched from behind and swung over the Black Captain's shoulder, but in five minutes his tears were stanched, and he was playing with the officer's accoutrements. All of which the Grey Goose saw with her own eyes, and heard afterwards that that bad boy had been whining to go back to the Black Captain ever since, which showed how hardened he was, and that nobody but Bonaparte himself could be expected to do him any good.

But those were "trying times." It was bad enough when the pickle of a large and respectable family cried for the Black Captain; when it came to the little Miss Jessamine crying for him, one felt that the sooner the French landed and had done with it the better.

The big Miss Jessamine's objection to him was that he was a soldier, and this prejudice was shared by all the Green. "A soldier," as the speaker from the town had observed, "is a bloodthirsty, unsettled sort of a rascal; that the peaceable, home-loving, bread-winning citizen can never conscientiously look on as a brother, till he has beaten his sword into a ploughshare, and his spear into a pruning-hook."

On the other hand there was some truth in what the Postman (an old soldier) said in reply; that the sword has to cut a way for us out of many a scrape into which our bread-winners get us when they drive their Ploughshares into fallows that don't belong to them. Indeed, whilst our most peaceful citizens were prosperous chiefly by means of cotton, of sugar, and of the rise and fall of the money market (not to speak of such saleable matters as opium, fire-arms, and "black ivory"), disturbances were apt to arise in India, Africa, and other outlandish parts, where the fathers of our domestic race were making fortunes for their families. And, for that matter, even on the Green, we did not wish the military to leave us in the lurch, so long as there was any fear that the French were coming.[23]

To let the Black Captain have little Miss Jessamine, however, was another matter. Her aunt would not hear of it; and then, to crown all, it appeared that the Captain's father did not think the young lady good enough for his son. Never was any affair more clearly brought to a conclusion.

But those were "trying times"; and one moon-light night, when the Grey Goose was sound asleep upon one leg, the Green was rudely shaken under her by the thud of a horse's feet. "Ga, ga!" said she, putting down the other leg, and running away.

By the time she returned to her place not a thing was to be seen or heard. The horse had passed like a shot. But next day, there was hurrying and scurrying and crackling at a very early hour all about the white house with the black beams, where Miss Jessamine lived. And when the sun was so low, and the shadows so long on the grass that the Grey Goose felt ready to run away at the sight of her own neck, little Miss Jane Johnson, and her "particular friend" Clarinda, sat under the big oak tree on the Green, and Jane pinched Clarinda's little finger till she found that she could keep a secret, and then she told her in confidence that she had heard from Nurse and Jemima that Miss Jessamine's niece had been a very naughty girl, and that that horrid wicked officer had come for her on his black horse, and carried her right away.

"Will she never come back?" asked Clarinda.

"Oh, no!" said Jane decidedly. "Bony never brings people back."

"Not never no more?" sobbed Clarinda, for she was weak-minded, and could not bear to think that Bony never never let naughty people go home again.

Next day Jane had heard more.

"He has taken her to a Green."

"A Goose Green?" asked Clarinda.

"No. A Gretna Green. Don't ask so many questions, child," said Jane; who, having no more to tell, gave herself airs.

Jane was wrong on one point. Miss Jessamine's niece did come back, and she and her husband were forgiven. The Grey Goose remembered it well, it was Michaelmastide, the Michaelmas before the Michaelmas before the Michaelmas—but, ga, ga! What does the date matter? It was autumn, harvest-time, and everybody was so busy prophesying and praying about the crops, that the young couple wandered through the lanes, and got blackberries for Miss Jessamine's celebrated crab and blackberry jam, and made guys of themselves with bryony-wreaths, and not a soul troubled his head about them, except the children, and the Postman. The children dogged the Black Captain's footsteps (his bubble reputation as an Ogre having burst), clamouring for a ride on the black mare. And the Postman would go somewhat out of his postal way to catch the Captain's dark eye, and show that he had not forgotten how to salute an officer.

But they were "trying times." One afternoon the black mare was stepping gently up and down the grass, with her head at her master's shoulder, and as many children crowded on to her silky back as if she had been an elephant in a menagerie; and the next afternoon she carried him away, sword and sabre-tach clattering war-music at her side, and the old Postman waiting for them, rigid with salutation, at the four cross roads.

War and bad times! It was a hard winter, and the big Miss Jessamine and the little Miss Jessamine (but she was Mrs. Black-Captain now) lived very economically that they might help their poorer neighbours. They neither entertained nor went into company, but the young lady always went up the village as far as the "George and Dragon" for air and exercise, when the London Mail[24] came in.

One day (it was a day in the following June) it came in earlier than usual, and the young lady was not there to meet it.

But a crowd soon gathered round the "George and Dragon," gaping to see the Mail Coach dressed with flowers and oak-leaves, and the guard wearing a laurel wreath over and above his royal livery. The ribbons that decked the horses were stained and flecked with the warmth and foam of the pace at which they had come, for they had pressed on with the news of Victory.

Miss Jessamine was sitting with her niece under the oak tree on the Green, when the Postman put a newspaper silently into her hand. Her niece turned quickly—

"Is there news?"

"Don't agitate yourself, my dear," said her aunt. "I will read it aloud, and then we can enjoy it together; a far more comfortable method, my love, than when you go up the village, and come out of breath, having snatched half the news as you run."

"I am all attention, dear aunt," said the little lady, clasping her hands tightly on her lap.

Then Miss Jessamine read aloud—she was proud of her reading—and the old soldier stood at attention behind her, with such a blending of pride and pity on his face as it was strange to see: —

> Downing Street,
>   June 22, 1815, 1 a.m.

"That's one in the morning," gasped the Postman; "beg your pardon, mum."

But though he apologized, he could not refrain from echoing here and there a weighty word. "Glorious victory,"—"Two hundred pieces of artillery,"—"Immense quantity of ammunition,"—and so forth.

"The loss of the British Army upon this occasion has unfortunately been most severe. It had not been possible to make out a return of the killed and wounded when Major Percy left headquarters. The names of the officers killed and wounded, as far as they can be collected, are annexed.

"I have the honor—"

"The list, Aunt! Read the list!"

"My love—my darling—let us go in and—"

"No. Now! Now!"

To one thing the supremely afflicted are entitled in their sorrow—to be obeyed—and yet it is the last kindness that people commonly will do them. But Miss Jessamine did. Steadying her voice, as best she might, she read on, and the old soldier stood bare-headed to hear that first Roll of the Dead at Waterloo, which began with the Duke of Brunswick, and ended with Ensign Brown.[25] Five-and-thirty British Captains fell asleep that day on the Bed of Honour, and the Black Captain slept among them.

◆ ◆ ◆

There are killed and wounded by war, of whom no returns reach Downing Street.

Three days later, the Captain's wife had joined him, and Miss Jessamine was kneeling by the cradle of their orphan son, a purple-red morsel of humanity, with conspicuously golden hair.

"Will he live, Doctor?"

"Live? God bless my soul, ma'am! Look at him! The young Jackanapes!"

Chapter II

And he wandered away and away
with Nature, the dear old Nurse.

Longfellow

The Grey Goose remembered quite well the year that Jackanapes began to walk, for it was the year that the speckled hen for the first time in all her motherly life got out of patience when she was sitting. She had been rather proud of the eggs—they were unusually large—but she never quite felt comfortable on them; and whether it was because she used to get cramp, and go off the nest, or because the season was bad, or what, she never could tell, but every egg was addled but one, and the one that did hatch gave her more trouble than any chick she had ever reared.

It was a fine, downy, bright yellow little thing, but it had a monstrous big nose and feet, and such an ungainly walk as she knew no other instance of in her well-bred and high-stepping family. And as to behaviour, it was not that it was either quarrelsome or moping, but simply unlike the rest. When the other chicks hopped and cheeped on the Green about their mothers' feet, this solitary yellow brat went waddling off on its own responsibility, and do or cluck what the speckled hen would, it went to play in the Pond.

It was off one day as usual, and the hen was fussing and fuming after it, when the Postman, going to deliver a letter to Miss Jessamine's door, was nearly knocked over by the good lady herself, who, bursting out of the house with her cap just off and her bonnet just on, fell into his arms, saying—

"Baby! Baby! Jackanapes! Jackanapes!"

If the Postman loved anything on earth, he loved the Captain's yellow-headed child, so propping Miss Jessamine against her own door-post, he followed the direction of her trembling fingers and made for the Green.

Jackanapes had had the start of the Postman by nearly ten minutes. The world—the round green world with an oak tree on it—was just becoming very interesting to him. He had tried, vigorously but ineffectually, to mount a passing pig the last time he was taken out walking; but then he was encumbered with a nurse. Now he was his own master, and might, by courage and energy, become the master of that delightful, downy, dumpy, yellow thing that was bobbing along over the green grass in front of him.

Forward! Charge! He aimed well, and grabbed it, but only to feel the delicious downiness and dumpiness slipping through his fingers as he fell upon his face. "Quawk!" said the yellow thing, and wobbled off sideways. It was this oblique movement that enabled Jackanapes to come up with it, for it was bound for the Pond, and obliged to come back into line. He failed again from top-heaviness, and his prey escaped sideway as before, and, as before, lost ground in getting back to the direct road to the Pond.

And at the Pond the Postman found them both, one yellow thing rocking safely on the ripples that lie beyond duck-weed, and the other washing his draggled frock with tears, because he too had tried to sit upon the Pond, and it wouldn't hold him.

Chapter III

If studious, copie fair what time hath blurred,
Redeem truth from his jawes; if souldier,
Chase brave employments with a naked sword
Throughout the world. Fool not; for all may have,
If they dare try, a glorious life, or grave.

◆   ◆   ◆

In brief, acquit thee bravely: play the man.
Look not on pleasures as they come, but go.
Defer not the least virtue: life's poore span
Make not an ell, by trifling in thy woe.
If thou do ill, the joy fades, not the pains.
If well: the pain doth fade, the joy remains.

George Herbert

Young Mrs. Johnson, who was a mother of many, hardly knew which to pity more; Miss Jessamine for having her little ways and her antimacassars rumpled by a young Jackanapes; or the boy himself, for being brought up by an old maid.

Oddly enough, she would probably have pitied neither, had Jackanapes been a girl. (One is so apt to think that what works smoothest works to the highest ends, having no patience for the results of friction.) That Father in God, who bade the young men to be pure, and the maidens brave, greatly disturbed a member of his congregation, who thought that the great preacher had made a slip of the tongue.

"That the girls should have purity, and the boys courage, is what you would say, good Father?"

"Nature has done that," was the reply; "I meant what I said."

In good sooth, a young maid is all the better for learning some robuster virtues than maidenliness and not to move the antimacassars. And the robuster virtues require some fresh air and freedom. As, on the other hand, Jackanapes (who had a boy's full share of the little beast and the young monkey in his composition) was none the worse, at his tender years, for learning some maidenliness—so far as maidenliness means decency, pity, unselfishness, and pretty behavior.

And it is due to him to say that he was an obedient boy, and a boy whose word could be depended on, long before his grandfather the General came to live at the Green.

He was obedient; that is he did what his great-aunt told him. But—oh dear! oh dear!—the pranks he played, which it had never entered into her head to forbid!

It was when he had just been put into skeletons (frocks never suited him) that he became very friendly with Master Tony Johnson, a younger brother of the young gentleman who sat in the puddle on purpose. Tony was not enterprising, and Jackanapes led him by the nose. One summer's evening they were out late, and Miss Jessamine was becoming anxious, when Jackanapes presented himself with a ghastly face all besmirched with tears. He was unusually subdued.

"I'm afraid," he sobbed; "if you please, I'm very much afraid that Tony Johnson's dying in the churchyard."

Miss Jessamine was just beginning to be distracted, when she smelt Jackanapes.

"You naughty, naught boys! Do you mean to tell me that you've been smoking?"

"Not pipes," urged Jackanapes; "upon my honour, Aunty, not pipes. Only segars like Mr. Johnson's! and only made of brown paper with a very very little tobacco from the shop inside them."

Whereupon, Miss Jessamine sent a servant to the churchyard, who found Tony Johnson lying on a tombstone, very sick, and having ceased to entertain any hopes of his own recovery.

If it could be possible that any "unpleasantness" could arise between two such amiable neighbours as Miss Jessamine and Mrs. Johnson—and if the still more incredible paradox can be that ladies may differ over a point on which they are agreed—that point was the admitted fact that Tony Johnson was "delicate," and the difference lay chiefly in this: Mrs. Johnson said that Tony was delicate—meaning that he was more finely strung, more sensitive, a properer subject for pampering and petting than Jackanapes, and that, consequently, Jackanapes was to blame for leading Tony into scrapes which resulted in his being chilled, frightened, or (most frequently) sick. But when Miss Jessamine said that Tony Johnson was delicate, she meant that he was more puling, less manly, and less healthily brought up than Jackanapes, who, when they got into mischief together, was certainly not to blame because his friend could not get wet, sit a kicking donkey, ride in a giddy-go-round, bear the noise of a cracker, or smoke brown paper with impunity, as he could.

Not that there was ever the slightest quarrel between the ladies. It never even came near it, except the day after Tony had been so very sick with riding Bucephalus in the giddy-go-round. Mrs. Johnson had explained to Miss Jessamine that the reason Tony was so easily upset, was the unusual sensitivity (as the doctor had explained it to her) of the nervous centres in her family—"Fiddlestick!" So Mrs. Johnson understood Miss Jessamine to say, but it appeared that she only said "Treaclestick!" which is quite another thing, and of which Tony was undoubtedly fond.

It was at the Fair that Tony was made ill by riding on Bucephalus. Once a year the Goose Green became the scene of a carnival. First of all, carts and caravans were rumbling up all along, day and night. Jackanapes could hear them as he lay in bed, and could hardly sleep for speculating what booths and whirligigs he should find fairly established, when he and his dog Spitfire went out after breakfast. As a matter of fact, he seldom had to wait so long for news of the Fair. The Postman knew the window out of which Jackanapes' yellow head would come, and was ready with his report.

"Royal Theayter, Master Jackanapes, in the old place, but be careful o' them seats, sir; they're ricketier than ever. Two sweets and a ginger-beer under the oak tree, and the Flying Boats is just a-coming along the road."

No doubt it was partly because he had already suffered severely in the Flying Boats that Tony collapsed so quickly in the giddy-go-round. He only mounted Bucephalus (who was spotted, and had no tail) because Jackanapes urged him, and held out the ingenious hope that the round-and-round feeling would very likely cure the up-and-down sensation. It did not, however, and Tony tumbled off during the first revolution.

Jackanapes was not absolutely free from qualms, having once mounted the Black Prince he stuck to him as a horseman should. During the first round he waved his hat, and observed with some concern that the Black Prince had lost an ear since last Fair; at the second, he looked a little pale but sat upright, though somewhat unnecessarily rigid; at the third round, he shut his eyes. During the fourth his hat fell off, and he clasped his horse's neck. By the fifth he had laid his yellow head against the Black Prince's mane, and so clung anyhow till the hobby-horses stopped, when the proprietor assisted him to alight, and he sat down rather suddenly and said he had enjoyed it very much.

The Grey Goose always ran away at the first approach of the caravans, and never came back to the Green till nothing was left of the Fair but footmarks and oyster-shells. Running away was her pet principle; the only system, she maintained, by which you can live long and easily, and lose nothing. If you run away when you see danger, you can come back when all is safe. Run quickly, return slowly, hold your head high, and gabble as loud as you can, and you'll preserve the respect of the Goose Green to a peaceful old age. Why should you struggle and get hurt, if you can lower your head and swerve, and not lose a feather? Why in the world should any one spoil the pleasure of life, or risk his skin, if he can help it?

"What's the use?"
Said the Goose.

Before answering which one might have to consider what world—which life—and whether his skin were a goose-skin; but the Grey Goose's head would never have held all that.

Grass soon grows over footprints, and the village children took the oyster-shells to trim their gardens with; but the year after Tony rode Bucephalus there lingered another relic of Fair—time, in which Jackanapes was deeply interested. "The Green" proper was originally only part of a straggling common, which in its turn merged into some wilder waste land where gipsies sometimes squatted if the authorities would allow them, especially after the annual Fair. And it was after the Fair that Jackanapes, out rambling by himself, was knocked over by the Gipsy's son riding the Gipsy's red-haired pony at break-neck pace across the common.

Jackanapes got up and shook himself, none the worse, except for being heels over head in love with the red-haired pony. What a rate he went at! How he spurned the ground with his nimble feet! How his red coat shone in the sunshine! And what bright eyes peeped out of his dark forelock as it was blown by the wind!

The Gipsy boy had had a fright, and he was willing enough to reward Jackanapes for not having been hurt, by consenting to let him have a ride.

"Do you mean to kill the little fine gentleman, and swing us all on the gibbet, you rascal?" screamed the Gipsy-mother, just as Jackanapes and the pony set off.

"He would get on," replied her son. "It'll not kill him. He'll fall on his yellow head, and it's as tough as a cocoa-nut."

But Jackanapes did not fall. He stuck to the red-haired pony as he had stuck to the hobby-horse; but oh, how different the delight of this wild gallop with flesh and blood! Just as his legs were beginning to feel as if he did not feel them, the Gipsy boy cried "Lollo!" Round went the pony so unceremoniously, that, with as little ceremony, Jackanapes clung to his neck, and he did not properly recover himself before Lollo stopped with a jerk at the place where they had started.

"Is his name Lollo?" asked Jackanapes, his hand lingering in the wiry mane.

"Yes."

"What does Lollo mean?"

"Red."

"Is Lollo your pony?"

"No. My father's." And the Gipsy boy led Lollo away.

At the first opportunity Jackanapes stole away again to the common. This time he saw the Gipsy-father, smoking a dirty pipe.

"Lollo is your pony, isn't he?" said Jackanapes.

"Yes."

"He's a very nice one."

"He's a racer."

"You don't want to sell him, do you?"

"Fifteen pounds," said the Gipsy-father; and Jackanapes sighed and went home again. That very afternoon he and Tony rode the two donkeys, and Tony managed to get thrown, and even Jackanapes's donkey kicked. But it was jolting, clumsy work after the elastic swiftness and the dainty mischief of the red-haired pony.

A few days later Miss Jessamine spoke very seriously to Jackanapes. She was a good deal agitated as she told him that his grandfather the General was coming to the Green, and that he must be on his very best behaviour during the visit. If it had been feasible to leave off calling him Jackanapes and to get used to his baptismal name of Theodore before the day after to-morrow (when the General was due), it would have been satisfactory. But Miss Jessamine feared it would be impossible in practice, and she had scruples about it on principle. It would not seem quite truthful, although she had always most fully intended that he should be called Theodore when he had outgrown the ridiculous appropriateness of his nickname. The fact was that he had not outgrown it, but he must take care to remember who was meant when his grandfather said Theodore.

Indeed for that matter he must take care all along. "You are apt to be giddy, Jackanapes," said Miss Jessamine.

"Yes Aunt," said Jackanapes, thinking of the hobby-horses.

"You are a good boy, Jackanapes. Thank God, I can tell your grandfather that. An obedient boy, an honourable boy, and a kind-hearted boy. But you are—in short, you are a Boy, Jackanapes. And I hope"—added Miss Jessamine, desperate with the results of experience—"that the General knows that Boys will be Boys."

What mischief could be foreseen, Jackanapes promised to guard against. He was to keep his clothes and his hands clean, to look over this catechism, not to put sticky things in his pockets, to keep that hair of his smooth—("It's the wind that blows it, Aunty," said Jackanapes—"I'll send by the coach for some bear's grease," said Miss Jessamine, tying a knot in her pocket-handkerchief)—not to burst in at the parlour-door, not to talk at the top of his voice, not to crumple his Sunday frill, and to sit quite quiet during the sermon, to be sure to say "sir" to the General, to be careful about rubbing his shoes on the door-mat, and to bring his lesson-books to his aunt at once that she might iron down the dogs' ears. The General arrived, and for the first day all went well, except that Jackanapes' hair was as wild as usual, for the hair-dresser had no bear's-grease left. He began to feel more at ease with his grandfather, and disposed to talk confidentially with him, as he did with the Postman. All that the General felt it would take too long to tell, but the result was the same. He was disposed to talk confidentially with Jackanapes.

"Mons'ous pretty place this," he said, looking out of the lattice on to the Green, where the grass was vivid with sunset, and the shadows were long and peaceful.

"You should see it in Fair-week, sir," said Jackanapes, shaking his yellow mop, and leaning back in his one of the two Chippendale arm-chairs in which they sat.

"A fine time that, eh?" said the General, with a twinkle in his left eye. (The other one was glass.)

Jackanapes shook his hair once more. "I enjoyed this last one best of all," he said. "I'd so much money."

"By George, it's not a common complaint in these bad times. How much had ye?"

"I'd two shillings. A new shilling Aunty gave me, and elevenpence I had saved up, and a penny from the Postman—*sir*!" added Jackanapes with a jerk, having forgotten it.

"And how did ye spend it—*sir*?" inquired the General.

Jackanapes spread his ten fingers on the arms of his chair, and shut his eyes that he might count the more conscientiously.

"Watch-stand for Aunty, threepence. Trumpet for myself, twopence, that's fivepence. Ginger-nuts for Tony, twopence, and a mug with a Grenadier on for the Postman, fourpence, that's elevenpence. Shooting-gallery a penny, that's a shilling. Giddy-go-round, a penny, that's one and a penny. Treating Tony, one and twopence. Flying Boats (Tony paid for himself), a penny, one and threepence. Shooting-gallery again, one and fourpence. Fat Woman, a penny, one and fivepence. Giddy-go-round again, one and sixpence. Shooting Gallery, one and sevenpence. Treating Tony, and then he wouldn't shoot, so I did, one and eightpence. Living Skeleton, a penny—no, Tony treated me, the Living Skeleton doesn't count. Skittles, a penny, one and ninepence. Mermaid (but when we got inside she was dead), a penny, one and tenpence. Theatre, a penny ('Priscilla Partington, or the Green Lane Murder.' A beautiful young lady, sir, with pink cheeks and a real pistol), that's one and elevenpence. Ginger-beer, a penny (I *was* so thirsty!), two shillings. And then the Shooting-gallery man gave me a turn for nothing, because, he said, I was a real gentleman, and spent my money like a man."

"So you do, sir, so you do!" cried the General. "Why, sir, you spend it like a prince. And now I suppose you've not got a penny in your pocket?"

"Yes, I have," said Jackanapes. "Two pennies. They are saving up." And Jackanapes jingled them with his hand.

"You don't want money except at Fair-times, I suppose?" said the General.

Jackanapes shook his mop. "If I could have as much as I want, I should know what to buy," said he.

"And how much do you want, if you could get it?"

"Wait a minute, sir, till I think what two pence from fifteen pounds leaves. Two from nothing you can't, but borrow twelve. Two from twelve, ten, and carry one. Please remember ten, sir, when I ask you. One from nothing you can't, borrow twenty. One from twenty, nineteen and carry one. One from fifteen, fourteen. Fourteen pounds nineteen and—what did I tell you to remember?"

"Ten," said the General.

"Fourteen pounds nineteen shillings and tenpence then, is what I want," said Jackanapes.

"Bless my soul, what for?"

"To buy Lollo with. Lollo means red, sir. The Gipsy's red-haired pony, sir. Oh, he *is* beautiful! You should see his coat in the sunshine! You should see his mane! You should see his tail! Such little feet, sir, and they go like lightning! Such a dear face, too, and eyes like a mouse! But he's a racer, and the Gipsy wants fifteen pounds for him."

"If he's a racer, you couldn't ride him. Could you?"

"No—o, sir, but I can stick to him. I did the other day."

"You did, did you? Well, I'm fond of riding myself, and if the beast is as good as you say, he might suit me."

"You're too tall for Lollo, I think," said Jackanapes, measuring his grandfather with his eye.

"I can double up my legs. I suppose. We'll have a look at him tomorrow."

"Don't you weigh a good deal?" asked Jackanapes.

"Chiefly waistcoats," said the General, slapping the breast of his military frock-coat. "We'll have the little racer on the Green the first thing in the morning. Glad you mentioned it, grandson. Glad you mentioned it."

The general was as good as his word. Next morning the Gipsy and Lollo, Miss Jessamine, Jackanapes, and his grandfather and his dog Spitfire, were all gathered at one end of the Green in a group, which so aroused the innocent curiosity of Mrs. Johnson, as she saw it from one of her upper windows, that she and the children took their early promenade rather earlier than usual. The General talked to the Gipsy, and Jackanapes fondled Lollo's mane, and did not know whether he should be more glad or miserable if his grandfather bought him.

"Jackanapes!"

"Yes, sir!"

"I've bought Lollo, but I believe you were right. He hardly stands high enough for me. If you can ride him to the other end of the Green, I'll give him to you."

How Jackanapes tumbled on to Lollo's back he never knew. He had just gathered up the reins when the Gipsy-father took him by the arm.

"If you want to make Lollo go fast, my little gentleman—"

"*I* can make him go!" said Jackanapes, and drawing from his pocket the trumpet he had bought in the Fair, he blew a blast both loud and shrill.

Away went Lollo, and away went Jackanape's hat. His golden hair flew out, an aureole from which his cheeks shone red and distended with trumpeting. Away went Spitfire, mad with the rapture of the race, and the wind in his silky ears. Away went the geese, the cocks, the hens, and the whole family of Johnson. Lucy clung to her mamma, Jane saved Emily by the gathers of her gown, and Tony saved himself by a somersault.

The Grey Goose was just returning when Jackanapes and Lollo rode back, Spitfire panting behind.

"Good, my little gentleman, good!" said the Gipsy. "You were born to the saddle. You've the flat thigh, the strong knee, the wiry back, and the light caressing hand; all you want to learn is the whisper. Come here!"

"What was that dirty fellow talking about, grandson?" asked the General.

"I can't tell you, sir. It's a secret."

They were sitting in the window again, in the two Chippendale armchairs, the General devouring every line of his grandson's face, with strange spasms crossing his own.

"You must love your aunt very much, Jackanapes?"

"I do, sir," said Jackanapes warmly.

"And whom do you love next best to your aunt?"

The ties of blood were pressing very strongly on the General himself, and perhaps he thought of Lollo. But love is not bought in a day, even with fourteen pounds nineteen shillings and tenpence. Jackanapes answered quite readily, "The Postman."

"Why the Postman?"

"He knew my father," said Jackanapes, "and he tells me about him, and about his black mare. My father was a soldier, a brave soldier. He died at Waterloo. When I grow up I want to be a soldier too."

"So you shall, my boy. So you shall."

"Thank you, Grandfather. Aunty doesn't want me to be a soldier for fear of being killed."

"Bless my life! Would she have you get into a feather-bed and stay there? Why, you might be killed by a thunderbolt, if you were a butter-merchant!"

"So I might. I shall tell her so. What a funny fellow you are, sir! I say, do you think my father knew the Gipsy's secret? The Postman says he used to whisper to his black mare."

"Your father was taught to ride as a child, by one of those horsemen of the East who swoop and dart and wheel about a plain like swallows in autumn. Grandson! Love me a little, too. I can tell you more about your father than the Postman can."

"I do love you," said Jackanapes. "Before you came I was frightened. I'd no notion you were so nice."

"Love me always, boy, whatever I do or leave undone. And—God help me—whatever you do or leave undone, I'll love you! There shall never be a cloud between us for a day; no, sir, not for an hour. We're imperfect enough, all of us, we needn't be so bitter; and life is uncertain enough at its safest, we needn't waste opportunities. Look at me! Here sit I, after a dozen battles and some of the worst climates in the world, and by yonder lych-gate lies your mother, who didn't move five miles, I suppose, from your aunt's apron-strings, —dead in her teens; my golden-haired daughter, whom I never saw."

Jackanapes was terribly troubled. "Don't cry, grandfather," he pleaded, his own blue eyes round with tears. "I will love you very much, and I will try to be very good. But I should like to be a soldier."

"You shall, my boy, you shall. You've more claims for a commission than you know of. Cavalry, I suppose; eh, ye young Jackanapes? Well, well; if you live to be an honour to your country, this old heart shall grow young again with pride for you; and if you die in the service of your country—God bless me, it can but break for ye!"

And beating the region which he said was all waistcoats, as if they stifled him, the old man got up and strode out on the Green.

Chapter IV

> Greater love hath no man than this, that a man lay down his life
> for his friends. John 15:13

Twenty and odd years later the Grey Goose was still alive, and in full possession of her faculties, such as they were. She lived slowly and carefully, and she lived long. So did Miss Jessamine; but the General was dead.

He had lived on the Green for many years, during which he and the Postman saluted each other with a punctiliousness that it almost drilled one to witness. He would have completely spoiled Jackanapes if Miss Jessamine's conscience would have let him; otherwise he somewhat dragooned his neighbours, and was as positive about parish matters as a ratepayer about the army. A stormy-tempered, tender-hearted soldier, irritable with the suffering of wounds of which he never spoke, whom all the village followed to his grave with tears.

The General's death was a great shock to Miss Jessamine and her nephew stayed with her for some little time after the funeral. Then he was obliged to join his regiment, which was ordered abroad.

One effect of the conquest which the General had gained over the affections of the village, was a considerable abatement of the popular prejudice against "the military." Indeed the village was now somewhat importantly represented in the army. There was the General himself, and the Postman, and the Black Captain's tablet in the church, and Jackanapes, and Tony Johnson, and a Trumpeter.

Tony Johnson had no more natural taste for fighting than for riding, but he was devoted as ever to Jackanapes, and that was how it came about that Mr. Johnson bought him a commission in the same cavalry regiment that the General's grandson (whose commission had been given him by the Iron Duke) was in, and that he was quite content to be the butt of the mess where Jackanapes was the hero; and that when Jackanapes wrote home to Miss Jessamine, Tony wrote with the same purpose to his mother; namely, to demand her congratulations that they were on active service at last, and were ordered to the front. And he added a postscript to the effect that she could have no idea how popular Jackanapes was, nor how splendidly he rode the wonderful red charger whom he had named after his old friend Lollo.

◆　◆　◆

"Sound Retire!"

A Boy Trumpeter, grave and with the weight of responsibilities and the accoutrements beyond his years, and stained, so that his mother would not have known him, with the sweat and dust of battle, did as he was bid; and then pushing his trumpet pettishly aside, adjusted his weary legs for the hundredth time to the horse, which was a world too big for him, and muttering, " 'Tain't a pretty tune," tried to see something of this his first engagement, before it came to an end.

Being literally in the thick of it, he could hardly have seen less or known less of what happened in that particular skirmish if he had been at home in England. For many good reasons; including dust and smoke, and that what attention he dared distract from his commanding officer was pretty well absorbed by keeping his hard-mouthed troop-horse in hand, under pain of execration by his neighbours in the *melee*. By and by, when the newspapers came out, if he could get a look at one before it was thumbed to bits, he would learn that the enemy had appeared from ambush in overwhelming numbers, and that orders had been given to fall back, which was done slowly and in good order, the men fighting as they retired.

Born and bred on the Goose Green, the youngest of Mr. Johnson's gardener's numerous offspring, the boy had given his family "no peace" till they let him "go for a soldier" with Master Tony and Master Jackanapes. They consented at last, with more tears than they shed when an elder son was sent to gaol for poaching, and the boy was perfectly happy in his life, and full of *esprit de corps*. It was this which was wounded by having to sound retreat for "the young gentlemen's regiment," the first time he served with it before the enemy, and he was also harassed by completely lost sight of Master Tony. There had been some hard fighting before the backward movement began, and he had caught sight of him once, but none since. On the other hand, all the pulses of his village pride had been stirred by one or two visions of Master Jackanapes whirling about on his wonderful horse. He had been easy to distinguish, since an eccentric blow had bared his head without hurting it, for his close golden mop of hair gleamed in the hot sunshine as brightly as the steel of the sword flashing round it.

Of the missiles that fell pretty thickly, the Boy Trumpeter did not take much notice. First, one cannot attend to everything, and his hands were full. Secondly, one gets used to anything. Thirdly, experience soon teaches one, in spite of proverbs, how few bullets find their billet. Far more unnerving is the mere suspicion of fear or even of anxiety in the human mass around you. The Boy was beginning to wonder if there were any dark reason for increasing pressure, and whether they would be allowed to move back more quickly, when the smoke in front lifted for a moment, and he could see the plain, and the enemy's line some two hundred yards away.

And across the plain between them, he saw Master Jackanapes galloping alone at the top of Lollo's speed, their faces to the enemy, his golden head at Lollo's ear.

But at this moment noise and smoke seemed to burst out on every side, the officer shouted to him to sound retire, and between trumpeting and bumping about on his horse, he saw and heard no more of the incidents of his first battle.

Tony Johnson was always unlucky with horses, from the days of the giddy-go-round onwards. On this day—of all days in the year—his own horse was on the sick list, and he had to ride an inferior, ill-conditioned beast, and fell off that, at the very moment when it was a matter of life or death to be able to ride away. The horse fell on him, but struggled up again, and Tony managed to keep hold of it. It was in trying to remount that he discovered, by helplessness and anguish, that one of his legs was crushed and broken, and that no feat of which he was master would get him into the saddle. Not able even to stand alone, awkwardly, agonizingly unable to mount his restive horse, his life was yet so strong within him! And on one side of him rolled the dust and smoke-cloud of his advancing foes, and on the other, that which covered his retreating friends.

He turned one piteous gaze after them, with a bitter twinge, not of reproach, but of loneliness; and then, dragging himself up by the side of his horse, he turned the other way and drew out his pistol, and waited for the end. Whether he waited seconds or minutes he never knew, before someone gripped him by the arm.

"*Jackanapes! GOD bless you!* It's my left leg. It you *could* get me on—"

It was like Tony's luck that his pistol went off at his horse's tail, and made it plunge; but Jackanapes threw him across the saddle.

"Hold on anyhow, and stick your spur in. I'll lead him. Keep your head down, they are firing high."

And Jackanapes laid his head down—to Lollo's ear.

It was when they were fairly off, that a sudden up-springing of the enemy in all directions had made it necessary to change the gradual retirement of our force into as rapid a retreat as possible. And when

Jackanapes became aware of this, and felt the lagging and swerving of Tony's horse, he began to wish he had thrown his friend across his own saddle, and left their lives to Lollo.

When Tony became aware of it, several things came into his head. 1. That the dangers of their ride for life were now more than doubled. 2. That if Jackanapes and Lollo were not burdened with him they would undoubtedly escape. 3. That Jackanapes' life was infinitely valuable, and his—Tony's—was not. 4. That this—if he could seize it—was the supremest of all the moments in which he had tried to assume the virtues which Jackanapes had by nature; and that if he could be courageous and unselfish now—

He caught at his own reins and spoke very loud—

"Jackanapes! It won't do. You and Lollo must go on. Tell the fellows I gave you back to them, with all my heart. Jackanapes, if you love me, leave me!"

There was a daffodil light over the evening sky in front of them, and it shone strangely on Jackanapes' hair and face. He turned with an odd look in his eyes that a vainer man than Tony Johnson might have taken for brotherly pride. Then he shook his mop, and laughed at him.

"*Leave you*? To save my skin? No, Tony, not to save my soul!"

Chapter V

Mr. Valiant *summoned. His will. His last words.*
Then said he, "I am going to my Father's. My Sword
I give to him that shall succeed me in my Pilgrimage, and
my Courage and Skill to him that can get it." . . . And
as he went down deeper, he said, "Grave, where is thy
Victory?" So he passed over, and all the Trumpets
sounded for him on the other side.

Bunyan's Pilgrim's Progress.

Coming out of a hospital-tent, at head-quarters, the surgeon cannoned against, and rebounded from another officer; a sallow man, not young, with a face worn more by ungentle experiences than by age; with weary eyes, that kept their own counsel, iron-grey hair, and a moustache that was as if a raven had laid its wing across his lips and sealed them.

"Well?"

"Beg pardon, Major. Didn't see you. Oh, compound fracture and bruises, but it's all right. He'll pull through."

"Thank God."

It was probably an involuntary expression, for prayer and praise were not much in the Major's line, as a jerk of the surgeon's head would have betrayed to an observer. He was a bright little man, with his feelings showing all over him but with gallantry and contempt of death enough for both sides of his profession; who took a cool head, a white handkerchief, and a case of instruments where other men went hot-blooded with weapons, and who was the biggest gossip, male or female, of the regiment. Not even the Major's taciturnity daunted him.

"Didn't think he'd had as much pluck about him as he has. He'll do all right if he doesn't fret himself into a fever about poor Jackanapes."

"Whom are you talking about?" asked the Major hoarsely.

"Young Johnson. He—"

"What about Jackanapes?"

"Don't you know? Sad business. Rode back for Johnson, and brought him in; but, monstrous ill-luck, hit as they rode. Left lung—"

"Will he recover?"

"No. Sad business. What a frame—what limbs—what health—and what good looks! Finest young fellow—"

"Where is he?"

"In his own tent," said the surgeon sadly.

The Major wheeled and left him.

◆ ◆ ◆

"Can I do anything else for you?

"Nothing, thank you. Except—Major! I wish I could get you to appreciate Johnson."

"This is not an easy moment, Jackanapes."

"Let me tell you, sir—*he* never will—that if he could have driven me from him, he would be lying yonder at this moment, and I should be safe and sound."

The Major laid his hand over his mouth, as if to keep back a wish he would have been ashamed to utter.

"I've known old Tony from a child. He's a fool on impulse, a good man and a gentleman in principle. And he acts on principle, which it's not every—some water, please! Thank you, sir. It's very hot, and yet one's feet get uncommonly cold. Oh, thank you, thank you. He's no fire-eater, but he has a trained conscience and a tender heart, and he'll do his duty when a braver and more selfish man might fail you. But he wants encouragement; and when I'm gone—"

"He shall have encouragement. You have my word for it. Can I do nothing else?"

"Yes, Major. A favour."

"Thank you, Jackanapes."

"Be Lollo's master, and love him as well as you can. He's used to it."

"Wouldn't you rather Johnson had him?"

The blue eyes twinkled in spite of mortal pain.

"Tony *rides* on principle, Major. His legs are bolsters, and will be to the end of the chapter. I couldn't insult dear Lollo, but if you don't care—"

"Whilst I live—which will be longer than I desire or deserve—Lollo shall want nothing, but—you. I have no little tenderness for—my dear boy, you're faint. Can you spare me for a moment?"

"No, stay—Major!"

"What? What?"

"My head drifts so—if you wouldn't mind."

"Yes! Yes!"

"Say a prayer by me. Out loud please, I am getting deaf."

"My dearest Jackanapes—my dear boy—"

"One of the Church Prayers—Parade Service, you know—"

"I see. But the fact is—God forgive me, Jackanapes—I'm a different sort of fellow to some of you youngsters. Look here, let me fetch—"

But Jackanapes' hand was in his, and it wouldn't let go.

There was a brief and bitter silence.

"'Pon my soul I can only remember the little one at the end."

"Please," whispered Jackanapes.

Pressed by the conviction that what little he could do it was his duty to do, the Major— kneeling—bared his head, and spoke loudly, clearly, and very reverently—

"The Grace of our Lord Jesus Christ—"

Jackanapes moved his left hand to his right one, which still held the Major's—

"—The love of God."

And with that—Jackanapes died.

Chapter VI

Und so ist der blaue Himmel grösser als jedes Gewölk darin,
und dauerhafter dazu.

Jean Paul Richter.

Jackanapes' death was sad news for the Goose Green, a sorrow just qualified by honourable pride in his gallantry and devotion. Only the Cobbler dissented, but that was his way. He said he saw nothing in it but foolhardiness and vainglory. They might both had been killed, as easy as not, and then where would ye have been? A man's life was a man's life, and one life was as good as another. No one would catch him throwing his away. And, for that matter, Mrs. Johnson could spare a child a great deal better than Miss Jessamine.

But the parson preached Jackanapes' funeral sermon on the text, "Whosoever will save his life shall lose it; and whosoever will lose his life for My sake will find it;" and all the village went and wept to hear him.

Nor did Miss Jessamine see her loss from the Cobbler's point of view. On the contrary, Mrs. Johnson said she never to her dying day should forget how, when she went to condole with her, the old lady came forward, with gentlewomanly self-control, and kissed her and thanked God that her dear nephew's effort had been blessed with success, and that this sad war had made no gap in her friend's large and happy home circle.

"But she's a noble, unselfish woman," sobbed Mrs. Johnson, "and she taught Jackanapes to be the same, and that's how it is that my Tony has been spared to me. And it must be sheer goodness in Miss Jessamine, for what can she know of a mother's feelings? And I'm sure most people seem to think that if you've a large family you don't know one from another anymore than they do, and that a lot of children are like a lot of store-apples, if one's taken it won't be missed."

Lollo—the first Lollo, the Gipsy's Lollo—very aged, draws Miss Jessamine's bath-chair slowly up and down the Goose Green in the sunshine.

The Ex-postman walks beside him, which Lollo tolerates to the level of his shoulder. If the Postman advances any nearer to his head, Lollo quickens his pace, and were the Postman to persist in the injudicious attempt, there is, as Miss Jessamine says, no knowing what might happen.

In the opinion of the Goose Green, Miss Jessamine had borne her troubles "wonderfully." Indeed, to-day, some of the less delicate and less intimate of those who see everything from the upper windows, say (well behind her back) that "the old lady seems quite lively with her military beaux again."

The meaning of this is, that Captain Johnson is leaning over one side of her chair, whilst by the other bends a brother officer who is staying with him, and who has manifested an extraordinary interest in Lollo. He bends lower and lower, and Miss Jessamine calls to the Postman to request Lollo to be kind enough to stop, whilst she is fumbling with something which always hangs by her side, and has got entangled with her spectacles.

It is a twopenny trumpet, bought years ago in the village Fair, and over it she and Captain Johnson tell, as best they can, between them, the story of Jackanapes' ride across the Goose Green; and how he won Lollo—the Gipsy's Lollo—the racer Lollo—dear Lollo—faithful Lollo—Lollo the never vanquished—Lollo the tender servant of his old mistress. And Lollo's ears twitch at every mention of his name.

Their hearer does not speak, but he never moves his eyes from the trumpet, and when the tale is told, he lifts Miss Jessamine's hand and presses his heavy black moustache in silence to her trembling fingers.

The sun, setting gently to his rest, embroiders the somber foliage of the oak tree with threads of gold. The Grey Goose is sensible of an atmosphere of repose, and puts up one leg for the night. The grass glows with a more vivid green, and in answer to a ringing call from Tony, his sisters, fluttering over the daisies in pale-hued muslins, come out of their ever-open door, like pretty pigeons from a dovecote.

And, if the good gossips' eyes do not deceive them, all the Miss Johnsons, and both the officers, go wandering off into the lanes, where bryony wreaths still twine about the brambles.

◆　◆　◆

A sorrowful story, and ending badly?

Nay, Jackanapes, for the end is not yet.

A life wasted that might have been useful?

Men who have died for men, in all ages, forgive the thought!

There is a heritage of heroic example and noble obligation, not reckoned in the Wealth of Nations, but essential to a nation's life; the contempt of which, in any people, may, not slowly, mean even its commercial fall.

Very sweet are the uses of prosperity, the harvests of peace and progress, the fostering sunshine of health and happiness, and length of days in the land.

But there be things—oh, sons of what has deserved the name of Great Britain, forget it not!—"the good of" which and "the use of" which are beyond all calculation of worldly goods and earthly uses: things such as Love, and Honour, and the Soul of Man, which cannot be bought with a price, and which do not die with death. And they who would fain live happily *ever* after, should not leave these things out of the lessons of their lives.

CHAPTER 5

Greedy Writing: *Mary's Meadow*

In Juliana Ewing's novel *Six to Sixteen* (1872), Emma, a student in the girls boarding school Bush House, observes that Eleanor Arkwright, a fellow student and one of the two major characters in the story, is what she calls a "greedy" reader.[1] She seems to mean that Eleanor reads with unusual deliberateness and highly focused concentration without regard to how much time it takes. She is selective in what she reads, and she reads as if she were slowly squeezing all the water from a sponge, making sure that she has gotten every drop that she can.

Ewing was herself a greedy reader as well as a greedy listener, as is apparent from many of her perceptive and detailed references to various books she had pored over—squeezing them for meaning—and detailed accounts she gave of such oral presentations as sermons she had heard. In a letter of 12 July 1874, to her sister Horatia K. F. Gatty (later Eden), she describes a sermon by one Dr. Edghill. Her account is remarkable for its specificity. She seemed to remember every detail of the sermon as well as the minister's individualistic way of delivering it. The letter ends with the following appraisal of the minister:

> He's not exactly an *equal* or a *finished* preacher for highly educated ears, but that sort of transparent candour which he has makes him *very* affecting when on his favourite topic, the inexhaustible love of God. His face when he quotes—"The Son of God Who loved *Me* and gave Himself for *Me*"—is like a man showing the Rock he has clung to himself in shipwreck.[2]

A greedy reader and listener she was, indeed, but of greater significance is that she was also a greedy writer. By the time she had written *Mary's*

Meadow, the last of her stories that were published serially in *Aunt Judy's Magazine* (November 1883–March 1884), she was adept at creating a literary sponge that would hold a great deal of the water of meaning, and she liberally infused *Mary's Meadow* with it. She was aware, of course, that a large segment of her readers was made up of children, who could squeeze but lightly for meaning. Even from that slight intellectual exertion, however, they would be satisfactorily rewarded, for on the most apparent level of meaning, *Mary's Meadow* is a simple and appealing story about a family of five children and their wonderful imaginations in playing the roles of a game that Mary created, their interest in and fondness for growing flowers, their love and respect for each other, their tastes in books, and their interaction with their mother and father.[3] The narrator, Mary, is somewhat older than her three brothers and her sister, but even so she is herself a child, which makes the work more endearing to readers who are themselves children.

It is, then, a story with children, about children, and told by a young girl. From their readings elsewhere, most of Ewing's young readers were probably already familiar with a stock character type who plays an important role in *Mary's Meadow*, the "Old Squire," who is grouchy, selfish, and miserly. Predictably, by the end of the story, he seems to be changed for the better from contact with the children, especially the narrator.

For children readers, one of the most attractive aspects of the story is a fierce-looking dog named Saxon that is not fierce at all but affectionate especially toward Mary and her siblings.[4] Saxon belongs to the Old Squire but loves the children more than he does his master and visits them frequently.[5]

Ewing's portrayal of the youngest of the five children, Christopher, is a little masterpiece of characterization that is created to delight young readers especially. Chris, as he is called, marches to a different drum and bugle corps (a single drummer would be inadequate for this unique little trooper). He is both lovable and mischievous, strikingly clever beyond his young age but with many of the endearing qualities of a little boy. The rather austere older woman of the family, Aunt Catherine (also called Lady Catherine), finds Chris charming and interesting and invites him, usually just him, to tea with her regularly. His parents and siblings are amazed and puzzled by this odd friendship. He, however, takes it in his stride, seldom revealing what he and Lady Catherine discuss, and accepting her friendship not as odd at all but as perfectly normal. There is much humor and human interest here at this level of the story, the level that is accessible to young readers.

The ending is all that would satisfy and please all those children who have read *Mary's Meadow* or had it read to them through the generations since it was first published in *Aunt Judy's Magazine*. After the happy surprise of the Old Squire's apologizing to Mary for his previous angry behavior toward her and then the unexpected revelation that he has been to a lawyer and has deeded the meadow to her, the final scene brings together Mary and her little brother, Chris, who informs Mary that he is in desperate need of a pet—in this instance, a hedgehog—to sleep by his bed as Saxon often sleeps by Mary's. What follows may well be considered by many readers, children included, as one of the most amusing and perhaps the most touching scene in *Mary's Meadow*:

> "Chris, Chris!" I said, "You should not be so sly. You're a real slyboots. Double–stockings and sly boots." And I took him on my lap.
>
> Chris put his arms round my neck, and buried his cheek against mine.
>
> "I won't be sly, Mary," he whispered; and then, hugging me as he hugs Lady Catherine, he added, "For I do love you; for you are a darling, and I do really think it always was yours."
>
> "What, Chris?"
>
> "If not," said Chris, "why was it always called MARY'S MEADOW?"[6]

Although *Mary's Meadow* is not obtrusively didactic, it does not lack the mandatory lesson of children's stories of the time. In fact, Mary begins her narrative by stating in concise form the moral that pervades almost every scene of the story: one must work hard to become unselfish, but achieving it is well worth the effort because unselfishness is the cornerstone of all virtues:

> Mother is always trying to make us love our neighbors as ourselves. She does despise us for greediness, or grudging, or snatching, or not sharing what we have got, or taking the best and leaving the rest, or helping ourselves first, or pushing forward, or praising Number One, or being Dogs in the Manger, or anything selfish. (p. 13)

In child rearing, sharing is probably the first and most basic lesson that parents try to teach their young children. *Mary's Meadow* fortifies and encourages that attempt to imbue children with the universal virtue of unselfishness.

As a greedy writer, however, Ewing was not content to write merely for the purpose of entertaining children and teaching them a good moral lesson. If she wrote for them, she also wrote for herself, a highly imaginative and skillful creative artist whose work is often multilayered with metaphors serving double duty to produce not just a child's story or poem but a work of literature that is brilliantly complex. *Mary's Meadow* is such a work.

There is evidence that as the years passed, Ewing may have considered the advantage of writing for the express purpose of attracting more mature readers. The popular poet and novelist Jean Ingelow (1820–97) praised Ewing's writings and advised her to seek a more inclusive reputation for herself. The fact that it was this author who brought the idea to her attention had considerable appeal to Ewing because Jean Ingelow had become well known at the time as a poet and novelist for mature readers as well as a writer of children's verse and stories. Her notoriety in both areas could not help but impress Ewing since her own reputation was limited to children's literature.

In a letter to her husband, Alexander ("Rex") Ewing, dated 16 May 1879, she indicated that one reason she was about to travel to London was that she wanted to visit with Jean Ingelow:

> I want to get several things done in London. Jean Ingelow has burst out rather about my writings, and wants me to do something "in the style of 'Madam Liberality,'" and let her try to get it into

> *Good Words*, as she thinks I ought to try for a wider audience. I
> shall certainly go and see her, and talk over matters.[7]

She further indicates that when she is finished writing what she is currently
working on, *We and the World*, she will "try and aim at something to give
me a better footing if I can."[8]

We and the World was published serially from November 1877 to
October 1879, and on the 8th of April 1880, Ewing dined with Jean
Ingelow at her residence in London with several distinguished guests
present.[9] Whatever advice Ingelow may have offered Juliana as to the
advantages of a career and notoriety based not upon a single area—
children's writings—but upon a wider base that included not only works
for children but also fiction and poetry expressly for a mature readership,
Ewing obviously concluded after due consideration that she could not
write as did her new friend, nor did she have any desire to do so.

From the time when she began writing for *Aunt Judy's Magazine*, she
knew precisely what she was doing. She had an accurate idea of what
her gifts were, and she was unusually aware of how to use them. She was
what critics call with enthusiastic approval a "conscious artist." She was
appreciative of Jean Ingelow's offer to help her to get something published
in *Good Words Magazine*, but she must have known that she possessed
a gift that Ingelow lacked. Consequently, she wrote no differently after
meeting with Ingelow, and she did nothing to change her image of a writer
for children. This is not to say, however, that only children read her works.
To be sure, she always had some adult readers who greatly appreciated the
beauty of her writings that ostensibly were for children but, when read
more deliberately, reveal complexity and artistic sophistication, readers
like Rudyard Kipling, John Ruskin, Henry James, and Arnold Bennett,
who perceived the universal appeal of her work.

During the period of her terminal illness late in 1884 and the early
months of 1885, family members began reading to her. Significantly, the
work she repeatedly asked to be read to her during these final days was
Mark Twain's *Adventures of Huckleberry Finn*, a new novel published
in December of 1884 in the United Kingdom (and in February 1885
in the United States). It was at that time generally considered a book
for children, especially boys, but Juliana recognized at once that it was

more than a boys' book. It drew her into its world of the great river, and she perceived that this author known as Mark Twain was a kindred spirit endowed with the same creative gift that she possessed: what I have called artistic duplicity. She could see that he had created a work for adults as well as for children at the center of which is a symbol that goes so deeply into the conscious and subconscious minds of even the most sophisticated of readers that they are moved even beyond the immediate ability to understand why.

It must have struck her with almost the power of an epiphany that what Mark Twain had achieved with the river in *Adventures of Huckleberry Finn* she had accomplished on a minor scale with the meadow in *Mary's Meadow*. Just as the river has a profound and magnetic appeal to Huck and Jim, into whose minds and imaginations its image secures a permanent place, so is Mary affected by the meadow near her home, and she takes it as her duty as "Little Mother" to be sure that the meadow will become as important to Arthur, Harry, Adela, and Chris as it has been for her.[10] To her, the meadow is the apotheosis of natural beauty within a sizeable but limited space. With her love of flowers, the extraordinary number of them in the meadow takes her breath away and paints upon her mind a picture that will never fade but will always be there to enhance her happiness or to pull her from the depths of despair. It is not a garden, she points out, but wilder and more natural. Yet it exhibits such variety in plants as nothing else she has ever seen:

> Wild roses, and white bramble, and hawthorn, and dogwood, with its curious red flowers; and nuts, and maple, and privet, and all sorts of bushes in the hedge, far more than one would think; and ferns, and the stinking iris, which has such splendid berries, in the ditch on the lower side . . . On the top of the field, it is dry, and blue succory grows, and grows out on the road beyond. The most beautiful blue possible, but so hard to pick. And there are Lent lilies, and lords and ladies, and ground ivy, which smells herby when you find it, trailing about and turning the colour of Mother's "aurora" wool in green winters; and sweet white violets, and blue dog violets, and primroses, of course, and two or three

kinds of orchis, all over the field cowslips, cowslips, cowslips—to
please the nightingale. (pp. 81–2)

What the meadow means to Mary and what she wishes it to mean also
to her brothers and sister is close to if not identical with what a similar
meadow meant to another child, eleven-year-old Thomas Berry, who
wrote about it many years later in Chapter 2, "The Meadow across the
Creek," of his book *The Great Work*:

> There across the creek was a meadow. It was an early afternoon
> in late May when I first wandered down the incline, crossed
> the creek, and looked out over the scene. The field was covered
> with white lilies rising above the thick grass. A magic moment,
> this experience gave to my life something that seems to explain
> my thinking at a more profound level than almost any other
> experience I can remember. It was not only the lilies. It was the
> singing of the crickets and the woodlands in the distance and the
> clouds in a clear sky . . . As the years pass this moment returns
> to me, and whenever I think about my basic life attitude and the
> whole trend of my mind and the causes to which I have given
> my efforts, I seem to come back to this moment and the impact
> it has had on my feeling for what is real and worthwhile in life.[11]

When Thomas Berry died in 2009, he was buried at his own request in
the meadow that he had seen and loved in his childhood. The following
statement was given at his memorial service: "It was the deep archetype
of the Meadow . . . that Thomas carried with him throughout his life. His
religious orientation, it seems to us, had its origin in the deep mystery
of the Meadow . . . The Meadow also influenced his intellectual life and
became the norm for his entire range of thinking. Whatever preserved
the Meadow was good; whatever opposed the Meadow was not."[12]

Ewing recognized even earlier than *Mary's Meadow* the possibilities
inherent in a field or meadow as a universal symbol, and she created one
in "Our Field," which appeared in the September 1876 issue of *Aunt Judy's
Magazine*. Like the later and longer *Mary's Meadow*, the story is narrated
by a young girl who tells of a field that she and her brothers discover. It

is the perfect place to play their games undisturbed, a place covered with flowers, hedges, mosses, and, most significantly, habituated by a bird, a lark (a nightingale in *Mary's Meadow*).

As in *Mary's Meadow*, a large dog, Perronet, plays an important role. One of the children rescues Perronet from drowning, and they all love the dog immediately. An affluent elderly man owns the field although he takes no interest in it. At the end of the story, the narrator comments that they "never saw him in Our Field. And I don't believe anybody could have such a field of their very own, and never come to see it, from one end of Summer to the other."[13] The point in both "Our Field" and *Mary's Meadow*, is that he or she to whom the image of the meadow or field has penetrated so deeply into the mind, heart, and imagination that it is a kind of standard to measure and determine what is truly meaningful and lasting in life—that is the person who "owns" it. Ewing has the children call their favorite place in the whole world "Our Field" because it is theirs in a real sense and for as long as they live. They shall never forget it whereas the man who has the deed to it is a stranger to it and is not connected to it. To have a deed is not in the truest sense to own. That is why in *Mary's Meadow* Chris tells his sister Mary that she has owned the meadow all along, even before the Old Squire gives her the deed to it. He, on the other hand, has never owned it even when it was legally his. But the field in "Our Field" is not just the children's in the story; it is "ours," that is, all of those who read the story and respond to this powerful central image, timeless, reverberating with all that is deep within us recalling the joy of peace, freedom, and beauty. It was John Ruskin's field, for he made it his when the words of Ewing's story painted on the mind of this great Victorian critic of literature and art a place of primal innocence and contentment. His reaction to "Our Field" was in the highest form of praise: he insisted that it was not a short story but a poem.[14]

In dedicating *Six to Sixteen* to her friend Eleanor Lloyd, Ewing made the point that the novel is not preachy on a subject that she had given a good deal of thought to, namely what she terms "a model education" for children, but she confesses that the book "does touch by the way on a few of the many strong opinions I have on the subject."[15] One of these opinions was that which she held on the "joys and benefits" to be derived from the pursuit of certain creative and character-molding hobbies. Her remarks in her dedication to *Six to Sixteen* touch on the deepest concern and conviction pervading her writings: how children should be guided and what they should be taught. Though she had none of her own, she was greatly concerned with the question of what is most valuable in the education of children. For the greedy reader, she answers that question in *Mary's Meadow*. In addition to the glorious fun that the children are having and in doing so learning more and more about flower gardening as they play the roles they have assumed—Traveller's Joy (Mary), John Parkinson (Arthur), Honest Root-gatherer (Harry), Weeding Woman (Adela), and Hose-in-Hose (Chris)—and as they pursue this hobby of gardening, they are learning the importance of being practical, being unselfish, being creative, being responsible, and being honest. In other words, they are being schooled in how to live. Their teacher, their "Little Mother," is learning along with them without any of them realizing the importance to their later lives of 1) the meadow, 2) their role-playing game, and 3) gardening.

Their texts, their schoolbooks, in this educational process are two in number. The first, the book that inspires Mary to put together the game of the Earthly Paradise, *Paradisi in Sole Paradisus Terrestris* by the English botanist John Parkinson (1567–1650), whose official title was Apothecary to King James I (and who dedicated the book to Queen Henrietta Maria), is no children's book. They discover it with delight in their father's large library, and because they are somewhat tired of the usual books for children, feeling that such books are often beneath them, they seek and receive his permission to read it. At one point, Arthur tells Mary: "Look here, Mary, I'm not going to read any books but grown-up ones unless it is an Adventure Book. I'm sick of books for young people, there's so much *stuff* in them." Mary explains: "We call it *stuff* when there seems to be going to be a story and it comes to nothing but talk; and we call it *stuff* when there is a very interesting picture, and you read to see what it is about, and the reading does not tell you, or tells you wrong" (pp. 28–9). The older children, Mary and Arthur, read in Parkinson's book though probably not through it, for even in its very large format, it is over 600 pages and printed in seventeenth-century English type not inviting to a nineteenth-century child reader. Its discussions cover close to 1,000 plants congenial to English soil and climate. Some 800 of these are illustrated on a little over a hundred full-page plates. Published in 1629, it soon became the masterwork for English gardeners, especially those primarily interested in flowers.

If it is Parkinson's book that gives Mary the idea of engaging her siblings through gardening by creating an "Earthly Paradise," as the children call it,[16] it is another book that stimulates her into moving from concentrating on a traditional garden to the meadow close to their house, the field that the children have been familiar with but not to the extent that Mary wants them to be. While away on a trip with Aunt Catherine and Chris, Mary's mother sends her a book by the French author Alphonse Karr (1808–90), *A Tour Round My Garden*. Published in 1855, Karr's book is briefer and thus much less intimidating than Parkinson's. It strongly sustains a theme—the nobility of unselfishness—so important to Ewing that it is to be found in many of her writings.

The narrator of *A Tour Round My Garden* is an avid gardener who describes his own practices but also tells entertaining stories within the main narrative. Since Mary quotes passages that occur in several different places, it is to be assumed that she read the entire book, and she has obviously been greatly swayed by the narrator's worldview, which consists of a series of ideas somewhat akin to those exhibited by Henry David Thoreau in *Walden* (1854), who exhibits sharp sarcasm aimed effectively at the absurdity of certain popular trends such as traveling.

Both *A Tour Round My Garden* and *Walden* stress that frequent traveling to distant places, so popular among the pretentious affluent, does not make one wiser or better. Karr's narrator, who "tours" not the world but merely his own garden, constantly contrasts himself with his friend, something of a fool, who as a tourist travels the world as if desperately seeking something he knows not what. Thoreau mimics the constant tourist by seemingly bragging about his travels: "I have travelled a good deal," he ostensibly boasts but then ends the sentence with the opposite of what is expected, not by giving an account of all the places in the wide world he has seen but by concluding with "in Concord," his rather small native town in Massachusetts.[17] The point that both authors make is that it is traveling inside oneself, self-exploration, that is infinitely rewarding and revealing, not feverishly going from one place in the world to another merely to be able to brag about how many places one has seen.

While Ewing's own view was in accord with what she found in Karr's book about travel, what most attracted her to *A Tour Round My Garden* was probably Karr's recurrent insistence that there is something noble about gardening, something that leads one into a better way of life. Of major importance to her was what Karr wrote about unselfishness in gardening, that is, generously sharing the enjoyment of plants with others by planting along pathways and in fields where people daily walk and may see the beauty of blooming flowers. To a greater extent than John Parkinson, Alphonse Karr posits in his book that he who plants with the thought of others in mind derives the greatest benefit and rewards. The sheer amount of quoting in *Mary's Meadow* from just a single source, namely, Karr's book, sets it off as extraordinary in that regard among her writings. Toward the end of Chapter 5, Mary quotes the following long passage from *A Tour Round My Garden*, a passage that Ewing no doubt felt expressed so well her own sentiment and the moral underpinnings of her story that it should be included, despite its length:

> At the extremity of my garden the vine extends in long porticoes, through the arcades of which may be seen trees of all sorts, and foliage of all colours. Here is an *azerolier* (a small medlar) which is covered in autumn with little scarlet apples, producing the richest effect. I have given away several grafts of this: far from deriving pleasure from the privation of others, I do my utmost to spread and render common and vulgar all the trees and plants that I prefer; it is as if I multiplied the pleasure and the chances of beholding them of all who, like me, really love flowers for their splendor, their grace, and their perfume. Those who, on the contrary, are jealous of their plants, and only esteem them in proportion with their conviction that nobody else possesses them, do not love flowers; and be assured that it is either chance or poverty which has made them collectors of flowers, instead of being collectors of pictures, cameos, medals, or any other thing that might serve as an excuse for indulging in all the joys of possession, seasoned with the idea that others do not possess.
>
> I have even carried the vulgarization of beautiful flowers further than this. I ramble about the country near my dwelling,

and seek the wildest and least frequented spots. In these, after clearing and preparing a few inches of ground, I scatter the seeds of my most favourite plants, which re-sow themselves, perpetuate themselves, and multiply themselves. At this moment, whilst the fields display nothing but the common red poppy, strollers find with surprise in certain wild nooks of our country, the most beautiful double poppies with the white, red, pink, carnation, and variegated blossoms.

At the foot of an isolated tree, instead of the little bind-weed, with its white flower, may sometimes be found the beautifully climbing convolvulus major, of all the lovely colours that can be imagined.

Sweet peas fasten their tendrils to the bushes, and cover them with the deliciously scented white, rose-colour, or white and violet butterflies.

It affords me immense pleasure to fix upon a wild rose in a hedge, and graft upon it red and white cultivated roses, sometimes simple roses of a magnificent gold yellow, then large Provence roses, or others variegated with red and white.

The rivulets in our neighbourhood do not produce on their banks these forget-me-nots, with their blue flowers, with which the rivulet of my garden is adorned: I mean to save the seed, and scatter it in my walks.

I have observed two young wild quince-trees in the nearest wood; next spring I will graft upon them two of the best kinds of pears.

And then, how I enjoy beforehand and in imagination, the pleasure and surprise which the solitary stroller will experience when he meets in his rambles with those beautiful flowers and those delicious fruits!

This fancy of mine may, one day or other, cause some learned botanist, who is herborizing in these parts a hundred years hence, to print a stupid and startling system. All these beautiful flowers will have become common in the country, and will give it an aspect peculiar to itself; and, perhaps, chance or the wind will

cast a few of the seeds of some of them amidst the grass which
shall cover my forgotten grave![18]

This lengthy passage from *A Tour Round My Garden* embodies the very
spirit of *Mary's Meadow*. It is about the reward that an avid gardener,
Alphonse Karr, received from anonymously serving, from doing for
others. Behind his act of kindness is the idea that Mary expresses in
the first sentence of her narrative: "Mother is always trying to make us
love our neighbors as ourselves" (p. 13). Whether the reader of *Mary's
Meadow* is a child or person of maturity and literary sophistication, he
or she is not likely to miss the theme that pervades all levels of the story:
love, love for all. There is a good reason why the character McKnight in
Rudyard Kipling's story "Fairy-Kist" refers to *Mary's Meadow* as "The
best, the kindest, the sweetest, the most eenocent tale ever the soul of
a woman gied birth to."[19] The reason is that *Mary's Meadow* is a story
of love, from the first sentence to the last, Mary's love for her younger
siblings and their love for her.

Considered from one angle, the literal, the meadow of the story is a
meadow, a beautiful meadow with flowers and plants of all sorts. Other
readers will perceive it as an archetype embodying associations that
penetrate deep into the imagination and the subconscious mind. Still
others will see the meadow as a symbol for Mary's family. As its gardener,
Mary cultivates its flowers, her siblings, bringing them along lovingly
and artfully as she learns to be "Little Mother." So, in this sense, the
chief gardener of the story is Mary. What motivates her always is her
love of flowers—her siblings—and using her guidebooks—Parkinson for
practical matters and Karr for the constant reminder of the importance
of self-denial—she "gardens" with love, always love, and patience, and
the skill that is wisdom. The result is that she fully earns the right to be
called and considered "Little Mother." At the end, the meadow is hers. It
is truly Mary's Meadow. It is a story for the ages, never to die, never to
become irrelevant.[20]

Mary's Meadow

Chapter 1

Mother is always trying to make us love our neighbors as ourselves. She does so despise us for greediness, or grudging, or snatching, or not sharing what we have got, or taking the best and leaving the rest, or helping ourselves first, or pushing forward or praising Number One, or being Dogs in the Manger, or anything selfish. And we cannot bear her to despise us!

We despise being selfish, too; but very often we forget. Besides, it is sometimes rather difficult to love your neighbour as yourself when you want a thing very much; and Arthur says he believes it is particularly difficult if it is your next-door-neighbour, and that that is why Father and the Old Squire quarreled about the footpath through Mary's Meadow.

The Old Squire is not really his name, but that is what people call him. He is very rich. His place comes next to ours, and it is much bigger, and he has quantities of fields, and Father has only got a few; but there are two fields beyond Mary's Meadow which belong to Father, though the Old Squire wanted to buy them. Father would not sell them, and he says he has a right of way through Mary's Meadow to go to his fields, but the Old Squire says he has nothing of the kind, and that is what they quarreled about.

Arthur says if you quarrel, and are too grown-up to punch each's heads, you go to law; and if going to law doesn't make it up, you appeal. They went to law, I know, for Mother cried about it; and I suppose it did not make it up, for the Old Squire appealed.

After that he used to ride about all day on his grey horse, with Saxon, his yellow bull-dog, following him, to see that we did not trespass on Mary's Meadow. I think he thought that if we children were there, Saxon would frighten us, for I do not suppose that he knew that we knew him. But Saxon used often to come with the Old Squire's Scotch Gardener to see our gardener, and when they were looking at the wall-fruit, Saxon used to come snuffing after us.

He is the nicest dog I know. He looks very savage, but he is only very funny. His lower jaw sticks out, which makes him grin, and some people think that he is gnashing his teeth with rage. We think it looks as if he were laughing—like Mother Hubbard's dog, when she brought home his coffin, and he wasn't dead—but it really is only the shape of his jaw. I loved Saxon the first day I saw him, and he likes me, and licks my face. But what he likes best of all are Bath Oliver Biscuits.

One day the Scotch Gardener saw me feeding him, and he pulled his red beard, and said, "Ye do weel to mak' hay while the sun shines, Saxon, my man. There's sma' sight o' young leddies and sweet cakes at hame for ye!" And Saxon grinned, and wagged his tale, and the Scotch Gardener touched his hat to me, and took him away.

The Old Squire's Weeding Woman is our nursery-maid's aunt. She is not very old, but she looks so, because she has lost her teeth, and is bent nearly double. She wears a large hood, and carries a big basket, which she puts down outside the nursery door when she comes to tea with Bessy. If it is a fine afternoon, and we are gardening, she lets us borrow the basket, and we play at being weeding women in each other's gardens.

She tells Bessy about the Old Squire. She says—"He do be a real old skinflint, the Old Zquire a be!" But she thinks it—"zim as if 'twas having ne'er a wife nor child for to keep the natur' in 'un, so his heart do zim to shrivel, like they walnuts Butler tells us of as a zets down for desart. The Old Zquire he mostly eats ne'er a one now's teeth be so bad. But a counts them every night when's desart's done. And a keeps 'em till the karnels be mowldy, and a keeps 'em till they be dust; and when the karnels is dust, a cracks aal the lot of 'em when desart's done, zo's no one mayn't have no good of they walnuts, since they be no good to he."

Arthur can imitate the Weeding Woman exactly, and he can imitate the Scotch Gardener too. Chris (that is Christopher, our youngest brother) is very fond of "The Zquire and the Walnuts." He gets nuts, or anything, like shells or bits of flower-pots, that will break, and something to hit with, and when Arthur comes to *"The karnels is dust,"* Chris smashes everything before him, shouting, *"A cracks aal the lot of 'em,"* and then he throws the bits all over the place, with *"They be no good to he."*

Father laughed very much when he heard Arthur do the Weeding Woman, and Mother could not help laughing too; but she did not like it, because she does not like us to repeat servants' gossip.

The Weeding Woman is a great gossip. She gossips all the time she is having her tea, and it is generally about the Old Squire. She used to tell Bessy that his flowers bloomed themselves to death, and the fruit rotted on the walls, because he would let nothing be picked, and gave nothing away, except now and then a grand present of fruit to Lady Catherine, for which the old lady returned no thanks, but only a rude message to say that his peaches were over-ripe, and he had better have sent the grapes to the Infirmary. Adela asked—"Why is the Old Squire so kind to Lady Catherine?" and Father said—"Because we are so fond of Lords and Ladies in this part of the country." I thought he meant the lords and ladies in the hedges, for we are very fond of them. But he didn't. He meant real lords and ladies.

There are splendid lords and ladies in the hedges of Mary's Meadow. I never can make up my mind when I like them best. In April and May, when they have smooth plum-coloured coats and pale green cowls, and push up out of last year's dry leaves, or in August and September, when their hoods have fallen away, and their red berries shine through the dusty grass and nettles that have been growing up round them all summer out of the ditch.

Flowers were one reason for our wanting to go to Mary's Meadow. Another reason was the nightingale. There was one that used always to sing there, and Mother had made us a story about it.

We are very fond of fairy books, and one of our greatest favourites is Bechstein's *As Pretty as Seven*. It has very nice pictures, and we particularly like "The Man in the Moon, and How He Came There;" but the story doesn't end well, for he came there by gathering sticks on Sunday, and then scoffing about it, and he has been there ever since. But Mother made us a new fairy tale about the nightingale in Mary's Meadow being the naughty woodcutter's only child, who was turned into a little brown bird that lives on in the woods, and sits on a tree on summer nights, and sings to its father up in the moon.

But after our Father and the Old Squire went to law, Mother told us we must be content with hearing the nightingale from a distance. We did not really know about the lawsuit then, we only understood that the Old Squire was rather crosser than usual; and we rather resented being warned not to go into Mary's Meadow, especially as Father kept saying we had a perfect right so to do. I thought that Mother was probably afraid of Saxon being set at us, and of course I had no fears about him. Indeed, I used to wish that it could happen that the Old Squire, riding after me as full of fury as King Padella in the *Rose and the Ring*, might set Saxon on me, as the lions were let loose to eat the Princess Rosalba. "Instead of devouring her with their great teeth, it was with kisses they gobbled her up. They licked her pretty feet, they nuzzled their noses in her lap," and she put her arms "around their tawny necks and kissed them." Saxon gobbles us with kisses, and nuzzles his nose, and we put our arms round his tawny neck. What a surprise it would be to the Old Squire to see him! And then I wondered if my feet were as pretty as Rosalba's, and I thought they were, and I wondered if Saxon would lick them, supposing that by any possibility it could ever happen that I should be barefoot in Mary's Meadow at the mercy of the Old Squire and his bull-dog.

One does not, as a rule, begin to go to bed by letting down one's hair, and taking off one's shoes and stockings. But one night I was silly enough to do this, just to see if I looked (in the mirror) at all like the picture of Rosalba in the *Rose and the Ring*. I was trying to see my feet as well as my hair, when I heard Arthur jumping the three steps in the middle of the passage between his room and mine. I had only just time to spring into the window-seat, and tuck my feet under me, when he gave a hasty knock, and bounced in with his telescope in his hand.

"Oh, Mary," he cried, "I want you to see the Old Squire, with a great-coat over his evening clothes, and a squash hat, marching up and down Mary's Meadow."

And he pulled up my blind, and threw open the window, and arranged the telescope for me.

It was a glorious sight. The moon was rising round and large out of the mist and dark against its brightness I could see the figure of the Old Squire pacing the pathway over Mary's Meadow.

Saxon was not there; but on a slender branch of a tree in the hedgerow sat the nightingale, singing to comfort the poor, lonely old Man in the Moon.

Chapter II

Lady Catherine is Mother's aunt by marriage, and Mother is one of the few people she is not rude to.

She is very rude, and yet she is very kind, especially to the poor. But she does kind things so rudely, that people now and then wish that she would mind her own business instead. Father says so, though Mother would say that that is gossip. But I think sometimes that Mother is thinking of Aunt Catherine when she tells us that in kindness it is not enough to be good to others, one should also learn to be gracious.

Mother thought she was very rude to *her* once, when she said, quite out loud, that Father is quite ill-tempered, and that if Mother had not the temperament of an angel, the house could never hold together. Mother was very angry, but Father did not mind. He says our house will hold together much longer than most houses, because he swore at the workmen and went to the law with the builder for using dirt instead of mortar, so the builder had to pull down what was done wrong, and do it right; and Father says he knows he has a bad temper, but he does not mean to pull the house over our heads at present, unless he has to get bricks out to heave at Lady Catherine if she becomes quite unbearable.

We do not like dear Father to be called bad-tempered. He comes home cross sometimes, and then we have to be very quiet, and keep out of the way; and sometimes he goes out rather cross, but not always. It was what Chris said about that that pleased Lady Catherine so much.

It was one day when Father came home cross, and was very much vexed to find us playing about the house. Arthur had got a new Adventure Book, and he had been reading to us about the West Coast of Africa, and natives, and tom-toms, and "going Fantee;" and James gave him a lot of old corks out of the pantry, and let him burn them in a candle. It rained, and we could not go out; so we all blacked our faces with burnt cork, and played at the West Coast in one of the back passages, and at James being the captain of a slave ship, because he tried to catch us when we beat the tom-toms too near him when he was cleaning the plate, to make him give us rouge and whitening to tattoo with.

Dear Father came home rather earlier than we expected, and rather cross. Chris did not hear the front door, because his ears were pinched up with tying curtain rings to them, and just at that minute he shouted, "I go Fantee!" and tore his pinafore right up the middle, and burst into the front hall with it hanging in two pieces by the armholes, his eyes shut, and a good grab of James's rouge-powder smudged on his nose, yelling and playing the tom-tom on what is left of Arthur's drum.

Father was very angry indeed, and Chris was sent to bed, and not allowed to go down to dessert; and Lady Catherine was dining at our house, so he missed her.

Next time she called, and saw Chris, she asked him why he had not been at dessert that night. Mother looked at Chris, and said, "Why was it, Chris? Tell Aunt Catherine." Mother thought he would say, "Because I tore my pinafore, and made a noise in the front hall." But he smiled, the grave way Chris does, and said, "Because Father came home cross." And Lady Catherine was pleased, but Mother was vexed.

I am quite sure Chris meant no harm, but he does say funny things. Perhaps it is because his head is rather large for his body, with some water having got into his brain when he was very little, so that we have to take care of him. And though he does say very odd things, very slowly, I do not think any one of us tries harder to be good.

I remember once Mother had been trying to make us forgive each other's trespasses, and Arthur would say that you cannot *make* yourself feel kindly to them that trespass against you; and Mother said if you make yourself do right, then at last you get to feel right; and it was very soon after this that Harry and Christopher quarreled, and would not forgive each other's trespasses in the least, in spite of all that I could do to try and make peace between them.

Chris went off in the sulks, but after a long time I came upon him in the toy-cupboard, looking rather pale and very large-headed, and winding up his new American top, and talking to himself.

When he talks to himself he mutters, so I could only just hear what he was saying, and he said it over and over again:

"*Dos first and feels afterwards.*"

"What are you doing, Chris?" I asked.

"I'm getting ready my new top to give to Harry. *Dos first and feels afterwards.*"

"I should like to punch his head," said Chris—and he said it in just the same sing-song tone—"but I'm getting the top ready. *Dos first and feels afterwards.*"

And he went on winding and muttering.

Afterwards he told me that the "feels" came sooner than he expected. Harry wouldn't take his top, and they made up their quarrel.

Christopher is very simple, but sometimes we think he is also a little sly. He can make very wily excuses about things he does not like.

He does not like Nurse to hold back his head and wash his face; and at last one day she let him go down-stairs with a dirty face, and then complained to Mother. So Mother asked Chris why he was so naughty about having his face washed, and he said, quite gravely, "I do think it would be *such* pity if the water got into my head again by accident." Mother did not know he had ever heard about it, but she said, "Oh, Chris! Chris! That's one of your excuses." And he said, "It's not my 'scusis. She lets a good deal get in—at my ears—and lather too."

But with all his whimsical ways, Lady Catherine is devoted to Christopher. She likes him far better than any of us, and he is very fond of her; and they say quite rude things to each other all along. And Father says that it is very lucky, for if she had not been so fond of Chris, and so ready to take him too, Mother would never have been persuaded to leave us when Aunt Catherine took them to the South of France.

Mother had been very unwell for a long time. She has so many worries, and Dr. Solomon said she ought to avoid worry, and Aunt Catherine said worries were killing her, and Father said "Pshaw!" and Aunt Catherine said, "Care killed the cat," and that a cat has nine lives, and a woman has only one; and then Mother got worse, and Aunt Catherine wanted to take her abroad, and she wouldn't go and then Christopher was ill, and Aunt Catherine said she would take him too, if only Mother would go with her; and Dr. Solomon said it might be the turning-point of his health, and Father said, "the turning-point which way?" But he thanked Lady Catherine, and they didn't quarrel; and so Mother yielded, and it was settled that they should go.

Before they went, Mother spoke to me, and told me I must be a Little Mother to the others whilst she was away. She hoped we should all try to please Father, and to be unselfish with each other; but she expected me to try far harder than the others, and never to think of myself at all, so that I might fill her place whilst she was away. So I promised to try and I did.

We missed Christopher sadly. And Saxon missed him. The first time Saxon came to see us after Mother and Chris went away, we told him all about it, and he looked very sorry. Then we said that he should be our brother in Christopher's stead, whilst Chris was away; and he looked very much pleased, and wagged his tail, and licked our faces all round. So we told him to come and see us very often.

He did not, but we do not think that it was his fault. He is chained up so much.

One day Arthur and I were walking down the road outside the Old Squire's stables, and Saxon smelt us, and we could hear him run and rattle his chain, and he gave deep, soft barks.

Arthur laughed. He said, "Do you hear Saxon, Mary? Now I dare say the Old Squire thinks he smells tramps and wants to bite them. He doesn't know that Saxon smells his new sister and brother, and wishes he could go out walking with them in Mary's Meadow."

Chapter III

Nothing comforted us so much whilst Mother and Chris were away as being allowed to play in the library.

We were not usually allowed to be there so often, but when we asked Father he gave us leave to amuse ourselves there at the time when Mother would have had us with her, provided that we did not bother him or hurt the books. We did not hurt the books, and in the end were allowed to go there as much as we liked.

We have plenty of books of our own, and we have new ones very often: on birthdays and at Christmas. Sometimes they are interesting, and sometimes they are disappointing. Most of them have pretty pictures. It was because we had been rather unlucky for some time, and had had disappointing ones on our birthdays, that Arthur said to me, "Look here, Mary, I'm not going to read any books now but grown-up ones, unless it is an Adventure Book. I'm sick of books for young people, there's so much *stuff* in them."

We call it *stuff* when there seems to be going to be a story and it comes to nothing but talk; and we call it *stuff* when there is a very interesting picture, and you read to see what it is about, and the reading does not tell you, or tells you wrong.

Both Arthur and Christopher had had disappointments in their books on their birthdays.

Arthur jumped at his book at first, because there were Japanese pictures in it, and Uncle Charley had just been staying with us, and had brought beautiful Japanese pictures with him, and had told us Japanese fairy tales, and they were as good as Bechstein. So Arthur was full of Japan.

The most beautiful picture of all was of a stork, high up in a tall pine tree, and the branches were most beautifully drawn; and there was a nest with young storks in it, and behind the stork and the nest and the tall pine the sun was blazing with all his rays. And Uncle Charley told us the story to it, and it was called "the Nest of the Stork."

So when Arthur saw a stork standing among pine needles in his new book he shouted with delight, though the pine needles were rather badly done, with thick strokes. But presently he said, "It's not nearly so good a stork as Uncle Charley's. And where's the stem of the pine? It looks as if the stork were on the ground and on the top of the pine tree too, and there's no nest. And there's no sun. And, oh! Mary, what do you think is written under it? '*Crane and water-reeds*.' Well, I do call that a sell!"

Christopher's disappointment was quite as bad. Mother gave him a book with very nice pictures, particularly of beasts. The chief reason she got it for him was that there was such a very good picture of a toad, and Chris is so fond of toads. For months he made friends with one in the garden. It used to crawl away from him, and he used to creep after it, talking to it, and then it used to half begin to crawl up the garden wall and stand so, on its hind legs, and let Chris rub its wrinkled back. The toad in the picture was exactly like Christopher's toad, and he ran about the house with the book in his arms begging us to read him the story about Dear Toady.

We were all busy but Arthur, and he said, "I want to go on with my water-wheel." But Mother said, "Don't be selfish, Arthur." And he said, "I forgot. All right, Chris; bring me the book." So they went and sat in the conservatory, not to disturb any one. But very soon they came back, Chris crying, and saying, "It couldn't be the right one, Arthur;" and Arthur frowning, and saying, "It is the right story; but it's *stuff*. I'll tell you what that book's good for, Chris. To paint the pictures. And you've got a new paint-box." So Mother said, "What's the matter?" And Arthur said, "Chris thinks I haven't read him the right story to his Toad Picture. But I have, and what do you think it's about? It's about the silliest little girl you can imagine—a regular mawk of a girl—and a frog. Not a toad, but a F. R. O. G. frog! A regular hop, skip, jumping frog!"

Arthur leaped round the room, but Chris cried bitterly. So Arthur ran up to him and kissed him, and said, "Don't cry, old chap. I tell you what I'll do. You get Mary to cut out a lot of the leaves of your book that have no pictures, and that will make it like a real scrap-book; and then I will give you a lot of my scraps and pictures to paste over what's left of the stories, and you will have such a painting-book as you never had in all your life before."

So we did. And Arthur was very good, for he gave Chris pictures that I know he prized, because Chris liked them. But the very first picture he gave him was the "Crane and Water-reeds."

I thought it so good of Arthur to be so nice with Chris that I wished I could have helped him over his water-wheel. He had put Japan out of his head since the disappointment, and spent all his play-time in making mills and machinery. He did grind some corn into flour once, but it was not at all white. He said that was because the bran was left in. But it was not only bran in Arthur's flour. There was a good deal of sand too, from his millstones being made of sandstone, which he thought would not matter. But it grinds off.

Down in the valley, below Mary's Meadow, runs the Ladybrook, which turns the old water-wheel of Mary's Mill. It is a very picturesque old mill, and Mother has made beautiful sketches of it. She caught the last cold she got before going abroad with sketching it—the day we had a most delightful picnic there, and went about in the punt. And from that afternoon Arthur made up his mind that his next mill should be a water-mill.

The reason that I am no good at helping Arthur about his mills is that I am stupid about machinery; and I was so vexed not to help him, that when I saw a book in the library which I thought would do so, I did not stop to take it out, for it was in four very large volumes, but ran off at once to tell Arthur.

He said, "What *is* the matter, Mary?"

I said, "Oh, Arthur! I've found a book that will tell you all about mills; and it is the nicest smelling book in the library.

"The nicest *smelling*? What's that got to do with mills?"

"Nothing, of course. But it's bound in russia, and I am so fond of the smell of russia. But that's nothing. It's a Miller's Dictionary, and it is in four huge volumes, 'with plates.' I should think you could look out all about every kind of mill there ever was a miller to."

"If the plates give sections and diagrams"—Arthur began, but I did not hear the rest, for he started off for the library at once, and I ran after him.

But when he got Miller's Dictionary on the floor, how he did tease me! For there was nothing about mills or millers in it. It was a Gardener's and Botanist's Dictionary, by Philip Miller; and the plates were plates of flowers very truly drawn, like the pine tree in Uncle Charley's Jap. Picture. There were some sections too, but they were sections of greenhouses, not of any kinds of mills or machinery.

The odd thing was that it turned out to be a kind of help to Arthur after all. For we got so much interested in it that it roused us up about our gardens. We are all very fond of flowers, I most of all, and at last Arthur said he thought that miniature mills were really rather humbugging things, and it would be much easier and more useful to build a cold frame to keep the choice auriculas and *half-hardies* in.

When we took up our gardens so hotly, Harry and Adela took up theirs, and we did a great deal, for the weather was fine.

We were surprised to find that the Old Squire's Scotch Gardener knew Miller's Dictionary quite well. He said, "It's a gran' wurrk!" (Arthur can say it just like him.)

One day he wished he could see it, and smell the russia binding; he said he liked to feel a nice smell. Father was away, and we were by ourselves, so we invited him into the library. Saxon wanted to come in too, but the gardener was very cross with him, and sent him out; and he sat on the mat outside and dribbled with longing to get in, and thudded his stiff tail whenever he saw any one through the doorway.

The Scotch Gardener enjoyed himself very much, and he explained a lot of things to Arthur, and helped us to put away the Dictionary when we had done with it.

When he took up his hat to go, he gave one long look all round the library. Then he turned to Arthur (and Saxon took advantage of this to wag his way in and join the party), and said, "It's a rare privilege, the free entry of a book chamber like this. I'm hoping, young gentleman, that you're not insensible of it?"

Then he caught sight of Saxon, and beat him out of the room with his hat.

But he came back himself to say, that it might just happen that he would be glad now and again to hear what was said about this or that plant (of which he would write down the botanical name) in these noble volumes.

So we told him that if he would bring Saxon to see us pretty often, we would look out anything he wanted to know about in Miller's Gardener's Dictionary.

Chapter IV

Looking round the library one day, to see if I could see any more books about gardening, I found the Book of Paradise.

It is a very old book, and very queer. It has a brown leather back—not russia—and stiff little gold flowers and ornaments all the way down, where Miller's Dictionary has gold swans in crowns, and ornaments.

There are a good many old books in the library, but they are not generally very interesting—at least not to us. So when I found that though this one had a Latin name on the title-page, it was written in English, and that though it seemed to be about Paradise, it was really about a garden, and quite common flowers, I was delighted, for I have always cared more for gardening and flowers than for any other amusement, long before we found Miller's Gardener's Dictionary. And the Book of Paradise is much smaller than the Dictionary, and easier to hold. And I like old, queer things, and it is very old and queer.

The Latin name is *Paradisi in sole, Paradisus terrestris*, which we do not any of us understand, though we are all learning Latin; so we call it the Book of Paradise. But the English name is—"Or a Garden of all sorts of pleasant flowers which our English ayre will permitt to be noursed up;" and on the top of every page is written "The Garden of Pleasant Flowers," and it says—"Collected by John Parkinson, Apothecary of London, and the King's Herbarist, 1629."

I had to think a minute to remember who was the king then, and it was King Charles I; so then I knew that it was Queen Henrietta to whom the book was dedicated. This was the dedication:

> "To the Queen's Most Excellent Majesty.
>
> "Madame, —Knowing your Majesty so much delighted with all the fair flowers of a Garden, and furnished with them as far beyond others as you are eminent before them; this my Work of a Garden long before this intended to be published, and but now only finished, seemed as it were destined to be first offered into your Highness's hands as of right, challenging the propriety of Patronage from all others. Accept, I beseech your Majesty, this speaking Garden, that may inform you in all the particulars of your store as well as wants, when you cannot see any of them fresh upon the ground: and it shall further encourage him to accomplish the remainder; who in praying that your Highness may enjoy the heavenly Paradise, after many years' fruition of this earthly, submitteth to be your Majesties,
>
> "In all humble devotion,
>
> "John Parkinson."

We like queer old things like this, they are so funny! I liked the Dedication, and I wondered if the Queen's Garden really was an Earthly Paradise, and whether she did enjoy reading John Parkinson's book about flowers in the winter time, when her own flowers were no longer "fresh upon the ground." And then I wondered what flowers she had, and I looked out a great many of our chief favourites, and she had several kinds of them.

We are particularly fond of Daffodils and she had several kinds of Daffodils, from the "Primrose Peerlesse," "of a sweet but stuffing scent," to "the least Daffodil of all," which the book says "was brought to us by a Frenchman called Francis le Vean, the honestest root-gatherer that ever came over to us."

The Queen had Cowslips too, though our gardener despised them when he saw them in my garden. I dug mine up in Mary's Meadow before Father and the Old Squire went to the law; but they were only common Cowslips, with only one Oxlip, by good luck. In the Earthly Paradise there were "double Cowslips, one within another." And they were called Hose-in-Hose. I wished I had Hose-in-Hose.

Arthur was quite as much delighted with the Book of Paradise as I. He said, "Isn't it funny to think of Queen Henrietta Maria gardening! I wonder if she went trailing up and down the walks looking like that picture of her we saw when you and I were in London with Mother about our teeth, and went to see the Loan Collection of Old Masters. I wonder if the Dwarf packed the flowers for her. I do wonder what Apothecary John Parkinson looked like when he offered his Speaking Garden into her Highness's hands. And what beautiful hands she had! Do you remember the picture, Mary? It was by Vandyck."

I remembered it quite well.

That afternoon the others could not amuse themselves, and wanted me to tell them a story. They do not like old stories too often, and it is rather difficult to invent new ones. Sometimes we do it by turns. We sit in a circle and one of us begins, and the next must add something, and so we go on. But that way does not make a good plot. My head was so full of the Book of Paradise that afternoon that I could not think of a story, but I said I would begin one. So I began:

"Once upon a time there was a Queen—"

"How was she dressed?" asked Adela, who thinks a good deal about dress.

"She had a beautiful dark blue satin robe."

"*Princesse* shape? Inquired Adela.

"No; Queen's shape," said Arthur. "Drive on, Mary."

"And lace ruffles falling back from her Highness's hands—"

"Sweet!" murmured Adela.

"And a high hat, with plumes, on her head, and—"

"A very low dwarf at her heels," added Arthur.

"Was there really a dwarf, Mary?" asked Harry.

"There was," said I.

"Had he a hump, or was he only a plain dwarf?"

"He was a very plain dwarf," said Arthur.

"Does Arthur know the story, Mary?"

"No, Harry, he doesn't; and he oughtn't to interfere till I come to a stop."

"Beg pardon, Mary. Drive on."

"The Queen was very much delighted with all the fair flowers, and she had a garden so full of them that it was called the Earthly Paradise."

There was a long drawn out and general "Oh!" of admiration.

"But though she was a Queen, she couldn't have flowers in the winter, not even in an Earthly Paradise."

"Don't you suppose she had a greenhouse, bye the bye, Mary?" said Arthur.

"Oh, Arthur," cried Harry. "I do wish you'd be quiet: when you know it's a fairy story, and that Queens of that sort never had greenhouses or anything like we have now."

"And so the King's Apothecary and Herbarist, whose name was John Parkinson—"

"I shouldn't have thought he would have had a common name like that," said Harry.

"Bessy's name is Parkinson," said Adela.

"Well, I can't help it; his name *was* John Parkinson."

"Drive on," said Arthur.

"And he made her a book, called the Book of Paradise, in which there were pictures and written accounts of her flowers, so that when she could not see any of them fresh upon the ground, she could read about them, and think about them, and count up how many she had."

"Ah, but she couldn't tell. Some of them may have died in the winter," said Adela.

"Ah, but some of the others may have got little ones at their roots," said Harry. "So that would make up."

I said nothing. I was glad of the diversion, for I could not think how to go on with the story. Before I quite gave in, Harry luckily asked, "Was there a Weeding Woman in the Earthly Paradise?"

"There was," said I.

"How was she dressed?" asked Adela.

"She had a dress the colour of common earth."

"*Princesse* shape?" Inquired Arthur.

"No; Weeding Woman shape. Arthur, I wish you wouldn't—"

"All right, Mary. Drive on."

"And a little shawl, that had partly the colour of grass, and partly the colour of hay."

"*Hay dear!*" Interpolated Arthur, exactly imitating a well-known sigh peculiar to Bessy's aunt.

"Was her bonnet like our Weeding Woman's bonnet?" asked Adela, in a disappointed tone.

"Much larger," said I, "and the colour of a marigold."

Adela looked happier. "Strings the same?" she asked.

"No. One string canary colour, and the other white."

"And a basket?" asked Harry.

"Yes, a basket, of course. Well, the Queen had all sorts of flowers in her garden. Some of them were natives of the country, and some of them were brought to her from countries far away, by men called Root-gatherers. There were very beautiful Daffodils in the Earthly Paradise, but the smallest of all the Daffodils—"

"A Dwarf, like the Hunchback?" said Harry.

"The Dwarf Daffodil of all was brought to her by a man called Francis le Vean."

"That was a *much* nicer name than John Parkinson," said Harry.

"And he was the honestest Root-gatherer that ever brought foreign flowers into the Earthly Paradise."

"Then I love him!" said Harry.

Chapter V

One sometimes thinks it is very easy to be good, and then there comes something which makes it very hard.

I liked being a Little Mother to others, and almost enjoyed giving way to them. "Others first; Little Mothers afterwards," as we used to say—till the day I made up that story for them out of the Book of Paradise.

The idea of it took our fancy completely, the others as well as mine, and though the story was constantly interrupted, and never came to any real plot or end, there were no Queens or dwarfs or characters of any kind in all Bechstein's fairy tales, or even in Grimm, more popular than the Queen of the Blue Robe and her Dwarf, and the Honest Root-Gatherer, and John Parkinson, King's Apothecary and Herbarist, and the Weeding Woman of the Earthly Paradise.

When I said, "Wouldn't it be a good new game to have an Earthly Paradise in our gardens, and to have a King's Apothecary and Herbarist to gather things and make medicine of them, and an Honest Root-Gatherer to divide the polyanthus plants and the bulbs when we take them up, and divide them fairly, and a Weeding Woman to work and make things tidy, and a Queen in a blue dress, and Saxon for the Dwarf"—the others set up such a shout of approbation that Father sent James to inquire if we imagined that he was going to allow his house to be turned into a bear-garden.

And Arthur said, "No. Tell him we're only turning it into a Speaking Garden, and we're going to turn our own gardens into an Earthly Paradise."

But I said, "Oh, James! Please don't say anything of the kind. Say we're very sorry, and we will be quite quiet."

And James said, "Trust me, Miss. It would be a deal more than my place is worth to carry Master Arthur's messages to his Pa."

"I'll be the Honestest Root-Gatherer," said Harry. "I'll take up Dandelion roots to the very bottom, and sell them to the King's Apothecary to make Dandelion tea of."

That's a good idea of yours, Harry," said Arthur. "I shall be John Parkinson—"

"*My* name is Francis le Vean," said Harry.

"King's Apothecary and Herbarist," continued Arthur, disdaining the interruption. "And I bet you my cloth of gold pansy to your black prince that Bessy's aunt takes three bottles of my dandelion and chamomile mixture for the 'swimmings,' bathes her eyes every morning with my elder-flower lotion to strengthen the sight, and sleeps every night on my herb pillow (if Mary will make me a flannel bag) before the week's out."

"I could make you a flannel bag," said Adela, "if Mary will make me a bonnet, so that I can be the Weeding Woman. You could make it of tissue-paper, with stiff paper inside, like all those caps you made for us last Christmas, Mary, dear, couldn't you? And there is some lovely orange-coloured paper, I know, and pale yellow, and white. The bonnet was marigold colour, was it not? And one string canary coloured and one white. I couldn't tie them, of course, being paper, but Bessy's aunt doesn't tie her bonnet. She wears it like a helmet to shade her eyes. I shall wear mine so, too. It will be all marigold, won't it, dear? Front *and* crown; and the white string going back over one shoulder and the canary string over the other. They might be pinned together behind, perhaps, if they were in my way. Don't you think so?"

I said "Yes," because if one does not say something, Adela never stops saying whatever it is she is saying, even if she has to say it two or three times over. But I felt so cross and so selfish, that if Mother *could* have known, she *would* have despised me!

For the truth was, I had set my heart on being the Weeding Woman. I thought Adela would want to be the Queen, because of the blue dress, and the plumed hat, and the lace ruffles. Besides, she likes picking flowers, but she never liked grubbing. She would not really like the Weeding Woman's work; it was the bonnet that had caught her fancy, and I found it hard to smother the vexing thought that if I had gone on dressing the Weeding Woman of the Earthly Paradise like Bessy's aunt, instead of trying to make the story more interesting by inventing a marigold bonnet with yellow and white strings for her, I might have had the part I wished to play in our new game (which certainly was of my devising), and Adela would have been better pleased to be the Queen than to be anything else.

As it was, I knew that if I asked her she would give up the Weeding Woman. Adela is very good, and she is very good-natured. And I knew, too, that it would not have cost her much. She would have given a sigh about the bonnet, and then have turned her whole attention to a blue robe, and how to manage the ruffles.

But even whilst I was thinking about it, Arthur said, "Of course, Mary must be the Queen, unless we could think of something else—very good—for her. If we could have thought of something, Mary, I was thinking how jolly it would be, when Mother comes home, to have had *her* for the Queen, with Chris for her Dwarf, and to give her flowers out of our Earthly Paradise."

"She would look just like a queen," said Harry.

"In her navy blue nun's cloth and Russian lace," said Adela.

That settled the question. Nothing could be so nice as to have Mother in the game, and the plan provided for Christopher also. I had no wish to be Queen, as far as that went. Dressing up, and walking about the garden would be no fun for me. I really had looked forward to clearing away big baskets full of weeds and rubbish, and keeping our five gardens and the paths between them so tidy as they had never been kept before. And I knew the weeds would have a fine time of it with Adela, as Weeding Woman, in a tissue-paper bonnet!

But one thing was more important than tidy gardens—not to be selfish.

I had been left as Little Mother to the others, and I had been lucky enough to think of a game that pleased them. If I turned selfish now, it would spoil everything.

So I said that Arthur's idea was excellent; that I had no wish to be Queen, that I thought I might, perhaps, devise another character for myself by and by; and that if the others would leave me alone, I would think about it whilst I was making Adela's bonnet.

The others were quite satisfied. Father says people always are satisfied with things in general, when they've got what they want for themselves, and I think that is true.

I got the tissue-paper and the gum; resisted Adela's extreme desire to be with me and talk about the bonnet, and shut myself up in the library.

I got out the Book of Paradise too, and propped it up in an arm-chair, and sat on a footstool in front of it, so that I could read in between whiles of making the bonnet. There is an index, so that you can look out the flowers you want to read about. It was no use our looking out flowers, except common ones, such as Harry would be allowed to get bits of out of the big garden to plant in our little gardens, when he became our Honest Root-gatherer.

I looked at the Cowslips again. I am very fond of them, and so, they say, are nightingales; which is, perhaps, why that nightingale we know lives in Mary's Meadow, for it is full of cowslips.

The Queen had a great many kinds, and there are pictures of most of them. She had the Common Field Cowslip, the Primrose Cowslip, the Single Green Cowslip, Curled Cowslips, or Galligaskins, Double Cowslips, or Hose-in-Hose, and the Franticke or Foolish Cowslip, or Jackanapes on Horsebacke.

I did not know one of them except the common cowslip, but I remembered that Bessy's aunt once told me that she had a double cowslip. It was the day I was planting common ones in my garden, when our gardener despised them. Bessy's aunt despised them too, and she said the double ones were only fit for a cottage garden. I laughed so much that I tore the canary-coloured string as I was gumming it on the bonnet, to think how I could tell her now that cowslips are Queen's flowers, the common ones as well as the Hose-in-Hose.

Then I looked out the Honeysuckle, it was page 404, and there were no pictures. I began at the beginning of the chapter; this was it, and it was as funnily spelt as the preface, but I could read it.

"Chap. CV. *Periclymemum*. Honysuckles.

"The Honisucle that groweth wilde in every hedge, although it be very sweeete, yet doe I not bring it into my garden, but let it rest in his owne place, in serue their senses that trauell by it, or haue no garden."

I had got so far when James came in. He said—"Letters, miss."

It was the second post, and there was a letter for me, and a book parcel; both from Mother.

Mother's letters are always delightful; and, like things she says, they often seem to come in answer to something you have been thinking about, and which you would never imagine she could know, unless she was a witch. This was the *knowing bit* in that letter:—"*Your dear father's note this morning did me more good than bottles of tonic. It is due to you, my trustworthy little daughter, to tell you of the bit that pleased me most. He says—'The children seem to me to be behaving unusually well, and I must say, I believe the credit belongs to Mary. She seems to have a genius for keeping them amused, which luckily means keeping them out of mischief.' Now, good Little Mother, I wonder how you yourself are being entertained?*

I hope the others are not presuming on your unselfishness? Anyhow, I send you a book for your own amusement when they leave you a bit of peace and quiet. I have long been fond of it in French, and I have found an English translation with nice little picture and send it to you. I know you will enjoy it, because you are so fond of flowers,"

Oh, how glad I was that I had let Adela be the Weeding Woman with a good grace, and could open my book parcel with a clear conscience!

I put the old book away and buried myself in the new one. I never had a nicer. It was called *A Tour Round my Garden*, and some of the little stories in it—like the Tulip Rebecca, and the Discomfited Florists—were very amusing indeed; and some were sad and pretty, like the Yellow Roses; and there were delicious bits, like the Enriched Woodman and the Connoisseur Deceived, but there was no "stuff" in it at all.

Some chapters were duller than others, and at last I got into a very dull one, about the vine, and it had a good deal of Greek in it, and we have just begun Greek.

But after the Greek, and the part about Bacchus and Anacreon (I did not care about *them*; they were not in the least like the Discomfited Florists, or the Enriched Woodman!) there came this, and I liked it the best of all:—

"At the extremity of my garden the vine extends in long porticoes, through the arcades of which may be seen trees of all sorts, and foliage of all colours. There is an *azerolier* (a small medlar) which is covered in autumn with little apples, producing the richest effect. I have given away several grafts of this; far from deriving pleasure from the privation of others, I do my utmost to spread and render common and vulgar all the trees and plants that I prefer; it is as if I multiplied the pleasure and the chances of beholding them of all who, like me, really love flowers for their splendor, their grace, and their perfume. Those who, on the contrary, are jealous of their plants, and only esteem them in proportion with their conviction that no one else possesses them, do not love flowers; and be assured that it is either chance or poverty which has made them collectors of flowers, instead of being collectors of pictures, cameos, medals, or any other thing that might serve as an excuse for indulging in all the joys of possession, seasoned with the idea that others do not possess.

"I have even carried the vulgarization of beautiful flowers farther than this.

"I ramble about the country near my dwelling, and seek the wildest and least frequented spots. In these, after clearing and preparing a few inches of ground, I scatter the seeds of my most favourite plants, which re-sow themselves, perpetuate themselves, and multiply themselves. At this moment, whilst the fields display nothing but the common red poppy, strollers find with surprise in certain wild nooks of our country, the most beautiful double poppies, with their white, red, pink, carnation, and variegated blossoms.

"At the foot of an isolated tree, instead of the little bindweed with its white flower, may sometimes be found the beautifully climbing convolvulus major, of all the lovely colours that can be imagined.

"Sweet peas fasten their tendrils to the bushes, and cover them with the deliciously-scented white, rose-colour, or white and violet butterflies.

"It affords me immense pleasure to fix upon a wild-rose in a hedge, and graft upon it red and white cultivated roses, sometimes single roses of a magnificent golden yellow, then large Provence roses, or others variegated with red and white.

"The rivulets in our neighbourhood do not produce on their banks those forget-me-nots, with their blue flowers, with which the rivulet of my garden is adorned; I mean to save the seed, and scatter it in my walks.

"I have observed two young wild quince trees in the nearest wood; next spring I will engraft upon them two of the best kinds of pears.

"And then, how I enjoy beforehand and in imagination, the pleasure and surprise which the solitary stroller will experience when he meets in his rambles with those beautiful flowers and these delicious fruits!

"This fancy of mine may, one day or another, cause some learned botanist who is herbarizing in these parts a hundred years hence, to print a stupid and startling system. All these beautiful flowers will have become common in the country, and will give it an aspect peculiar to itself; and, perhaps, chance or the wind will cast a few of the seeds or some of them amidst the grass which shall cover my forgotten grave!"

This was the end of the chapter, and then there was a vignette, a very pretty one, of a cross-marked, grass-bound grave.

Some books, generally grown-up ones, put things into your head with a sort of rush, and now it suddenly rushed into mine—"*That's what I'll be!* I can think of a name hereafter- but that's what I'll do. I'll take seeds and cuttings, and off-shoots from our garden, and set them in waste places, and hedges, and fields, and I will make an Earthly Paradise of Mary's Meadow."

Chapter VI

The only difficulty about my part was to find a name for it. I might have taken the name of the man who wrote the book—it is Alphonse Karr— just as Arthur was going to be called John Parkinson. But I am a girl, so it seemed silly to take a man's name. And I wanted some kind of title, too, like King's Apothecary and Herbarist, or Weeding Woman, and Alphonse Karr does not seem to have had any by-name of that sort.

I had put Adela's bonnet on my head to carry it safely, and was still sitting thinking, when the others burst into the library.

Arthur was first, waving a sheet of paper; but when Adela saw the bonnet, she caught hold of his arm and pushed forward.

"Oh, it's sweet! Mary, dear, you're an angel. You couldn't be better if you were a real milliner and lived in Paris. I'm sure you couldn't."

"Mary," said Arthur, "remove that bonnet, which by no means becomes you, and let Adela take it into a corner and gibber over it to herself. I want you to hear this."

"You generally do want the platform," I said, laughing. "Adela, I am very glad you like it. Tomorrow, if I can find a bit of pink tissue-paper, I think I could gum on little pleats round the edge of the strings as a finish."

I did not mind how gaudily I dressed the part of Weeding Woman now.

"You are good, Mary. It will make it simply perfect; and kilts don't you think? Not box pleats?"

Arthur groaned.

"You shall have which you like, dear. Now, Arthur, what is it?"

Arthur shook out his paper, gave it a flap with the back of his hand, as you do with letters when you are acting, and said: "It's to Mother, and when she gets it, she'll be a good deal astonished, I fancy."

When I had heard the letter, I thought so too:

> "To the Queen's Most Excellent Maiestie—
>
> "My Dear Mother, —This is to tell you that we have made you Queen of the Blue Robe, and that your son Christopher is a dwarf, and we think you'll both be very much pleased when you hear it. He can do as he likes about having a hump back. When you come home we shall give faire flowers into your Highnesse hands—that is if you'll do what I'm going to ask you, for nobody can grow flowers out of nothing. I want you to write to John—write straight to him, don't put it in your letter to Father—and tell him that you have given us leave to have some of the seedlings out of the frames, and that he's to dig us up a good big clump of daffodils out of the shrubbery—and we'll divide them fairly, for Harry is the Honestest Root-gatherer that ever came over to us. We have turned the whole of our gardens into a *Paradisi in sole Paradisus terrestris,* if you can construe that; but we must have something to make a start. He's got no end of bedding things over that are doing nothing in the Kitchen Garden and might just as well be in our Earthly Paradise. And please tell him to keep us a tiny pinch of seed at the bottom of every paper when he is sowing the annuals. A little goes a long way, particularly of poppies. And you might give him a hint to let us have a flower-pot or two now and then (I'm sure that he takes ours if he finds any of our dead

window-plants lying about), and that he needn't be so mighty mean about the good earth in the potting-shed, or the labels either, they're dirt cheap. Mind you write straight. If only you let John know that the gardens don't entirely belong to him, you'll see that what's spare from the big garden would more than set us going; and it shall further encourage him to accomplish the remainder, who in praying that your Highnesse may enjoy the heavenly Paradise after the many years fruition of this earthly,

"Submitteth to be, Your Maiestie's,

"In all humbled devotion,

"John Parkinson,

"King's Apothecary and Herbarist.

"P. S. —It was Mary's idea."

"My *dear* Arthur!" said I.

"Well, I know it's not very well mixed," said Arthur. "Not half so well as I intended at first. I meant to write it all in the Parkinson style. But then, I thought, if I put the part about John in queer language and old spelling, she mightn't understand what we want. But every word of the end comes out of the Dedication; I copied it the other day, and I think she'll find it a puzzlewig when she comes to it."

After which Arthur folded his paper and put it into an envelope which he licked copiously, and closed the letter with a great deal of display. But then his industry coming to an abrupt end, as it often did, he tossed it to me, saying: "You can address it, Mary." So, I enclosed it in my own letter to thank Mother for the book, and I fancy she did write to our gardener, for he gave us a good lot of things, and was much more good-natured than usual.

After Arthur had tossed his letter to me, he clasped his hands over his head and walked up and down thinking. I thought he was calculating what he should be able to get out of John, for when you are planning about a garden, you seem to have to do so much calculating. Suddenly he stopped in front of me and threw down his arms. "Mary," he said, "if Mother were at home, she *would* despise us for selfishness, wouldn't she just?"

"I don't think it's selfish to want spare things for our gardens, if she gives us leave," said I.

"I'm not thinking of that," said Arthur; "and you're not selfish, you never are; but she would despise me, and Adela, and Harry, because we've taken your game, and got our parts, and you've made that preposterous bonnet for Adela to be the Weeding Woman in—much she'll weed!"

"I *shall* weed," said Adela.

"Oh, yes! You'll weed,—Groundsel!—and leave Mary to get up the docks and dandelions, and clear away the heap. But never mind. Here we've taken Mary's game, and she hasn't even got a part."

"Yes," said I, "I have; I have got a capital part. I have only to think of a name."

"How shall you be dressed?" asked Adela.

"I don't know yet," said I. "I have only just thought of the part."

"Are you sure it's a good-enough one?" asked Harry, with a grave and remorseful air; "because, if not, you must take Francis le Vean. Girls are called Frances sometimes."

I explained, and I read aloud the bit that had struck my fancy.

Arthur got restless half-way through, and took out the Book of Paradise. His letter was on his mind. But Adela was truly delighted.

"Oh, Mary," she said. "It is lovely. And it just suits you. It suits you much better than being a Queen."

"Much better," said I.

"You'll be exactly the reverse of me," said Harry. "When I'm digging up, you'll be putting in."

"Mary," said Arthur from the corner where he was sitting with the Book of Paradise in his lap, "'what have you put a mark in the place about honeysuckle for?"

"Oh, only because I was just reading there when James brought the letters."

"John Parkinson can't have been quite so nice a man as Alphonse Karr," said Adela; "not so unselfish. He took care of the Queen's gardens, but he didn't think of making the lanes and hedges nice for poor wayfarers."

I was in the rocking chair, and I rocked harder to shake up something that was coming into my head. Then I remembered.

"Yes, Adela, he did—a little. He wouldn't root up the honeysuckle out of the hedges (and I suppose he wouldn't let his root-gatherers grub it up, either); he didn't put it in the Queen's Gardens, but left it wild outside—"

"To serve their senses that travel by it, or have no garden," interrupted Arthur, reading from the book, "and, oh, Mary, that reminds me—*travel—travellers*. I've got a name for your part just coming into my head. But it dodges out again like a wire-worm through a three-pronged fork. *Travel—traveller—travellers*—what's the common name for the—oh, dear! the what's his name that scrambles about in the hedges. A flower—you know?"

"Deadly nightshade?" said Harry.

"Deadly fiddlestick!—"

"Bryony?" I suggested.

"Oh, no; It begins with a 'c.'"

"Clematis?" said Adela.

"Clematis. Right you are, Adela. And the common name for Clematis is Traveller's Joy. And that's the name for you, Mary, because you're going to serve their senses that travel by hedges and ditches and perhaps have no garden."

"Travellers Joy," said Harry. "Hooray!"

"Hooray!" said Adela, and she waved the Weeding Woman's bonnet.

It was a charming name, but it was too good for me, and I said so.

Arthur jumped on the rockers and rocked me to stop my talking. When I was far back, he took the point of my chin in his two hands and lifted up my cheeks to be kissed, saying in his very kindest way, "It's not a bit too good for you—it's you all over."

Then he jumped off as suddenly as he had jumped on, and as I went back with a bounce, he cried, "Oh, Mary! Give me back that letter. I must put another postscript and another puzzlewig. 'P.P.S. —Excellent Majesty: Mary will still be our Little Mother on all common occasions, as you wished, but in the Earthly Paradise, we call her 'Traveller's Joy.'"

Chapter VII

There are two or three reasons why the part of Traveller's Joy suited me very well. In the first place it required a good deal of trouble, and I like taking trouble. Then John was willing to let me do many things he would not have allowed the others to do because he could trust me to be careful and to mind what he said.

On each side of the long walk in the kitchen garden there are flowers between you and the vegetables, herbaceous borders, with nice big clumps of things that have suckers, and off-shoots and seedlings at their feet.

"The long walk's the place to steal from if I wasn't an *honest* Root-gatherer," said Harry.

John had lovely poppies there that summer. When I read about the poppies Alphonse Karr sowed in the wild nooks of his native country, it made me think of John's French poppies and peony poppies, and ranunculus poppies, and carnation poppies, some very large, some quite small, some round and neat, some full and ragged like Japanese chrysanthemums, but all of such beautiful shades of red, rose, crimson, pink, pale blush, and white, that if they had but smelt like carnations instead of smelling like laudanum, when you have the toothache, they would have been quite perfect.

In one way they are nicer than carnations. They have such lots of seed, and it is so easy to get. I asked John to let me have some of the heads. He could not possibly want them all, for each head has enough in it to sow two or three yards of a border. He said I might have what seeds I liked, if I used scissors, and did not drag things out of the ground by pulling. But I was not to let the young gentlemen go seed gathering. "Boys be so destructive," John said.

After a time, however, I persuaded him to let Harry transplant seedlings of the things that sow themselves and come up in the autumn, if they came up a certain distance from the parent plants. Harry got a lot of things for our Paradise in this way; indeed, he would not have got much otherwise except wild flowers; and, as he said, "How can I be your Honest Root-gatherer if I mayn't gather anything up by the roots?"

I can't help laughing sometimes to think of the morning when he left off being our Honest Root-gatherer. He did look so funny, and so like Chris.

A day or two before, the Scotch Gardener had brought Saxon to see us, and a new kind of mouldiness that had got into his grape vines to show to John.

He was very cross at Saxon for walking on my garden. (And I am sure I quite forgave him, for I am so fond of him, and he knew no better, poor dear!) But, though he kicked Saxon, the Scotch Gardener was kind to us. He told us that the reason our gardens do not do so well as the big garden, and that my *Jules Margottin* has not such big roses as John's *Jules Margottin* is because we have never renewed the soil.

Arthur and Harry got very much excited about this. They made the Scotch Gardener tell them what good soil ought to be made of, and all the rest of the day they talked of nothing but *compost*. Indeed Arthur would come into my room and talk about compost after I had gone to bed.

Father's farming man was always much more good-natured to us than John ever was. He would give us anything we wanted. Warm milk when the cows were milked, or sweet-pea sticks, or bran to stuff the dolls' pillows. I've known him take his hedging-bill, in his dinner hour, and cut fuel for our beacon fire, when we were playing at a French Invasion. Nothing could be kinder.

Perhaps we do not tease him so much as we tease John. But when I say that, Arthur says, "Now, Mary, that's just how you explain away things. The real difference between John and Michael is, that Michael is good-natured and John is not. Catch John showing me the duck's nest by the pond, or letting you into the cow-house to kiss the new calf between the eyes—if he were farm man instead of gardener!"

And the night Arthur sat in my room, talking about compost, he said, "I shall get some good stuff out of Michael, I know; and Harry and I see our way to road-scrapings if we can't get sand; and we mean to take precious good care John doesn't have all the old leaves to himself. It's the top-spit that puzzles us, and loam is the most important thing of all."

"What is top-spit?" I asked.

"It's the earth you get when you dig up squares of grass out of a field like the paddock. The new earth that's just underneath. I expect John got a lot when he turfed that new piece by the pond, but I don't believe he'd spare us a flower pot full to save his life."

"Don't quarrel with John, Arthur. It's no good."

"I won't quarrel with him if he behaves himself," said Arthur, "but we mean to have some top-spit somehow."

"If you aggravate him, he'll only complain of us to Father."

"I know," said Arthur hotly, "and beastly mean of him, too, when he knows what Father is about this sort of thing."

"I know it's mean. But what's the good of fighting when you'll only get the worst of it?"

"Why to show that you're in the right, and that you know you are," said Arthur. "Good-night, Mary. We'll have a compost heap of our own this autumn, mark my words."

Next day, in spite of my remonstrances, Arthur and Harry came to open war with John, and loudly and long did they rehearse their grievances, when we were out of Father's hearing.

"Have we ever swept our own walks, except that once, long ago, when the German women came round with threepenny brooms?" asked Arthur, throwing out his right arm, as if he were making a speech. "And think of all the years John has been getting leaf mould for himself out of our copper beech leaves, and now refuses us a barrow-load of loam!"

The next morning but one, Harry was late for breakfast, and then it seemed that he was not dressing; he had gone out,—very early, one of the servants said. It frightened me, and I went out to look for him.

When I came upon him in our gardens, it was he who was frightened.

"Oh, dear," he exclaimed, "I thought you were John."

I have often seen Harry dirty—very dirty—but from the mud on his boots to the marks on his face where he had pushed the hair out of his eyes with earthy fingers, I never saw him quite so grubby before. And if there had been a clean place left in any part of his clothes well away from the ground, that spot must have been soiled by a huge and very dirty sack under the weight of which his poor little shoulders were bent nearly to his knees.

"What are you doing, Honest Root-gatherer?" I asked; "are you turning yourself into a hump-backed dwarf?"

"I'm not honest, and I'm not a Root-gatherer just now," said Harry, when he had got breath after setting down his load. He spoke shyly and a little surlily, like Chris when he is in mischief.

"Harry, what's that?"

"It's a sack I borrowed from Michael. It won't hurt it. It's had mangel-wurzels in already."

"What have you got in it now? It looks dreadfully heavy."

"It *is* heavy, I can tell you," said Harry, with one more rub of his dirty fingers over his face.

"You look half dead. What is it?"

"It's top-spit;" and Harry began to discharge his load on the walk.

"Oh, Harry; where did you get it?"

"Out of the paddock. I've been digging up turfs and getting this out, and putting the turfs back, and stamping them down not to show, ever since six o'clock. It *was* hard work; and I was so afraid of John coming. Mary, you won't tell tales?"

"No, Harry. But I don't think you ought to have taken it without Mother's leave."

"I don't think you can call it stealing," said Harry. "Fields are a kind of wild places anyhow, and the paddock belongs to Father, and it certainly doesn't belong to John."

"No," said I doubtfully.

"I won't get any more; it's dreadfully had work," said Harry, but as he shook the sack out and folded it up, he added (in a rather satisfied tone), "I've got a good deal."

I helped him to wash himself for breakfast, and half-way through he suddenly smiled and said, "John Parkinson will be glad when he sees *you-know-what*, Mary, whatever the other John thinks of it."

But Harry did not cut any more turfs without leave, for he told me that he had a horrid dream that night of waking up in prison with a warder looking at him through a hole in the door of his cell, and finding out that he was in penal servitude for stealing top-spit from the bottom of the paddock, and Father would not take him out of prison, and that Mother did not know about it.

However, he and Arthur made a lot of compost. They said we couldn't possibly have a Paradise without it.

It made them very impatient. We always want the spring and summer and autumn and winter to get along faster than they do. But this year Arthur and Harry were very impatient with summer.

They were nearly caught one day by Father coming home just as they had got through the gates with Michael's old sack full of road scrapings, instead of sand (we have not any sand growing near us, and silver sand is rather dear), but we did get leaves together and stacked them to rot into leaf mould.

Leaf mould is splendid stuff, but it takes a long time for the leaves to get mouldy, and it takes a great many too. Arthur is rather impatient, and he used to say—"I never saw leaves stick on to branches in such a way. I mean to get into some of these old trees and give them a good shaking to remind them what time of year it is. If I don't we shan't have anything like enough leaves for our compost."

Chapter VIII

Mother was very much surprised by Arthur's letter, but not so much puzzled as he expected. She knew Parkinson's *Paradisus* quite well, and only wrote to me to ask, "What are the boys after with the old books? Does your Father know?"

But when I told her that he had given us leave to be in the library, and that we took great care of the books, and how much we enjoyed the ones about gardening, and all that we were getting to do, she was very kind indeed, and promised to put on a blue dress and lace ruffles and be Queen of our Earthly Paradise as soon as she came home.

When she did come home, she was much better, and so was Chris. He was delighted to be our Dwarf, but he wanted to have a hump, and he would have such a big one that it would not keep in its place, and kept slipping under his arm and into all sorts of queer positions.

Not one of us enjoyed our new game more than Chris did, and he was always teasing me to tell him the story I had told the others, and to read out the names of the flowers which "the real Queen" had in her "real paradise." He made Mother promise to try to get him a bulb of the real Dwarf Daffodil as his next birthday present, to put in his own garden.

"And I'll give you some compost," said Arthur. "It'll be ever so much better than a stupid book with 'stuff' in it."

Chris did seem much stronger. He had colour in his cheeks, and his head did not look so large. But he seemed to puzzle over things in it as much as ever, and he was just as odd and quaint.

One warm day I had taken the *Tour round my Garden* and was sitting near the bush in the little wood behind our house, when Chris came after me with a Japanese fan in his hand and sat down cross-legged at my feet. As I was reading, and Mother has taught us not to interrupt people when they are reading, he said nothing, but there he sat.

"What is it, Chris?" said I.

"I am discontented," said Chris.

"I'm very sorry," said I.

"I don't think I'm selfish, particularly, but I'm discontented."

"What about?"

"Oh, Mary, I do wish I had not been away when you invented Paradise. Then I should have had a name in the game."

"You've got a name, Chris. You're the Dwarf."

"Ah, but what was the Dwarf's name?"

"I don't know," I admitted.

"No; that's just it. I've only one name, and Arthur and Harry have two. Arthur is a Pothecary" (Chris could never be induced to accept Apothecary as one word), "and he's John Parkinson as well. Harry is Honest Root-gatherer, and he is Francis le Vean. If I'd not been away, I should have had two names.

"You can easily have two names," said I. We'll call the Dwarf Thomas Brown."

Chris shook his big head.

"No, no. That wasn't his name; I know it wasn't. It's only stuff. I want another name out of the old book."

I dared not tell him that the Dwarf was not in the old book. I said:

"My dear Chris, you really are discontented; we can't all have double names. Adela has only one name, she is Weeding Woman and nothing else; and I have only one name, I'm Traveller's Joy, and that's all."

"But you and Adela are girls," said Chris, complacently. "The boys have two names." I suppressed some resentment, for Christopher's eyes were beginning to look weary, and said: "Shall I read to you for a bit?" "No, don't read. Tell me things out of the old book. Tell me about the Queen's flowers. Don't tell me about daffodils, they make me think what a long way off my birthday is, and I'm quite discontented enough."

And Chris sighed, and lay down on the grass, with one arm under his head, and his fan in his hand; and, as well as I could remember, I told him all about the different varieties of Cowslips, down to the Franticke, or Foolish Cowslip, and he became quite happy.

Dear Father is rather short-sighted, but he can hold a round glass in his eye without cutting himself. It was the other eye which was next to Chris at prayers the following morning; but he saw his legs, and the servants had hardly got out of the hall before he shouted, "Pull up your stockings, Chris!" —and then to Mother, "Why do you keep that sloven of a girl Bessy, if she can't dress the children decently? But I can't conceive what made you put that child into knickerbockers, he can't keep his stockings up."

"Yes, I can," said Christopher, calmly, looking at his legs.

"Then what have you got 'em down for?" shouted Father.

"They're not all down," said Chris, his head still bent over his knees, till I began to fear he would have a fit.

"One of 'em is, anyhow. I saw it at prayers. Pull it up."

"Two of 'em are," said Christopher, never lifting his admiring gaze from his stockings. "Two of them are down, and two of them are up, quite up, quite tidy."

Dear Father rubbed his glass and put it back into his eye.

"Why, how many stockings have you got on?"

"Four," said Chris, smiling serenely at his legs; "and it isn't Bessy's fault. I put 'em on myself, every one of them."

At this minute James brought in the papers, and Father only laughed, and said, "I never saw such a chap," and began to read. He is very fond of Christopher, and Chris is never afraid of him.

I was going out of the room, and Chris followed me into the hall, and drew my attention to his legs, which were clothed in four stockings; one pair, as he said, being drawn tidily up over his knees, the other pair turned down with some neatness in folds a little above his ankles.

"Mary," he said, "I'm contented now."

"I'm very glad, Chris. But do leave off staring at your legs. All the blood will run into your head."

"I wish things wouldn't always get into *my* head, and nobody else's," said Chris, peevishly as he raised it; but when he looked back at his stockings, they seemed to comfort him again.

"Mary, I've found another name for myself."

"Dear Chris! I'm so glad."

"It's a real one, out of the old book. I thought of it entirely by myself."

"Good Dwarf. What is your name?"

"*Hose-in-Hose*," said Christopher, still smiling down upon his legs.

Chapter IX

Alas for the hose-in-hose!

I laughed over Christopher and his double stockings, and I danced for joy when Bessy's aunt told me that she had got me a fine lot of roots of double cowslips. I never guessed what misery I was about to suffer, because of the hose-in-hose.

I had almost forgotten that Bessy's aunt knew double cowslips. After I became Traveller's Joy I was so busy with wayside planting that I had thought less of my own garden than usual, and had allowed Arthur to do what he liked with it as part of the Earthly Paradise (and he was always changing his plans), but Bessy's aunt had not forgotten about it, which was very good of her.

The Squire's Weeding Woman is old enough to be Bessy's aunt, but she has an aunt of her own, who lives seven miles on the other side of the Moor, and the Weeding Woman does not get to see her very often. It is a very out-of-the-way village, and she has to wait for chances of a cart and team coming and going from one of the farms, and so get a lift.

It was the Weeding Woman's aunt who sent me the hose-in-hose.

The weeding woman told me—"Aunt be mortal fond of her flowers, but she've no notions of gardening, not in the ways of a gentleman's garden. But she be after 'em all along, so well as the roomatiz in her back do let her, with an old shovel and a bit of stuff to keep the frost out, one time, and the old shovel and a bit of stuff to keep 'em moistened from the drought, another time; cuddling of 'em like Christians. 'Ee zee, Miss, Aunt be advanced in years; her family be off her mind, zum married, zum buried; and it zim as if her flowers be like new children for her, spoilt children, too, as I zay, and most fuss about they that be least worth it, zickly uns and contrary uns, as parents will. Many's time I do say to she—'Th' Old Zquire's garden, now, 'twould zim strange to thee, sartinly 'twould! How would 'ee feel to see Gardener zowing's spring plants by the hunderd, and a-throwing of 'em away by the score when beds be vull, and turning of un out for bedding plants, and throwing they away when he 'eve made his cuttings?' And she 'low she couldn't abear it, no more 'n see Herod a mass-sakering of the Innocents. But if 'ee come to Bible, I do say Aunt put me in mind of the par'ble of the talents, she do, for what you give her she make ten of, while other folks be losing what they got. And 'tis well too, for if 'twas not for givin' of un away, seeing's she lose nothin', and can't abear to destry nothin', and never takes un up but to set un again, six in place of one, as I say, with such a mossel of a garden, 'Aunt, where would you be?' And she 'low she can't tell, but the Lard would provide. 'Thank He,' I says, 'you be so out o' way, and 'ee back so bad, and past trevelling, zo there be no chance of 'ee ever seein' Old Zquire's Gardener's houses and they stove plants;' for if Gardener give un a pot, sure's death her'd set it in the chimbly nook on frosty nights, and put bed-quilt over un, and any cold corner would do for she."

At this point the Weeding Woman became short of breath, and I managed to protest against taking so many plants of the hose-in-hose.

"Take un and welcome, my dear, take un and welcome," replied Bessy's aunt. "I did say to Aunt to keep two or dree, but 'One be aal I want,' her says, 'I'll have so many agin in a few years, dividin' of un in autumn,' her says. 'Thee've one foot in grave, Aunt,' says I, 'it don't altogether become 'ee to forecast autumns,' I says, 'when next may be your latter end, 's like as not.' 'Niece,' her says, 'I be no ways presuming. His will be done,' her says, 'but if I'm spared, I'll rear un, and if I'm took, 'twill be where I sha'n't want un. Zo let young lady have un,' her says. And there a be!"

When I first saw the nice little plants, I did think of my own garden, but not for long. My next and final thought was—"Mary's Meadow!"

Since I became Traveller's Joy, I had chiefly been busy in the hedge-rows by the high-roads, and in waste places like the old quarry, and very bare and trampled bits, where there seemed to be no flowers at all.

You cannot say that of Mary's Meadow. Not to be a garden, it is one of the most flowery places I know. I did once begin a list of all that grows in it, but it was in one of Arthur's old exercise-books, which he had "thrown in," in a bargain we had, and there were very few blank pages left. I had thought a couple of pages would be more than enough, so I began with rather full accounts of the flowers, but I used up the book long before I had written out one half of what blossoms in Mary's Meadow.

Wild roses, and white bramble, and hawthorn, and dogwood, with its curious red flowers; and nuts, and maple, and privet, and all sorts of bushes in the hedge, far more than one would think; and ferns, and the stinking iris, which has such splendid berries, in the ditch—the ditch on the lower side where it is damp and where I meant to sow forget-me-nots, like Alphonse Karr, for there are none there as it happens. On the other side, at the top of the field, it is dry, and blue succory grows, and grows out on the road beyond. The most beautiful blue possible, but so hard to pick. And there are Lent lilies, and lords and ladies, and ground ivy, which smells herby when you find it, trailing about and turning the colour of Mother's "aurora" wool in green winters; and sweet white violets, and blue dog violets, and primroses, of course, and two or three kinds of orchis, and all over the field cowslips, cowslips, cowslips—to please the nightingale.

And I wondered if the nightingale would find out the hose-in-hose, when I had planted six of them in the sunniest, cosiest corner of Mary's Meadow.

For this was what I resolved to do, though I kept my resolve to myself for which I was afterwards very glad. I did not tell the others because I thought that Arthur might want some of the plants for our Earthly Paradise, and I wanted to put them all in Mary's Meadow. I said to myself, like Bessy's great aunt, that "if I were spared," I would go next year and divide the roots of the six, and bring some off-sets to our gardens, but I would keep none back now. The nightingale should have them all.

We had been busy in our gardens, and in the roads and bye-lanes, and I had not been in Mary's Meadow for a long time before the afternoon when I put my little trowel, and a bottle of water, and the six hose-in-hose into a basket, and was glad to get off quietly and alone to plant them. The highways and hedges were very dusty, but there it was very green. The nightingale had long been silent. I do not know where he was, but the rooks were not at all silent; they had been holding a parliament at the upper end of the field this morning, and were now all talking at once, and flapping about the tops of the big elms which were turning bright yellow, whilst down below a flight of starlings had taken their place and sat in the prettiest circles; and groups of hedge-sparrows flew and mimicked them. And in the fields round about the sheep baaed, and the air, which was very sweet, was so quiet that these country noises were the only sounds to be heard, and they could be heard from very far away.

I had found the exact spot I wanted, and had planted four of the hose-in-hose, and watered them from the bottle, and had the fifth in my hand, and the sixth still in the basket, when all these nice noises were drowned by a loud harsh shout which made me start, and sent the flight of starlings into the next field, and made the hedge-sparrows jump into the hedge.

And when I looked up, I saw the Old Squire coming towards me, and storming and shaking his fist at me as he came. But with the other hand he held Saxon by the collar, who was struggling to get away from him and to go to me.

I had so entirely forgotten about Father's quarrel with the Squire, that when the sight of the old gentleman in a rage suddenly reminded me, I was greatly stupefied and confused, and really did not at first hear what he said. But when I understood that he was accusing me of digging cowslips out of his field, I said at once (and pretty loud, for he was deaf) that I was not digging up anything, but was planting double cowslips to grow up and spread amongst the common ones.

I suppose it did sound rather unlikely, as the Old Squire knew nothing about our game, but a thing being unlikely is no reason for calling truthful people liars, and that was what the Old Squire called me.

It choked me, and when he said I was shameless, and that he had caught me with the plants upon me, and yelled to me to empty my basket, I threw away the fifth and sixth hose-in-hose as if they had been adders, but I could not speak again. He must have been beside himself with rage, for he called me all sorts of names, and said I was my father's own child, a liar and a thief. Whilst he was talking about sending me to prison (and I thought of Harry's dream, and turned cold with fear), Saxon was tugging to get to me, and at last he got away and came rushing up.

Now I knew that the Old Squire was holding Saxon back because he thought Saxon wanted to worry me as a trespasser, but I don't know whether he let Saxon go at last because he thought I deserved to be worried, or whether Saxon got away of himself. When his paws were almost on me, the Old Squire left off abusing me, and yelled to the dog, who at last, very unwillingly, went back to him, but when he just got to the Squire's feet he stopped, and pawed the ground in the funny way he sometimes does, and looked up at his master as much as to say, "You see it's only play," and then turned round and raced back to me as hard as he could lay legs to ground. This time he reached me, and jumped to lick my face, and I threw my arms round his neck and burst into tears.

When you are crying and kissing at the same time, you cannot hear anything else, so what more the Old Squire said I do not know.

I picked up my basket and trowel at once, and fled homewards as fast as I could go, which was not very fast, so breathless was I with tears and shame and fright.

When I was safe in our grounds, I paused and looked back. The Old Squire was still there, shouting and gesticulating, and Saxon was at his heels, and over the hedge two cows were looking at him, but the rooks and the starlings were far off in distant trees and fields.

And I sobbed afresh when I remembered that I had been called a liar and a thief, and had lost every one of my hose-in-hose; and this was all that had come of trying to make an Earthly Paradise of Mary's Meadow, and of taking upon myself the name of Traveller's Joy.

Chapter X

I told no one. It was bad enough to think of by myself. I could not have talked about it. But every day I expected that the Old Squire would send a letter or a policeman, or come himself, and rage and storm, and tell Father.

He never did; and no one seemed to suspect that anything had gone wrong, except that Mother fidgeted because I looked ill, and would show me to Dr. Solomon. It is a good thing doctors tell you what they think is the matter, and don't ask you what you think, for I could not have told him about the Squire. He said I was below par, and that it was our abominable English climate, and he sent me a bottle of tonic. And when I had taken half the bottle, and had begun to leave off watching for the policeman, I looked quite well again. So I took the rest, not to waste it, and thought myself very lucky. My only fear now was that Bessy's aunt might ask after the hose-in-hose. But she never did.

I had one more fright, where I least expected it. It had never occurred to me that Lady Catherine would take an interest in our game, and want to know what we had done, and what we were doing, and what we were going to do, or I should have been far more afraid of her than of Bessy's aunt. For the Weeding Woman has a good deal of delicacy, and often begs pardon for taking liberties; but if Aunt Catherine takes an interest, and wants to know, she asks one question after another, and does not think whether you like to answer or not.

She took an interest in our game after one of Christopher's luncheons with her.

She often asks Chris to go there to luncheon, all by himself. Father is not very fond of his going, chiefly, I fancy, because he is so fond of Chris, and misses him. Sometimes, in the middle of luncheon, he looks at Christopher's empty place, and says, "I wonder what those two are talking about over their pudding. They are the queerest pair of friends." If we ask Chris what they have talked about, he wags his head, and looks very well pleased with himself, and says, "Lots of things. I tell her things, and she tells me things." And that is all we can get out of him.

A few weeks afterwards, after I lost the hose-in-hose, Chris went to have luncheon with Aunt Catherine, and he came back rather later than usual.

"You must have been telling each other a good deal to-day, Chris," I said.

"I told her lots," said Chris complacently. "She didn't tell me nothing, hardly. But I told her lots. My apple fritter got cold whilst I was telling it. She sent it away, and had two hot ones, new, on purpose for me."

"What *did* you tell her?"

"I told her your story; she liked it very much. And I told her Daffodils, and about my birthday; and I told her Cowslips—all of them. Oh, I told her lots. She didn't tell me nothing."

A few days later, Aunt Catherine asked us to tea—all of us—me, Arthur, Adela, Harry, and Chris. And she asked us all about our game. When Harry said, "I dig up, but Mary plants—not in our garden, but in wild places, and woods, and hedges, and fields," Lady Catherine blew her nose very loud, and said, "I should think you don't do much digging and planting in that field your father went to law about?" and my teeth chattered so with fright that I think Lady Catherine would have heard them if she hadn't been blowing her nose. But, luckily for me, Arthur said, "Oh, we never go near Mary's Meadow now; we're so busy." And then Aunt Catherine asked what made us think of my name, and I repeated most of the bit from Alphonse Karr, for I knew it by heart now; and Arthur repeated what John Parkinson says about the "honisucle that growth wilde in euery hedge," and how he left it there "to serue their senses that trauell by it, or have no garden;" and then he said, "So Mary is called Traveller's Joy, because she plants flowers in the hedges, to serve their senses that travel by them."

"And who serves them that have no garden?" asked Aunt Catherine, sticking her gold glasses over her nose, and looking at us.

"None of us do," said Arthur after thinking for a minute.

"Humph!" said Aunt Catherine.

Next time Chris was asked to luncheon, I was asked too. Father laughed at me and teased me, but I went.

I was very much amused by the airs which Chris gave himself at table. He was perfectly well-behaved, but, in his quiet old-fashioned way, he certainly gave himself airs. We have only one man indoors—James; but Aunt Katherine has three—a butler, a footman, and a second footman. The second footman kept near Christopher, who sat opposite Aunt Catherine (she made me sit on one side), and seemed to watch to attend upon him; but if Christopher did want anything, he always ignored this man, and asked the butler for it and called him by his name.

After a bit, Aunt Catherine began to talk about the game again.

"Have you got any one to serve them that have no garden, yet?" she asked.

Christopher shook his head, and said, "No."

"Humph," said Aunt Catherine; "better take me into the game."

"Could you be of any use?" asked Christopher. "Toast and water, Chambers."

The butler nodded, as majestically as Chris himself, to the second footman, who flew to replenish the silver mug, which had been Lady Catherine's when she was a little girl. When Christopher had drained it (he is a very thirsty boy), he repeated the question: "Do you think you could be of any use?"

Mr. Chambers, the butler, never seems to hear anything that people say, except when they ask for something to eat or drink; and he does not often hear that, because he watches to see what you want, and gives it of himself, or sends it by the footman. He looks just as if he was having his photograph taken, staring at a point on the wall and thinking of nothing; but when Christopher repeated his question I saw Chambers frown. I believe he thinks Christopher presumes on Lady Catherine's kindness, and does not approve of it.

It is quite the other way with Aunt Catherine. Just when you would think she must turn angry, and scold Chris for being rude, she only begins to laugh, and shakes like a jelly (she is very stout), and encourages him. She said:

"Take care all that toast and water doesn't get into your head, Chris."

She said that to vex him, because, ever since he heard that he had water on the brain, Chris is very easily affronted about his head. He was affronted now, and began to eat his bread-and-butter pudding in silence, Lady Catherine still shaking and laughing. Then she wiped her eyes, and said—

"Never mind, old man, I'm going to tell you something. Put the sugar and cream on the table, Chambers, and you needn't wait."

The men went out very quietly, and Aunt Catherine went on—

"Where do you think I was yesterday? In the new barracks—a place I set my face against ever since they began to build it, and spoil one of my best peeps from the Rhododendron Walk. I went to see a young cousin of mine, who was fool enough to marry a poor officer, and have a lot of little boys and girls, no handsomer than you, Chris."

"Are they as handsome?" said Chris, who had recovered himself, and was selecting currants from his pudding, and laying them aside for a final *bonne bouche*.

"Humph! Perhaps not. But they eat so much pudding, and wear out so many boots, that they are all too poor to live anywhere except in barracks."

Christopher laid down his spoon, and looked as he always looks when he is hearing a sad story.

"Is barracks like the workhouse, Aunt Catherine?" he asked.

"A good deal like the workhouse," said Aunt Catherine. Then she went on—"I told her Mother I could not begin calling at the barracks. There are some very low streets close by, and my coachman said he couldn't answer for his horses with bugles, and perhaps guns, going off when you least expect them. I told her I would ask them to dinner; and I did but, they were engaged. Well, yesterday I changed my mind, and I told Harness that I meant to go to the barracks, and the horses would have to take me. So we started. When we were going along the upper road, between the high hedges, what do you think I saw?"

Chris had been going on with his pudding again, but he paused to make a guess.

"A large cannon, just going off?"

"No. If I'd seen that, you wouldn't have seen any more of me. I saw masses of wild clematis scrambling everywhere, so that the hedge looked as if somebody had been dressing it up in tufts of feathers."

As she said this, Lady Catherine held out her hand to me across the table very kindly. She has a fat hand, covered with rings, and I put my hand into it.

"And what do you think came into my head?" she asked.

"Toast and water," said Chris maliciously.

"No, you monkey. I began to think of hedge flowers, and travellers, and Traveller's Joy."

Aunt Catherine shook my hand here, and dropped it.

"And you thought how nice it was for the poor travellers to have such nice flowers," said Chris, smiling, and wagging his head up and down.

"Nothing of the kind," said Aunt Catherine, brusquely. "I thought what lots of flowers the travellers had already, without Mary planting any more; and I thought not one traveller in a dozen paid much attention to them—begging John Parkinson's pardon—and how much more in want of flowers people 'that have no garden' are; and then I thought of that poor girl in those bare barracks, whose old home was one of the prettiest places, with the loveliest garden in all Berkshire."

"Was it an Earthly Paradise?" asked Chris.

"It was, indeed. Well, when I thought of her inside those brick walls, looking out on one of those yards they march about in, now they've cut down all the trees, and planted sentry boxes, I put my best bonnet out of the window, which always spoils the feather, and told Harness to turn his horses' heads, and drive home again."

"What for?" said Chris, as brusquely as Lady Catherine.

"I sent for Hobbs."

"Hobbs the Gardener?" said Chris.

"Hobbs the Gardener; and I told Chambers to give him the basket from the second peg, and then I sent him into the conservatory to fill it. Mary, my dear, I am very particular about my baskets. If ever I lend you my diamonds, and you lose them, I may forgive you—I shall know *that* was an accident; but if I lend you a basket, and you don't return it, don't look me in the face again. I always write my name on them, so there's no excuse. And I don't know a greater piece of impudence—and people are wonderfully impudent now-a-days—than to think that because a thing only cost fourpence, you need not be at the trouble of keeping it clean and dry, and of sending it back."

"Some more toast and water, please," said Chris.

Aunt Catherine helped him and continued—"Hobbs is a careful man—he has been with me ten years—he doesn't cut flowers recklessly as a rule, but when I saw that basket I said, 'Hobbs, you've been very extravagant.' He looked ashamed of himself, but he said, 'I understood they was for Miss Kitty, m'm. She's been used to nice gardens, m'm.' Hobbs lived with them in Berkshire before he came to me."

"It was very nice of Hobbs," said Chris, emphatically.

"Humph!" said Aunt Catherine, "the flowers were mine."

"Did you ever get to the barracks?" asked Chris, "and what was they like when you did?"

"They were about as unlike Kitty's old home as anything could well be. She has made her rooms pretty enough, but it was easy to see she is hard up for flowers. She's got an old rose-coloured Sevres bowl that was my Grandmother's, and there it was, filled with bramble leaves and Traveller's Joy (which *she* calls Old Man's Beard; Kitty always would differ from her elders!), and a soup-plate full of forget-me-nots. She said two of the children had half drowned themselves and lost a good straw hat in getting them for her. Just like their mother, as I told her."

"What did she say when you brought out the basket?" asked Chris, disposing of his reserve of currants at one mouthful, and laying down his spoon.

"She said, 'Oh! oh! oh!' till I told her to say something more amusing, and then she said, 'I could cry for joy!' and 'Tell Hobbs he remembers all my favourites.'"

Christopher here bent his head over his empty plate, and said grace (Chris is very particular about his grace), and then got down from his chair and went up to Lady Catherine, and threw his arms round her as far as they would go, saying, "You are good. And I love you. I should think she thinked you was a fairy godmother."

After they had hugged each other, Aunt Catherine said, "Will you take me into the game, if I serve them that have no garden?"

Chris and I said "Yes" with one voice.

"Then come into the drawing-room," said Aunt Catherine, getting up and giving a hand to each of us. "And Chris shall give me a name."

Chris pondered a long time on this subject, and seemed a good deal disturbed in his mind. Presently he said, "I *won't* be selfish. You shall have it."

"Shall have what, you oddity?"

"I'm not a oddity, and I'm going to give you the name that I invented for myself. But you'll have to wear four stockings, two up and two down."

"Then you may keep *that* name to yourself," said Aunt Catherine. Christopher looked relieved.

"Perhaps you'd not like to be called "Old Man Beard?"

"Certainly not!" said Aunt Catherine.

"It *is* more of a boy's name," said Chris. "You might be the Franticke or Foolish Cowslip, but it is Jack an Apes on Horseback, too, and that's a boy's name. You shall be Daffodil, not a dwarf daffodil, but a big one, because you are big. Wait a minute—I know what you shall be. You shall be Nonsuch. It's a very big one, and it means none like it. So you shall be Nonsuch, for there's no one like you."

On which Christopher and Lady Catherine hugged each other afresh.

◆   ◆   ◆

"Who told most to-day?" asked Father when we got home.

"Oh, Aunt Catherine. Much most," said Christopher.

Chapter XI

The height of our game was in autumn. It is such a good time for digging up, and planting, and dividing, and making cuttings, and gathering seeds, and sowing them too. But it went by very quickly, and when the leaves began to fall they fell very quickly, and Arthur never had to go up the trees and shake them.

After the first hard frost we quite gave up playing at the Earthly Paradise; first, because there was nothing we could do, and second, because a lot of snow fell, and Arthur had a grand idea of making snow statues all along the terrace, so that Mother could see them from the drawing-room windows. We worked very hard, and it was very difficult to manage legs without breaking; so we made most of them Romans in togas, and they looked very well from a distance, and lasted a long time, because the frost lasted.

And, by degrees, I almost forgot that terrible afternoon in Mary's Meadow. Only when Saxon came to see us I told him that I was very glad that no one understood his bark, so that he could not let out what had become of the hose-in-hose.

But when the winter was past, and the snow-drops came out in the shrubbery, and there were catkins on the nut trees, and the missel-thrush we had been feeding in the frost sat out on mild days and sang to us, we all of us began to think of our gardens again, and to go poking about "with our noses in the borders," as Arthur said, "as if we were dogs snuffing after truffles." What we really were "snuffing after" were the plants we had planted in autumn, and which were poking and sprouting and coming up in all directions.

Arthur and Harry did real gardening in the Easter holidays, and they captured Adela now and then and made her weed. But Christopher's delight was to go with me to the waste places and hedges, where I had planted things as Traveller's Joy, and to get me to show them to him where they had begun to make a Spring start, and to help him to make up rambling stories, which he called "Supposings," of what the flowers would be like, and what this or that traveller would say when he saw them. One of his favourite *supposings* was—"Supposing a very poor man was coming along the road with his dinner in a handkerchief; and supposing he sat down under the hedge to eat it; and supposing it was cold beef, and he had no mustard; and supposing there was a seed on your nasturtium plants, and he knew it wouldn't poison him; and supposing he ate it with his beef, and it tasted nice and hot, like a pickle, wouldn't he wonder how it got there?"

But when the primroses had been out a long time, and the cowslips were coming into bloom, to my horror Christopher began "supposing" that we should find hose-in-hose in some of the fields, and all my efforts to put this idea out of his head, and to divert him from the search, were utterly in vain.

Whether it had anything to do with his having had water on the brain I do not know, but when once an idea got into Christopher's head, there was no dislodging it. He now talked of hose-in-hose constantly. One day he announced that he was "discontented" once more, and should remain so until he had "found a hose-in-hose." I enticed him to a field where I knew it was possible to secure an occasional oxlip, but he only looked pale, shook his head distressingly, and said, "I don't think nothin' of oxlips." Coloured primroses would not comfort him. He professed to disbelieve in the time-honoured prescription, "Plant a primrose upside down, and it will come up a polyanthus," and refused to help me to make the experiment. At last the worst came. He suddenly spoke, with smiles—"I *know* where we'll find hose-in-hose! In Mary's Meadow. It's the fullest field of cowslips there is. Hurrah! Supposing we find hose-in-hose, and supposing we find green cowslips, and supposing we find curled cowslips or galligaskins, and supposing—"

But I could not bear it. I fairly ran away from him, and shut myself up in my room and cried. I knew it was silly, and yet I could not bear the thought of having to satisfy everybody's curiosity, and describe that scene in Mary's Meadow that had wounded me so bitterly, and explain why I had not told of it before.

I cried, too, for another reason. Mary's Meadow had been dear to us all, ever since I could remember. It was always our favourite field. We had coaxed our nurses there, when we could induce them to leave the high-road, or when, luckily for us, on account of an epidemic, or for some reason or another, they were forbidden to go gossiping into the town. We had "pretended" fairies in the nooks of the delightfully neglected hedges, and we had found fairy-rings to prove our pretendings true. We went there for flowers; we went there for mushrooms and puff balls; we went there to hear the nightingale. What cowslip balls and what cowslip tea-parties it had afforded us! It is fair to the Old Squire to say that we were sad trespassers, before he and Father quarreled and went to law. For Mary's Meadow was a field with every quality to recommend it to childish affections.

And now I was banished from it, not only by the quarrel, of which we had really not heard much, or realized it as fully, but by my own bitter memories. I cried afresh to think I should never go again to the corner where I always found the earliest violets, and then I cried to think that the nightingale would soon be back and how that very morning when I opened my window, I had heard the cuckoo and could tell that he was calling from just about Mary's Meadow.

I cried my eyes into such a state, that I was obliged to turn my attention to making them fit to be seen; and I had spent quite half-an-hour in bathing them and breathing on my handkerchief, and dabbing them, which is more soothing, when I heard Mother calling me. I winked hard, drew a few long breaths, rubbed my cheeks, which were so white they showed up my red eyes, and ran downstairs. Mother was coming to meet me. She said—"Where is Christopher?"

It startled me. I said, "He was with me in the garden, about—oh, about an hour ago; have you lost him? I'll go and look for him."

And I snatched up a garden hat, which shaded my swollen eyelids, and ran out. I could not find him anywhere, and becoming frightened, I ran down the drive, calling him as I went, and through the gate, and out into the road.

A few yards farther on I met him.

That child is most extraordinary. One minute he looks like a ghost; an hour later his face is beaming with a radiance that seems absolutely to fatten him under your eyes. That was how he looked just then as he came towards me, smiling in an effulgent sort of way, as if he were the noonday sun—no less, and carrying a small nosegay in his hand.

When he came within hearing he boasted, as if he had been Caesar himself—

"I went; I found it; I've got them."

And as he held his hand up, and waved the nosegay—I knew all. He had been to Mary's Meadow, and the flowers between his fingers were hose-in-hose.

Chapter XII

"I won't be selfish, Mary," Christopher said. "You invented the game, and you told me about them. You shall have them in water on your dressing table; they might get lost in the nursery. Bessy is always throwing things out. Tomorrow I shall go and look for galligaskins."

I was too glad to keep them from Bessy's observation, as well as her unparalleled powers of destruction, which I knew well. I put them into a slim glass on my table, and looked stupidly at them, and then out of the window at Mary's Meadow.

So they had lived—and grown—and settled there—and were now in bloom. *My* plants.

Next morning I was sitting, drawing, in the school room window, when I saw the Old Squire coming up the drive. There is no mistaking him when you can see him at all. He is a big, handsome old man, with white whiskers, and a white hat, and white gaiters, and he generally wears a light coat, and a flower in his buttonhole. The flower he wore this morning looked like—, but I was angry with myself for thinking of it, and I went on drawing again, as well as I could, for I could not help wondering why he was coming to our house. Then it struck me he might have seen Chris trespassing, and he might be coming at last to lay a formal complaint.

Twenty minutes later James came to tell me that Father wished to see me in the library, and when I got there, Father was just settling his eye-glass in his eye, and the Old Squire was standing on the hearth-rug with a big piece of paper in his hand. And then I saw that I was right, and that the flowers in his button-hole were hose-in-hose.

As I came in he laid down the paper, took the hose-in-hose out of his buttonhole in his left hand, and held out his right hand to me, saying: "I'm more accustomed to public speaking than to private speaking, Miss Mary. But—will you be friends with me?"

In Mary's Meadow my head had got all confused because I was frightened. I was not frightened to-day, and I saw the whole matter in a moment. He had found the double cowslips, and he knew now that I was neither a liar nor a thief. I was glad, but I could not feel very friendly to him. I said, "You can speak when you are angry."

Though he was behind me, I could feel Father coming nearer, and I knew somehow that he had taken out his glass again to rub it and put it back, as he does when he is rather surprised or amused. I was afraid he meant to laugh at me afterwards, and he can tease terribly, but I could not have helped saying what came into my head that morning if I had tried. When you have suffered a great deal about anything, you cannot sham, not even politeness.

The Old Squire got rather red. Then he said, "I am afraid I am very hasty, my dear, and say very unjustifiable things. But I am very sorry, and I beg your pardon. Will you forgive me?"

I said, "Of course, if you're sorry, I forgive you, but you have been a very long time in repenting."

Which was true. If I had been cross with one of the others, and had borne malice for five months, I should have thought myself very wicked. But when I said it, I felt sorry, for the old gentleman made no answer. Father did not speak either, and I began to feel very miserable. I touched the flowers, and the Old Squire gave them to me in silence. I thanked him very much, and then I said—

"I am very glad you know about it now . . . I'm very glad they lived. . . . I hope you like them? . . . I hope, if you do like them, that they'll grow and spread all over your field."

The Old Squire spoke at last. He said, "It is not my field any longer."

I said, "Oh, why?"

"I have given it away; I have been a long time in repenting, but when I did repent I punished myself. I have given it away.

It overwhelmed me, and when he took up the big paper again, I thought he was going, and I tried to stop him, for I was sorry I had spoken unkindly to him, and I wanted to be friends.

"Please don't go," I said. "Please stop and be friends. And oh, please, please don't give Mary's Meadow away. You mustn't punish yourself. There's nothing to punish yourself for. I forgive you with all my heart, and I'm sorry I spoke crossly. I have been so very miserable, and I was so vexed at wasting the hose-in-hose, because Bessy's great aunt gave them to me, and I've none left. Oh, the unkindest thing you could do to me now would be to give away Mary's Meadow."

The Old Squire had taken both my hands in his, and now he asked very kindly: "Why, my dear, why don't you want me to give away Mary's Meadow?"

"Because we are so fond of it. And because I was beginning to hope that now we're friends, and you know we don't want to steal your things or to hurt your field, perhaps you would let us play in it sometimes, and perhaps have Saxon to play with us there. We are so very fond of him too."

"You are fond of Mary's Meadow?" said the Old Squire.

"Yes, yes! We have been fond of it all our lives. We don't think there is any field like it, and I don't believe there can be. Don't give it away. You'll never get one with such flowers in it again. And now there are hose-in-hose, and they are not at all common. Bessy's aunt's aunt has only got one left, and she's taking care of it with a shovel. And if you'll let us in, we'll plant a lot of things and do no harm, we will indeed. And the nightingale will be here directly. Oh, don't give it away!"

My head was whirling now with the difficulty of persuading him, and I did not hear what he said across me to my father. But I heard Father's reply—"Tell her yourself, sir."

On which the Old Squire stuffed the big paper into my arms, and put his hand on my head and patted it.

"I told you I was a bad hand at talking, my dear, he said, "but Mary's Meadow is given away, and that's the Deed of Gift which you've got in your arms, drawn up as tight as any rascal of a lawyer can do it, and that's not so tight, I believe, but what some other rascal of a lawyer could undo it. However, they may let you alone. For I've given it to you, my dear, and it is yours. So you can plant, and play, and do what you please there. 'You and your heirs and assigns, for ever,' as the rascals say."

It was my turn now to be speechless. But as I stared blankly in front of me, I saw that Father had come round, and was looking at me through his eye-glass. He nodded to me, and said: "Yes, Mary, the Squire has given Mary's Meadow to you, and it is yours."

◆   ◆   ◆

Nothing would induce the Old Squire to take it back, so I had to have it, for my very own. He said he had always been sorry he had spoken so roughly to me, but he could not say so, as he and Father were not on speaking terms. Just lately he was dining with Lady Catherine, to meet her cousins from the barracks, and she was telling people after dinner about our game (rather mean of her, I think, to let out our secret at a dinner party), and when he heard about my planting things in the hedges, he remembered what I had said. And next day he went to the place to look, and there were the hose-in-hose.

Oh, how delighted the others were when they heard the Mary's Meadow belonged to me.

"It's like having an Earthly Paradise given to you, straight off!" said Harry.

"And one that doesn't want weeding," said Adela.

"And, oh, Mary, Mary!" cried Arthur. "Think of the yards and yards of top-spit. It does rejoice me to think I can go to you now when I'm making compost, and need not be beholden to that old sell-up-your-grandfather

John for as much as would fill Adela's weeding basket, and that's about as small an article as anyone can make-believe with."

"It's very heavy when it's full," said Adela.

"Is everything hers?" asked Christopher. "Is the grass hers, and the trees hers, and the hedges hers, and the rooks hers, and the starlings hers, and will the nightingale be hers when he comes home, and if she could dig through to the other side of the world, would there be a field the same size in Australia that would be hers, and are the sheep hers, and—"

"For mercy's sake stop that catalogue, Chris," said Father. "Of course the sheep are not hers; they were moved yesterday. By the bye, Mary, I do not know what you propose to do with your property, but if you like to let it to me, I'll turn some sheep in tomorrow, and I'll pay you so much a year, which I advise you to put into the Post Office Savings Bank."

I couldn't fancy Mary's Meadow always without sheep, so I was too thankful; though at first I could not see that it was fair that dear Father should let me have his sheep to look pretty in my field for nothing and pay me, too. He is always teasing me about my field, and he teases me a good deal about the Squire, too. He says we have set up another queer friendship in the family, and that the Old Squire and I are as odd a pair as Aunt Catherine and Chris.

I am very fond of the Old Squire now, and he is very kind to me. He wants to give me Saxon, but I will not accept him. It would be selfish. But the Old Squire says I had better take him, for we have quite spoilt him for a yard dog by petting him, till he has not a bit of savageness left in him. We do not believe that Saxon ever was savage; but I daren't say so to the Old Squire, for he does not like you to think you know better than he does about anything. There is one other subject on which he expects to be humoured, and I am careful not to offend him. He cannot tolerate the idea that he might be supposed to have yielded to Father the point about which they went to law, in giving Mary's Meadow to me. He is always lecturing me on encroachments, and the abuse of privileges, and warning me to be very strict about trespassers on the path through Mary's Meadow; and now that the field is mine, nothing will induce him to walk in it without asking my leave. That is his protest against the decision from which he meant to appeal.

Though I have not accepted Saxon, he spends most of his time with us. He likes to come for the night, because he sleeps on the floor of my room, instead of a kennel, which must be horrid, I am sure. Yesterday, the Old Squire said, "One of these fine days, when Master Saxon does not come home till morning, he'll find a big mastiff in his kennel, and will have to seek a home for himself where he can."

Chris has been rather whimsical lately. Father says Lady Catherine spoils him. One day he came to me, looking very peevish, and said, "Mary, if a hedgehog should come and live in one of your hedges, Michael says he would be yours, he's sure. If Michael finds him, will you give him to me?"

"Yes, Chris, but what do you want with a hedgehog?"

"I want him to sleep by my bed," said Chris. "You have Saxon by your bed; I want something by mine. I want a hedgehog. I feel discontented without a hedgehog. I think I might have something the matter with my brain if I didn't get a hedgehog pretty soon. Can I go with Michael and look for him this afternoon?" And he put his hand to his forehead.

"Chris, Chris!" I said, "you should not be so sly. You're a real slyboots. Double stockings and slyboots." And I took him on my lap.

Chris put his arms round my neck and buried his cheek against mine.

"I won't be sly, Mary," he whispered; and then, hugging me as he hugs Lady Catherine, he added, "For I do love you; for you are a darling, and I do really think it always was yours."

"What, Chris?"

"If not," said Chris, "why was it always called Mary's Meadow?"

C H A P T E R   6

Telling the Truth Slant: Ewing's Poetry

Tell all the truth but tell it slant—
Success in Circuit lies
Too bright for our infirm Delight
The Truth's superb surprise
As Lightning to the Children eased
With explanation kind
The Truth must dazzle gradually
Or every man be blind—

Emily Dickinson (1830–86)

There is no question but that Juliana Ewing was devoutly religious. Her niece, Christabel Maxwell, has pointed out the extent to which the church—primarily that pastored by her father in Ecclesfield—was central in her aunt's life, so much so that she was not satisfied unless she found a church to attend no matter where she happened to be:

> Throughout her life Juliana's actions were governed by her devotion to the Church of England. The church at Ecclesfield stood supreme, but wherever she went she interested herself in ecclesiastical matters. When she took a holiday, her first concern was to find a church where she could worship; and this activity was not reserved for Sundays. On more than one occasion her mother protested. In 1863 Julie [Juliana] found a church at Scarborough which she visited so assiduously that she succumbed eventually to a chill and forced her mother into wishing that the clergyman and "his smart church, and his eight o'clock service, and his choir practice were in Jericho!" Nor was this devotion a

matter of lip-service only. She took its teachings to her heart and regulated her life accordingly.[1]

In considering the life of one who was so pious, it would be natural to assume that her religion was the controlling factor in how she responded to what she read, especially when she reacted negatively to a piece of writing and declared her extreme displeasure with it as in the following example. A friend recommended to her a novel that appeared in 1880 and was a sensation at the time, *Mehalah: A Story of the Salt Marshes* by Sabine Baring-Gould (1834–1924). She read it and was appalled. Never mind that its author was an Anglican priest, a respected theologian, and a hymn writer one of whose hymns, "Onward Christian Soldiers," was and still is exceedingly popular. And never mind that this novel of his, *Mehalah*, was being praised and linked to that great work *Wuthering Heights* by no less a literary light than Algernon Charles Swinburne. To her friend who recommended *Mehalah* to her, Juliana wrote:

> I want to tell you that I have at last—on your recommendation— read Mehalah. I thought I would politely slur over the fact that I am not charmed by it—but on the whole I think I will tell you why. For the reasons for which I don't like it are general ones; I should apply them to any work of art, and I think it would be a help to you to do the same. That is if you agree with my first principles . . . A writer may of course paint human nature as it seems to him, and one may or may not see with him. If he dogmatises from his own point of view, one has of course a right to dispute his conclusions, and reflect on his premises! In Mehalah human beings are painted solely as animals. There is not one indication that I have been fortunate enough to find that any one of the people whose fortunes form the narrative has a hope, an aim, or even a capacity above the necessities and the lusts of the flesh. One wants whiskey—one wants money—one wants a woman—one wants a husband—a great many of them want dumplings and gravy (and they seem the most respectable), for the ones who want liquor don't care how they get it—the one who wants a husband will take any husband—and the man who wants

a special woman in his supreme outburst of—I won't profane the word Love, which has as much to do with it as with dumplings and gravy—of desire—says he would fain get her once into his arms, and then strangle her and cast her from him.[2]

Ewing was concerned that *Mehalah* was not the only work of literature currently being offered to the public in which the human spirit was depicted as unrelievedly depraved. She thought it absurd that human beings were consistently portrayed as little more than animals. Her displeasure with this twisted and oversimplified version of human nature is obvious not only in the letter quoted above but also in another letter, this one dated 17 January 1882, to her husband. In this letter she suggests that "The Fleshly School of Poetry" was responsible for fomenting the writing and publication of novels such as *Mehalah* and *Sophy of Kravonia* by Anthony Hope, which appeared the same year, 1880.[3] Seldom does one encounter in her letters the level of passion with which she explains in this letter what is wrong, badly wrong, with novels such as *Sophy* and *Mehalah*:

> Some novels lately—Sophy and Mehalah—deeply recommended to me, have made me aghast. I'm not very young, nor do I think very priggish; but I do decline to look at life and its complexities solely and entirely from a point of view that (bar Christian names and the English language) would do equally well for a pig or a monkey. If I am no more than a Pig, I'm a fairly "learned" pig, and will back myself to get some small piggish pleasures out of this mortal style, before I go to the Butcher!! But—IF—I am something different, and very much higher, I won't ignore my birthright, or sell it for Hogwash, because it involves the endurance of some pain, and the exercise of some faith and hope and charity! . . . [In the novel *Mehalah*,] the focus point of the hero's (!) desire would at quarter sessions, or assizes, go by the plain names of outrage and murder, and he succeeds in drowning himself with the girl who hates him lashed to him by a chain. In not one other character in the book is there an indication that life has an aim beyond the lusts of the flesh, and the most respectable

characters are tenants whose desires are summed up in the desire
of more suet pudding and gravy!!! To anyone who KNOWS the
poor! who knows what faiths and hopes (true or untrue) support
them in consumption and cancer, in hard lives and dreary deaths,
the picture is as untrue as it is (to me!) disgusting.[4]

This letter stands out from among all those published in Eden's book
as probably having the most marks of conviction, that is, exclamation
points. Juliana placed them there to indicate clearly her unusually strong
feelings and not just for the purpose of intensifying the dramatic impact
of her sentences. They are, in her case, marks of disgust and agitation,
but it is noteworthy that it was not primarily her religion that caused
this reaction. She was not condemning the novels *Sophy* and *Mehalah*
because she considered them indecent and thus an affront to her
Christian upbringing but mainly because she considered them artificial.
They offended her because they violated the ethic of her art. It was the
Juliana Ewing who was a devotee and a practitioner of that art who was
offended because, as she put it in the last sentence quoted above of her
letter to her husband, "the picture" presented in these two novels was
"untrue" and therefore to her "disgusting." The two novels did not present
the truth. In his astute treatment of Ewing, U. C. Knoepflmacher refers to
her as "a truth teller," a three-word description that penetrates to her very
heart and soul.[5] For her, *Sophy* and *Mehalah* did not depict "real people
and "real things," as Rudyard Kipling so admiringly said of her works,
but created an oversimplified and therefore unrealistic view of humanity
(she called it "animalism") that the authors were outrageously trying to
pass off as a depiction of real life, a literary lie. Heated with the anger of
insult, she planned to write a novel to be titled *The Things That are Seen*,
which would be, in effect, what she called in a letter to a friend "a protest
against animalism,"[6] in actuality, a protest against bad art that does not
portray things as they are seen.

She did not write that novel, however, and the reason is highly
significant: she found that her emotions were so deeply involved in her
objections to the disgusting artificiality of *Sophy* and *Mehalah* that she
would herself run the risk of writing bad art, that is, of writing what
would turn into a tract rather than a novel. She was not in the business of

writing tracts. She was aware of what makes for good fiction and poetry, and didacticism was not part of the formula. She knew that no matter how strong an author's desire is to express his or her stirred emotions, those emotions have to be reined in for the purpose of writing effectively, convincingly. The true artist, she contended, is aware of and practices at all times what she called "the law of reticence," which

> young writers of talent break almost invariably. No class of literature is a more striking example of the blunder of throwing away powder and shot than tracts—and I sometimes wonder if any recognised form of literature has more in its power. It is almost next to drama for what it has to work upon, the highest hopes, the deepest sufferings of humanity . . . and a real artist needs strong warrants of Conscience when he dips into those primary colours. In a fit of enthusiasm Ruskin wanted to lay a tax on all colours but black, Prussian blue, Vandyke brown, and Chinese white. I suspect it would be greatly to the advantage of our art if to depict some of the deepest emotions and experiences of humanity were forbidden . . . till years of discretion. "Make your white precious" is a quaint saying of Ruskin's which I often recall when I write.[7]

If she were a "truth teller," she was also a conscious artist who refused to obey her emotions if they threatened to turn her writing into what she called pejoratively "goody-goodyism." In her book devoted to her sister's biography and letters, Horatia Eden states that Juliana's faithful adherence to the law of reticence is what "gives the highest value to all her work" and spares her writings from "any approach to cant or goody-goodyism."[8] Devout as she was, she was not a goody-goodyism writer, nor could she abide those who were. She told the truth, but in a certain way, as Emily Dickinson put it, not straight out but "slant," by indirection. Reticence and the truth revealed indirectly characterize all of Ewing's work, but it is in her poetry that these two principles are most obvious.

That which is largely responsible for making them work is the method of narration she discovered to be best suited for her fairy tales, and she used it as well in many of her poems. In a letter to her mother (31 January 1869), she described this technique:

> All real "fairy tales" should be written as if they were oral traditions, taken down from the lips of a "story teller." This is where modern ones . . . fail, and the extent to which I have had to cut out reflections, abandon epithets, and shorten sentences, since I began, very much confirms my ideas.[9]

In other words, what she discovered through experience was that in order to tell the truth "slant," she would have to delete her own "reflections" and to move the narrative voice away from herself to someone else or something else. Her most successful poems do precisely that: in the five poems included in this book, the first is narrated by a squirrel, the second by a child (a little girl), the third also narrated by a child but a slightly older girl, the fourth partly by a body of water (a stream), and the fifth by a little boy who has been very ill.

She accomplished through these narrators a form of communication that could be aptly designated as "unintended wisdom," an ingenious way of conveying some established truth but doing so indirectly, which is to say, without the speaker's being aware of what he or she (or it) has actually achieved by way of passing on wisdom. It is the speaker, not the author, who does not intend to express the wisdom that is nevertheless expressed. The squirrel in "Boy and Squirrel" refuses to accept as wisdom what his white-tail grandfather tells him, and he contemptuously calls that wisdom "chaff." He is thus a foolishly naïve narrator who has not yet learned through hard experience that boys are, indeed, no friends to squirrels and that—the greater truth that Ewing wishes to express— the young would benefit greatly by taking heed of what the aged tell them. Therefore, the squirrel as narrator ironically offers the reader the opposite of wisdom believing all the time that he is expressing wisdom. The technique is roughly the same as that employed by Mark Twain in *Adventures of Huckleberry Finn*. When Huck Finn speaks of going to hell because he has helped a slave run away to freedom, he sincerely believes he has sinned beyond redemption, the truth being to him that slaves belong to their owners. What he is actually doing, however, is unintendedly revealing the truth that it is slavery that is wrong and that he is right in acting as he did. It is no coincidence that in her final days when she was confined to her bed, Juliana's favorite book to be read to her was *Huckleberry Finn*. Mark Twain and she discovered essentially the same effective way of telling the truth "slant."

As in Mark Twain's novel, so in much of the poetry of Juliana Ewing, humor and irony are frequently byproducts in the conveyance of unintended wisdom. In "Boy and Squirrel," incongruity fosters humor, a squirrel using expressions like "my dear friend," referring to "ladies' flounces" and to his "wary grandfather" —a talking squirrel who speaks to the boy with words that a cultured and rather sophisticated human would use and yet the total failure of even this elegant language to communicate, for boy and squirrel are fated to be worlds apart. The humor, therefore, is infiltrated by sadness. The poem evokes a smile, but the sad truth cannot be hidden. The boy is, indeed, a danger to the squirrel and always will be. Here as is often the case, Ewing's is the poetry of the sad smile, for that is what many of her poems evoke.

The sad part of the smile aroused by reading "Master Fritz" is likely to be even more pronounced, for although it has all the trappings of a delightful little poem about two children playing house, a situation that nearly always stimulates in readers the pleasure of fond memories, the larger message conveyed is a biting truth. The little girl is simply telling about her play-mate friend and next-door neighbor Fritz, what he is like, what he says to her, and how she reacts to him.

Unlike some of Ewing's other writings, "Master Fritz" is accessible to children of a certain age and reading level, and to them, whether they read the poem for themselves or it is read to them, a distinct message of truth emerges. A child is likely to perceive that Fritz is not really good to Grethel but selfish, and therefore unfair to his little neighbor and friend, who is not selfish but generous. To a child, the contrast between them would be obvious. On that level, the poem deals with what Ewing considered the ultimate vice, selfishness, which is unfortunately practiced all too often by those of all ages. On the simplest level of meaning, then, the poem contains a wise admonition for children to be unselfish, that is, not like Fritz.

But "Master Fritz" is also a superb example of Ewing's artistic duplicity, for there is a deeper and more stinging message that soaks into the consciousness of the adult reader and there electrifies with the shock of recognition: Master Fritz is the embodiment of a type of adult, found widely, especially among Victorian husbands. The child reader will not understand this, but to those older, the inescapable truth is that this poem puts on trial a culture in which the wife is expected to be adoringly submissive to the husband, unquestioning, obedient, and giving in every sense of the word, and the husband is the "master" of the household, totally owning all that he shares with his wife, who merely has the management of his possessions. Ewing brilliantly and scathingly puts into Fritz's mouth every aspect of the cultural concept of the dominant male not uncommon in the Victorian era but never totally obsolete even today in some cultures. It is a poem of authorial resentment but not a tract, for—as it should be remembered—Ewing was not in the business of writing tracts. She demonstrated her expertise in telling the truth "slant" by having a little girl narrator in "Master Fritz" unintendedly bring to light all that she herself wanted to reveal.

An ordinarily amusing situation is established early in "A Sweet Little Dear" with the narrator, a little girl somewhat older than Grethel in "Master Fritz," ostensibly bragging on herself as being "remarkable" and "sensitive" and, of course, very pretty. It does not take long, however, before what humor there is fades because she herself makes it clear that she is not a likable child with winning ways and charming innocence. Rather, the portrait that Ewing paints of her is of the prototypical spoiled brat. Details about her in the poem—her total self-absorption, her selfishness, her lack of sympathy for her mother's illness, her boredom producing insatiability for more of everything and then her quick loss of interest in what she wants, asks for, and is given—the presentation of all these negative aspects of her personality and behavior in the poem have the effect of alienating the child, Jane, from the reader. Not all children are precious little darlings, and it becomes clear fairly early that the poem's title, "A Sweet Little Dear," is blatantly ironic.

If the child is hopelessly spoiled, the mother seems misguided and foolish. Determination to understand her child and to tolerate her behavior seem to have taken the place in her mind of the practical importance of disciplining her. Bored and restless, Jane likes to hop around the room creating a disturbance that causes her mother's head to ache, but rather than correct the child, she says nothing and suffers the pain. When the nurse instructs Jane "go and play, dear, and let your Mamma rest," the mother counters the nurse's order to the child and tells her to remain, for Jane has asked a rather insipid question of the sort typical of a child and the mother tells the nurse:

> Dear Nurse, lift me up, and put a pillow to my back, I know you
> mean to be kind; But she does ask such remarkable questions,
> and while I've strength to speak, don't let me check the inquiring
> mind.

Obviously, Jane's mother has read in one of her books about child rearing that a parent should never stifle a child's "inquiring mind" by refusing to answer all of his or her questions. Not only the advice but also the phrase has been engraved on her mind: her Jane has an inquiring mind. On another occasion when Jane feels "as if I wanted something new to amuse me," her indulgent mother explains to her that she is anxious for something new because she has "got such an active brain." This sweet little dear with the inquiring mind and active brain is in reality the opposite of what her mother wants her to be (and has talked herself into believing that she is).

It is difficult to sympathize with a doting, indulgent mother and to feel that a badly spoiled, selfish child is cute and lovable, but as unlikable as Jane is and as foolish as her mother seems to be, in the final analysis this is a sad poem. Creating that final effect—sadness—despite all the reader-alienating details about the two main characters is something of an achievement for Ewing. She brings it off subtly, by having Jane remark on some action of her mother's or repeat something that her mother has said that is truly telling and strikes home—the heart—although the daughter certainly does not intend what she says to have the impact that it has. Perhaps the most effective of those comments is in her recounting a visit from the clergyman's wife:

> And I'm a sacred responsibility to my parents—(it was what the
> clergyman's wife at the seaside said),
>   And a solemn charge, and a fair white page, and a tender bud,
> and a spotless nature of wax to be molded . . .
>   There was a lot more, and she left two books as well, and
> I think she called me a Privilege, and Mamma said "Yes," and
> began to cry.

How can we account for the mother's tears? Maybe they are tears of
joy. Perhaps the clergyman's wife made her very happy in stressing how
important little Jane is and what a wonderful opportunity the mother
has to guide this sweet little dear into glorious womanhood. We might
conjure up other theories explaining why the mother cries, but Ewing is
careful that there be no misunderstanding as to the real reason, which
is revealed through the voice of truth in the poem, the Nurse. In a state
of irritation at what the clergyman's wife said, the Nurse knows why the
mother is crying and reveals it: she is worried, so worried that her nerves
are as tight and as sensitive as the strings of a violin, or as the Nurse puts
it: "she is weak as a kitten and worried to fiddlestrings."

The poem ends on this same note of the mother's deteriorating
health because of her worry. Jane has heard her confess to her worrying:
"She worries about me all night, till she's nearly mad." This is a woman
who feels intense pressure on her to raise a promising child the right
way, to mold her as if she were wax, nature's wax, to be sure that the
white blank page of her personality has the right words written on it,
to be certain that this promising bud blooms into the beautiful flower
it should become. This is a woman who cannot find enough time in a
day to read all the books on correct child rearing that are given to her to
read or recommended to her. This is a woman who is constantly hearing
from others how special her child is, how pretty and bright and what a
"privilege" it is for her, the mother, to have been chosen to mold and guide
this angel in human form. This is a woman who above all else is afraid,
as she puts it on one occasion, that she will not "be all a mother ought"
to be. And deep within her heart, she realizes that all is not going well.
For the child is unhappy and does not know why. The mother, feeling the
extreme pressure from others and from herself to succeed, is somehow

failing, and the implication is that she is worrying herself into the grave. The poem is deeply saddening.[10]

In the letter quoted earlier of 31 January 1869, to her mother, Ewing revealed her intent to compose fairy tales as if they were "oral traditions taken down from the lips of a 'story teller.'"[11] "The Mill Stream" is not a fairy tale per se, but Ewing was an experimenter in both fiction and poetry, and "The Mill Stream" is an experiment in a genre closely related to fairy tales, the myth in poetic form.

Ewing was drawn to myths because of her fondness for folklore of all sorts and because the myth nearly always manifests a message or lesson that has to do with right thinking and moral behavior, a necessary ingredient, she insisted, for all forms of literature, especially her own writing. The myth, therefore, offered her a ready vehicle for including a lesson without running the risk of didacticism, to which she was almost fanatically opposed. Myths tell the truth "slant."[12]

One of the two narrative voices in "The Mill Stream" functions much like the chorus in Greek tragedy, reporting what happens to the stream as a result of its hunger for more power and prestige. The other voice is identified in the poem as that of "the brook." It is the brook or stream personified, made into a speaker, perhaps a mythic figure, a god incarnated in the stream as was Vishnu in the Ganges or Hapi in the Nile, but a distinctly lesser figure with big dreams of doing big things: hungering to be more important, yearning to break the bonds that fetter him, aching to be great and powerful, hating the part he has been assigned to play in nature. For one with such potential as he has, he thinks, his role is demeaning. So, he complains and expresses his wishes. The result is that his unbounded ambitions, articulated with such insistency and arrogance, are heard, and "the spirits of the storm and the blast" are loosened, giving him the freedom he so thirsted for, but causing his obliteration. The lesson of the myth is that once it takes root, the drive for self-satisfaction is insatiable and destructive.[13]

Perhaps the most obvious technical aspect of the poem is its obtrusive rhyme scheme of couplets with a cadence deliberately created to make for a rhythm so compelling that the work cries out to be read aloud or recited.

> One of a hundred little rills—
> Born in the hills,
> Nourished with dews by the earth, and with tears by the sky,
>   Sang—Who is so mighty as I?
>   The farther I flow
>   The bigger I grow.
>   I, who was born but a little rill,
>   Now turn the big wheel of the mill."

If it seems odd and incongruous that a poetic myth ending tragically and with a strong moral warning that ambition without wisdom is self-destructive—if it seems odd that it is written with such a rhyme scheme and with such insistent rhythm, it would be well to remember that Juliana Ewing, whose reputation to this day is as a writer of children's stories and poems, was exceedingly accomplished in the practice of artistic duplicity. Consequently, when it seems that a poem such as "The Mill Stream" must have been written largely for children because it has such a catchy rhythm and frequent rhymes, a little further probing will reward one with the discovery that how the poem is written is an integral part of what it says.

The rhythm of the poem is a representation of the rhythm of nature. As a part of the natural world, the mill stream is governed by its rhythm, but it is not content to remain within such bounds but inspires to break out of it because of arrogant ambition. As the stream indicates, it considers itself too great to be bound by the limits imposed on it, those restrictions symbolized in the poem by the restrictive structure of couplets. The stream rebels against the couplets, one might say, but the rebellion fails. The couplets remain to the end, and the rhythm of nature prevails. The stream has been obliterated. It requires little imagination to recognize that this myth, like myths in general, teaches an important lesson related to human behavior. It conveys that truth as any gifted truth-teller should convey it—slant.

Standing out starkly in Juliana Ewing's relatively short life of forty-three years, two months, and twenty-one days is the number of times that she was recovering from ill health, not just slight illnesses and certainly not imagined ones but those involving real suffering. She was, therefore, by sheer experience an expert in the problems of convalescence.[14] It is scarcely a surprise, then, that she would write a poem about this phase of human experience, "Convalescence," but how she went about writing it is remarkable.

Readers familiar with the various types of poems will recognize at once that "Convalescence" is an example of the Browningesque dramatic monologue. The sole speaker is a boy recovering from an illness, and his audience is his little sister, whose presence is indicated first by the fact that the speaker addresses her directly—"Hold my hand, little sister, and nurse my head." Then later in the poem he reacts to something she says to him by his answering her directly: "Don't beg my pardon; I beg yours." Tired of being "better" but still not being well, the boy tells of his encounter with a sea captain and the advice he received from the older man.

The speaker is not a child but an early adolescent, old enough to read pretty well, to spell "convalescent," to remember that his doctor used the word "established," and to communicate at a level generally too advanced for a young child. He is at that impressionable age when men who have fought in the war become his heroes because he values bravery above all else. When he finally speaks with the sea captain after seeing him twice before "out walking with two sticks," he learns that "he was in the war. / And he fought." The implication is that the captain was wounded in combat, for, as the speaker tells his sister, "he's been ill ever since, and that's why he is not afloat but ashore." The boy knows all this because, as he says, "I asked him." When he tells his sister, "I like him," he is indulging in understatement, for it is clear that he is powerfully drawn for some reason to this old veteran of combat.

As is sometimes the case in dramatic monologues, a character that the speaker talks about is delineated as fully as the main character, making that person as important as the speaker.[15] Thus in "Convalescence," the speaker and the sea captain are of equal importance, for as the captain tells the boy: "We ought to be friends, because we're both convalescents." The boy's attraction to the older man is more than ordinary hero worship; it is the result of a phenomenon, a psychological transference of himself into this man that he has just met who already means so much to him. He does not merely want to be like the sea captain. When he looks at the sea captain, he is looking at himself in the future.

Similarly, the captain takes an unusual interest in the convalescing boy because he sees himself in him as he once was. He responds to the boy with patience and kindness, even agreeing to come to tea at the boy's house the next day. As we read the poem, then, we are witnessing what the speaker will be when he is a man and what the man was when he was a boy. The boy is drawn to the captain because he intuits this identity with himself; the older man is drawn to the boy for the same reason. They are the same person at radically different ages, a stunning variation on the doppelganger theme. It is one of Juliana Ewing's most ingenious achievements and exhibit A of her artistic duplicity, for beneath the simple poetic account of a boy who learns a valuable lesson of life from a sea captain is an imaginative tour de force.

As in many of Browning's dramatic monologues, so in Ewing's "Convalescence," the focus is on characterizing the speaker by skillfully having him characterize himself through his own words. The poem is more dramatic than is usual among such monologues, however, because a fundamental change takes place in the speaker before our very eyes while he is addressing his sister. That is, the boy is already in the process of becoming the captain by taking on the captain's inclusive brand of courage and thereby ridding himself of his former selfishness. Through this dramatic change in the boy speaker, the theme of the poem is projected. It concerns the close connection between the virtue of courage and the virtue of unselfishness, the one nourishing the other.

Before he saw and became acquainted with his older self, the speaker thought of courage solely in terms of derring-do, that is, the willingness to take risks, to be bold in one's actions despite the possible consequences. His older self, however, has learned that real courage involves more than that. The captain teaches him that true courage includes something else, "For the courage that dares, and the courage that bears, are really one and the same." From his conversation with the captain about "bearing" bravely whatever life puts on him, he realizes that his failure to suffer without complaint the restrictions a state of convalescence placed on him and his failure to react stoically to the physical discomfort he was experiencing have made him, in a sense, a selfish coward. From his older double, he comes to realize that courage is the double of unselfishness. The result is an important change in him. In the latter part of the poem, he expresses his regret that he has been so demanding during his illness and his present state of recovery, that he has worn out with his demands those who have cared for him. He is especially concerned with his little sister and instructs her to "have a gallop on Jack." He tells her that he will do his best to bear his headache and to be patient while she is gone, for the captain has also taught him that if he learns to be patient, he will also learn to be courageous in the full sense of the term.

"Convalescence" is an extraordinary poem in terms of its message or theme, the unusual but perceptive observation that two of what humankind considers virtues, valued highly by all who dwell on the best within us, overlap to such a degree that if one of these virtues is developed, the other will follow. But Juliana Ewing's exhibition in originality did not stop there, for "Convalescence" is, among her poems, the showpiece of virtuosity in how its theme is developed.

Boy and Squirrel

Oh boy, down there, I can't believe that what they say is true!
We squirrels surely cannot have an enemy in you;
We have so much in common, my dear friend, it seems to me
That I can really feel for you, and you can feel for me.

Some human beings might not understand the life we lead;
If we asked Dr. Birch to play, no doubt he'd rather read;
He hates all scrambling restlessness, and
    chattering, scuffling noise;
If he could catch us we should fare no better than you boys.

Fine ladies, too, whose flounces catch and tear on every stump,
What joy have they in jagged pines, who neither skip nor jump?
Miss Mittens never saw my tree-top home—so unlike hers;
What wonder if her only thought of squirrels is of furs?

But you, dear boy, you know so well the bliss of climbing trees,
Of scrambling up and sliding down, and rocking in the breeze,
Of cracking nuts and chewing cones, and
    keeping cunning hoards,
And all the games and all the sport and fun a wood affords.

It cannot be that you would make a prisoner of me,
Who hate yourself to be cooped up, who love so to be free;
An extra hour indoors, I know, is punishment to you;
You make *me* twirl a tiny cage? It never can be true!

Yet I've a wary grandfather, whose tail is white as snow.
He thinks he knows a lot of things we young ones do not know;
He says we're safe with Doctor Birch, because he is so blind,
And that Miss Mittens would not hurt a fly, for she is kind.

But you, dear boy, who know my ways, he bids me fly from you,
He says my life and liberty are lost unless I do;

That you, who fear the Doctor's cane, will fling big sticks at me,
And tear me from my forest home, and from my favourite tree.

The more we think of what he says, the more we're sure its "chaff,"
We sit beneath the shadow of our bushy tails and laugh;
Hey, presto! Friend, come up, and let us hide and seek and play.
If you could spring as well as climb, what fun we'd have to-day!

June 1877

Master Fritz

Fritz and I are not brother and sister, but we're next-
    door neighbours; for we both live next door.
I mean we both live next door to each other;
    for I live at number three, and Fritz and
    Nickel the dog live at number four.
In summer we climb through the garret
    windows and sit together on the leads,
And if the sun is too hot Mother lends us one
    big kerchief to put over both our heads.
Sometimes she gives us tea under the myrtle tree
    in the big pot that stands in the gutter.
(One slice each, and I always give Fritz the
    one that has the most butter.)
In winter we sit on the little stool by the stove at number four;
For when it's cold Fritz doesn't like to go
    out to come in next door.
It was one day in spring that he said, "I should like
    to have a house to myself with you, Grethel, and
    Nickel." And I said. "Thank you, Fritz."
And he said, "If you'll come in at tea-time and sit by the
    stove, I'll tell you tales that'll frighten you into fits.
About boys who ran away from their homes,
    and were taken by robbers, and ran after by
    wolves, and altogether in a dreadful state.

I saw the pictures of it in a book I was looking in, to
    see where perhaps I should like to emigrate.
I've not quite settled whether I shall, or be cast away
    on a desert island, or settle down nearer home;
But you'd better come in and hear about it, and then,
    wherever it is, you'll be sure to be ready to come."
So I took my darling Katerina in my
    arms, and we went in to tea.
I love Katerina, though she lost her head long ago, poor
    thing; but Fritz made me put her off my knee,
For he said, "When you're hushabying that silly old
    doll I know you are not attending to me.

Now look here, Grethel, I think
I have made up my mind that we won't go far;
For we can have a house, and I can be master
    of it just as well where we are.
Under the stairs would be a good place for
    a house for us if there's room.
It's very dirty, but you're the housewife now, and
    you must sweep it out well with the broom.
I shall expect you to keep my house very comfortable, and
    have my meals ready when there's anything to eat;
And when Nickel and I come back from playing
    outside, you may peep out and pretend you're
    watching for us coming up the street.
You've kept your apple, I see—I've eaten mine—well,
    it will be something to make a start,
And I'll put by some of my cake, if you'll keep some of
    yours, and remember Nickel must have part.
I call it your cake and your apple, but of course now
    you're my housewife everything belongs to me;
But I shall give you the management of it, and you
    must make it go as far as you can amongst three.
And if you make nice feasts every day for me and
    Nickel, and never keep us waiting for our food,

And always do everything that I want, and attend to
    everything I say, I'm sure I shall almost always be good.
And if I am naughty now and then, it'll most likely
    be your fault; and if it isn't, you mustn't mind;
For even if I seem to be cross, you ought to
    know that I mean to be kind.
And I'm sure you'll like combing Nickel's hair for my sake;
    it'll be something for you to do, and it bothers me so!
But it must be done regularly, for if it's not, his
    curls tangle into lugs as they grow.
I think that's all, dear Grethel, for I love you so
    much that I'm sure to be easy to please.
Only remember—it's a trifle—but when I want you,
    never keep that headless doll on your knees.
I'd much rather not have her in my house—there, don't
    cry! If you will have her, I suppose it must be;
Though I can't think what you want with Katerina
    when you've got Nickel and me."
So I said, "Thank you, dear Fritz, for letting me bring her, for I
    I've had her so long I shouldn't like to part with her now;
And I'll try and do everything you want as well
    as I can, now you've told me how."
But next morning I heard Fritz's garret-window
    open, and he put out his head,
And shouted, "Grethel! Grethel! I want you. Be
    quick! Haven't you got out of bed?"
I ran to the window and said, "What is it, dear Fritz?" and
    he said, "I want to tell you that I've changed my mind.
Hans Wandermann is here, and he says there are real
    sapphires on the beach; so I'm off to see what I can find."
"Oh, Fritz!" I said, "can I come too?" but he said,
    "You'd better not; you'll only be in the way.
You can stop quietly at home with Katerina, and
    you may have Nickel, too, if he'll stay."
But Nickel wouldn't. I give him far more of my cake
    than Fritz does, but he likes Fritz better than me.

So dear Katerina and I had breakfast together
   on the leads under the old myrtle tree.

August 1877

.

A Sweet Little Dear

I always *was* a remarkable child; so old for my age, and
   such a sensitive nature!—Mamma often says so.
And I am the sweetest little dear in my blue ribbons, and
   quite a picture in my Pompadour hat!—Mrs. Brown
   told her so on Sunday, and that's how I know.
And I am a sacred responsibility to my parents—(it was
   what the clergyman's wife at the seaside said),
And a solemn charge, and a fair white page, and a tender
   bud, and a spotless nature of wax to be moulded;
   —but the rest of it has gone out of my head.
There was a lot more, and she left two books as
   well, and I think she called me a Privilege, and
   Mamma said, "Yes," and began to cry.
And Nurse came in with luncheon on a tray, and
   put away the books, and said she was as weak as
   a kitten, and worried to fiddlestrings, as any one
   with common sense could see with half an eye.
I was hopping round the room, but I stopped and said, "My
   kitten's not weak, and I don't believe anybody could
   see with only half an eye. Could they, Mamma?"
And Nurse said, "Go and play, my dear, and let your Mamma
   rest;" but Mamma said, "No, my love, stay where you are.
Dear Nurse, lift me up, and put a pillow to my
   back. I know you mean to be kind;
But she does ask such remarkable questions, and while I've
   strength to speak, don't let me check the inquiring mind.
If I should fail to be all a mother ought—oh,
   how my head throbs when the dear child
   jumps!" and then Nurse said, "Ugh!

When you're worried into your grave, she'll have no mother
    at all, and 'll have to tumble up as other folks do.
There's the poor master at his wits' end—a child's not
    all a grown person has to think of— and Miss Jane
    would do well enough if she'd less of her own way;
But there's more children spoilt with care than the
    want of it, and more mothers murdered than
    there's folks hanged for, and that's what I say.
Children learns what you teach 'em, and Miss Jane's
    old enough to have learned to wait upon you:
And if her mother thought less of her and she thought
    more of her mother, it would be better for her, too."
But Nurse is a nasty cross old thing—I hate her; and I
    hate the doctor, for he wanted me to be left behind
When Mamma went to the sea for her health;
    but I begged and begged till she promised I
    should go, for Mamma is always kind.
And she bought me a new wooden spade and a basket,
    and a red and green ship with three masts, and a
    one-and-sixpenny telescope to look at the sea;
But when I got to the sands, I thought I'd rather
    be on the esplanade, for there was a little
    girl there who was looking at me,
Dressed in a navy-blue suit and a sailor hat, with fair
    hair tied with ribbons; so I told Mamma,
And she got me a suit, ready-made (but she said it was
    dreadfully dear), and a hat to match, in the Pebble
    Brooch Repository and Universal Bazaar.
It faded in the sun, and came all to pieces in
    the wash; but I was tired of it before.
For the esplanade is very dull, and the little girl with
    fair hair had got sand-boots and a shrimping-
    net and was playing on the shore.
And when my sand-boots came home, and I'd
    got a better net than hers, she went donkey-
    riding, and I knew it was to tease me,

But Nurse was so cross, and said if they sent a
    man in a herring-boat to the moon for what
    I wanted that nothing would please me.
So I said the seaside was a very disagreeable
    place, and I wished I hadn't come,
And I told Mamma so, and begged her to try
    and get well soon, to take us all home.
But now we've got home, it's very hot, and I'm afraid of
    the wasps; and I'm sure it was cooler at the sea,
And the Smiths won't be back for a fortnight,
    so I can't even have Matilda to tea.
I don't care much for my new doll—I think I'm too old for
    dolls now; I like books better, though I didn't like the last,
And I've read all I have: I always skip the dull parts, and when
    you skip a good deal, you get through them so fast.
I like toys if they're the best kind, with works; though
    when I have had one good game with them, I
    don't much care to play with them again.
I feel as if I wanted something new to amuse me, and
    Mamma says it's because I've got such an active brain.
Nurse says I don't know what I want, and I
    know I don't, and that's just what it is.
It seems so sad a young creature like me should
    feel unhappy, and not know what's amiss;
But Nurse never thinks of my feelings any more than the cruel
    nurse in the story about the little girl who was so good.
And if I die early as she did, perhaps then people
    will be sorry I've been misunderstood.
I shouldn't like to die early, but I should like people to be
    sorry for me, and to praise me when I was dead:
If I could only come to life again when they had missed
    me very much, and I'd heard what they said
Of course that's impossible, I know, but I
    wish I knew what to do instead!
It seems such a pity that a sweet little dear
    like me should ever be sad.

And Mamma says she buys everything I want, and has taught
    me everything I will learn, and reads every book, and takes
    every hint she can pick up, and keeps me with her all day
    and worries about me all night, till she's nearly mad;
And if any kind person can think of any better way to
    make me happy, we shall both of us be glad.

September 1877

The Mill Stream

One of a hundred little rills—
Born in the hills,
Nourished with dews by the earth, and with tears by the sky,
Sang—"Who so mighty as I?
The farther I flow
The bigger I grow.
I, who was born but a little rill,
Now turn the big wheel of the mill,
Though the surly slave would rather stand still.
Old, and weed-hung, and grim,
I am not afraid of him;
For when I come running and dance on his toes,
With a creak and a groan the monster goes.
And turns faster and faster,
As he learns who is master,
Round and round,
Till the corn is ground,
And the miller smiles as he stands on the bank,
And knows he has me to thank.
Then when he swings the fine sacks of flour,
I feel my power;
But when the children enjoy their food,
I know that I'm not only great but good!"

Furthermore sang the brook—
"Who loves the beautiful, let him look!
Garlanding me in shady spots
The Forget-me-nots
Are blue as the summer sky:
Who so lovely as I?
My King-cups of gold
Shine from the shade of the alders old,
Stars of the stream!—
At the water-rat's threshold they gleam.
From below
The Frog-bit spreads me its blossoms of snow,
And in masses
The Willow-herb, the flags, and the grasses,
Reeds, rushes, and sedges,
Flower and fringe and feather my edges.
To be beautiful is not amiss,
But to be loved is more than this;
And who more sought than I,
By all that run or swim or crawl or fly?
Sober shell-fish and frivolous gnats,
Tawny-eyed water-rats;
The poet with rippling rhymes so fluent,
Boys with boats playing truant,
Cattle wading knee-deep for water;
And the flower-plucking parson's daughter.
Down in my depths dwell creeping things
Who rise from my bosom on rainbow wings,
For—too swift for a school-boy's prize—
Hither and thither above me dart the
    prismatic-hued dragon-flies.
At my side the lover lingers,
And with lack-a-daisical fingers,
The Weeping Willow, woe-begone,
Strives to stay me as I run on."

There came an hour
When all this beauty and love and power
Did Seem
But a small thing to that Mill Stream.
And then his cry
Was, "Why, oh! Why
Am I thus surrounded
With checks and limits, and bounded
By bank and border
To keep me in order,
Against my will?
I, who was born to be free and unfettered—a mountain rill!
But for these jealous banks, the good
Of my gracious and fertilizing flood
Might spread to the barren highways,
And fill with Forget-me-nots countless neglected by-ways.
Why should the rough-barked Willow forever lave
Her feet in my cooling wave;
When the tender and beautiful Beech
Faints with midsummer heat in the
    meadow just out of my reach?
Could I but rush with unchecked power,
The miller might grind a day's corn in an hour.
And what are the ends
Of life, but to serve one's friends?"

A day did dawn at last,
When the spirits of the storm and the blast,
Breaking the bands of the winter's frost and snow,
Swept from the mountain source of the stream,
    and flooded the valley below.
Dams were broken and weirs came down;
Cottage and mill, country and town,
Shared in the general inundation,
And the following desolation.
Then the Mill Stream rose in its might,

And burst out of bounds to left and to right,
Rushed to the beautiful Beech,
In the meadow far out of reach.
But with such torrents the poor tree died,
Torn up by the roots and laid on its side.
The cattle swam till they sank,
Trying to find a bank.
Never more shall the broken water-wheel
Grind the corn to make the meal,
To make the children's bread.
The miller was dead.

When the setting sun
Looked to see what the Mill Stream had done
In its hour
Of unlimited power,
And what was left when that had passed by,
Behold the channel was stony and dry.
In uttermost ruin,
The Mill Stream had been its own undoing.
Furthermore, it had drowned its friend:
This was the end.

August 1881

Convalescence

Hold my hand, little Sister, and nurse my head,
    whilst I try to remember the word,
What was it?—that the doctor says is now fairly
    established both in me and my bird.
C-O-N-*con*, *with a con*, S-T-A-N-*stan*, *with a*
    stan--NO! That's Constantinople, that is
The capital of the country where rhubarb-and-
    magnesia comes from, and I wish they would
    keep it in that country, and not send it to this.

C-O-N-*con*-how my head swims! Now I've got
    it! C-O-N-V-A-L-E-S-C-E-N-C-E.
Convalescence! And that's what the doctor says is now
    fairly established both in my blackbird and me.
He says it means that you are better, and
    that you'll be well by and by.
And so the Sea-captain says, and he says we ought to be
    friends, because we're both convalescents—at least we're all
    three convalescents, my blackbird, and the Captain and I.
He's a sea-captain, not a land-captain, but,
    all the same, he was in the war,
And he fought,—for I asked him,—and he's been ill ever
    since, and that's why he's not afloat, but ashore;
And why somebody else has got his ship; and she
    behaved so beautifully in the battle, and he loves her
    quite as much as his wife, and rather better than the
    rest of his relations, for I asked him; and now he's
    afraid she will never belong to him anymore.
I like him. I've seen him three times out walking
    with two sticks when I was driving in the bath-
    chair, but I never talked to him till to-day.
He'd only one stick and a telescope, and he let
    me look through it at the big ship that was
    coming round the corner into the bay.
He was very kind, and let me ask questions. I said, "Are
    you a sea-captain?" and he said, "Yes." And I said,
    "How funny it is about land things and sea things!
There are captains and sea-captains, and weeds and
    sea-weeds, and serpents and sea-serpents. Did
    you ever meet one, and is it really like the dragons
    on our very old best blue tea-things?"
But he never did. So I asked him, "Have you got convalescence?
    Does your doctor say it is fairly established? Do your
    eyes ache if you try to read, and your neck if you draw,
    and your back if you sit up, and your head if you talk?

Don't you get tired of doing nothing, and worse
    tired still if you do anything; and does
    everything wobble about when you walk?
Wouldn't you rather go back to bed? I think I would. Don't
    you wish you were well? Wouldn't you rather be ill than
    only better? I do hate convalescence, don't you?"
Then I stopped asking, and he shut up his telescope, and
    sat down on the shingle, and said, "When you come
    to my age, little chap, you won't think 'What is it I
    had rather have?' but, 'What is it I've got to do?'
'What have I got to do or to bear; and how
    can I do it or bear it best?'
That's the only safe point to make for, my lad.
    Make for it, and leave the rest!"
I said, "But *wouldn't* you rather be in battles than in
    bed, with your head aching as if it would split?"
And he said, "Of course I would; so would most
    men. But, my little convalescent, that's not it.
What would *you* think of a man who was ordered into battle,
    and went grumbling and wishing he were in bed?"
What should I think of the fellow? Why, I
    should know he was a coward," I said.
"And if he were confined to bed," said the Sea-captain,
    "and lay grumbling and wishing he were in
    battle, I should give him no better a name;
For the courage that dares and the courage that
    bears are really one and the same."
Hold my hand, little Sister, and nurse my head,
    for I'm thinking, and I very much fear
You've had no good of being well since I was ill; I've led
    you such a life; but indeed I am obliged to you, dear!
Is it true that Nurse has got something the matter
    with her legs, and that Mary has gone home
    because she's worn out with nursing,
And won't be fit to work for months? (Will *she* be convalescent,
    because it was such hard work waiting on *me*?) And

did cook say, "So much grumbling and complaining
    is nigh as big a sin as swearing and cursing?"
I wish I hadn't been so cross with poor Mary,
    and I wish I hadn't given so much trouble
    about my medicine and my food.
I didn't think about her. I only thought what a bother
    it was. I wish I hadn't thought so much about being
    miserable, that I never thought of trying to be good.
I believe the Sea-captain is right, and I shall tell him
    so to-morrow when he comes here to tea;
He's going to look at my blackbird's leg, and if it
    is really set, he wants me to let it go free.
He says captivity is worse than convalescence,
    and so I should think it must be.
Are you tired, little Sister? You feel shaky. Don't beg my
    pardon; I beg yours. I've not let you out of my sight for
    weeks. Get your things on, and have a gallop on Jack. Ride
    round this way and let me see you. I won't say a word about
    wishing I was going too; and if my head gets bad whilst
    you're away, I will bear it my very best till you come back.
Tell me one thing before you start. If I learn to be patient, shall
    I learn to be brave, do you think? The Sea-captain says so.
He says, "Self-command is the making of a man," and he's
    a finely-made man himself, so he ought to know.
Perhaps, if I try hard at Convalescence now, I may become a
    brave sea-captain hereafter, and take my beautiful ship into
    battle, and bring her out again with flying colours and fame,
If the courage that dares and the courage that
    bears *are* really one and the same.

May 1883

Notes

Introduction

1 Gillian Avery, *Mrs. Ewing* (New York: Henry Z. Walck, 1964), p. 13.

2 Concerning the death of Captain Holloway, Kipling wrote in his autobiography: "Then the old Captain died, and I was sorry, for he was the only person in that house, as far as I can remember, who ever threw me a kind word." *Something of Myself: For My Friends Known and Unknown*, The Writings in Prose and Verse of Rudyard Kipling (New York: Scribner's, 1937), vol. 36, p. 7.

3 Kipling, *Something of Myself*, p. 10. See also Kipling's short story "Baa Baa Black Sheep" for further details of his time in the House of Desolation.

4 Kipling, *Something of Myself*, p. 8.

5 Kipling, *Something of Myself*, pp. 8–9.

6 *Lady Gregory's Journals, 1916–1930*, Lennox Robinson, ed. (New York: Macmillan, 1947), p. 271.

7 Juliana Ewing, *Six to Sixteen: A Story for Girls* (London: Society for Promoting Christian Knowledge, n. d.), p. 239. All page references to *Six to Sixteen* are to this edition and hereafter are given in the text.

8 For a discussion of the "Kipling creed," see William B. Dillingham, *Being Kipling* (New York: Palgrave Macmillan, 2008), pp. 124–5.

9 Kipling, "In Partibus," *The Cambridge Edition of the Poems of Rudyard Kipling*, ed. Thomas Pinney (Cambridge: Cambridge University Press, 2013), II, pp. 1319–21.

10 To be sure, Kipling was always drawn to groups that shared his values, but they were never cliques in the sense that they are described in *Six to Sixteen*. In such of his stories as the four involving a Masonic Lodge, Faith and Works No. 5837 E. C., for example, service to others, or unselfishness, is the *raison d'etre* for the group.

11 A phantom woman dressed in white and said to have been murdered haunts the area of land known as "Lady's Brig" in Perth close to Balmyre Farm.

12 Horatia K. F. Eden, *Juliana Horatia Ewing and Her Books* (London: Society for Promoting Christian Knowledge, 1896), p. 62.

13 Eden, *Juliana Horatia Ewing*, p. 69.

14 Eden, *Juliana Horatia Ewing*, pp. 178–9.

15 Eden writes: "Sometimes—particularly in tales that came out as serials, when she wrote from month to month, and had no opportunity for correcting the composition as whole—she was apt to give undue prominence to minor details, and throw her high lights on to obscure corners instead of concentrating them on the center point" (*Juliana Horatia Ewing*, pp. 16–17).

16 Kipling, *Something of Myself*, p. 127.

17 Kipling, *Something of Myself*, p. 126.

18 Kipling, *Something of Myself*, p. 209.

19 Ewing does not devote as much technical detail to the "intellectual hobby" of "natural science collecting" as she does to the other three, sewing, sketching, and gardening, but it is an important subject in the novel and is referred to in various places. For example, Margery states: "Once we made ourselves into a Field Naturalists Club. We girls gave up our 'spare dress wardrobe' for a museum. We subdivided the shelves, and proposed to make a perfect collection of the flora and entomology of the neighbourhood. Eleanor and I really did continue to add specimens whilst the boys were at school; but they came home at Christmas devoted, body and soul, to the drama" (p. 235). A little later, she writes of collecting as "a very sociable pursuit when one has . . . fellow naturalists" (p. 237). Major Buller, one of the two guardians of Margery, spends a great deal of his spare time—most of it, according to Theresa, his wife—enlarging his collection of insects, which he likes very much to talk about. Theresa accuses him of being "wrapt up in insects and things" (p. 108). To one degree or another most of the main characters of *Six to Sixteen* are collectors of natural science specimens, but ironically the one most successful is the young Jack Arkwright, the younger brother, who stumbles onto "some water-weed in a dock-leaf" that turns out to be a hitherto undiscovered form of alga, indeed, "it was described and figured in the *Phycological Quarterly*, and received the specific name of *Arkwrightii*, and Jack's double triumph was complete" (p. 254).

20 Eden, *Juliana Horatia Ewing*, pp. 80–1.

21 Eden, *Juliana Horatia Ewing*, pp. 186–7.

22 Rudyard Kipling, "An Interview with Mark Twain," *Pioneer*, 1890.

23 Kipling, *Something of Myself*, p. 209.

24 Kipling, *Something of Myself*, p. 96.

25 The eight stories in which she appears are as follows: "Three and—an Extra," "Mrs. Hauksbee Sits Out," "The Education of Otis Yeere," "A Second-Rate Woman," "The Rescue of Pluffles," "Consequences," "Kidnapped," and "A Supplementary Chapter."

26 Charles Allen, *Kipling Sahib: India and the Making of Rudyard Kipling* (London: Little, Brown, 2007), p. 232.

27 Andrew Lycett, *Rudyard Kipling* (London: Weidenfeld & Nicolson, 1999), p. 42.

28 Harry Ricketts, *Rudyard Kipling: A Life* (New York: Carroll & Graf, 1999), p. 96.

29 Allen, *Kipling Sahib*, p. 231.

30 Lycett, *Rudyard Kipling*, pp. 132, 133.

31 Ricketts, *Rudyard Kipling*, p. 96.

32 Angus Wilson, *The Strange Ride of Rudyard Kipling: His Life and Works* (New York: Viking, 1977), p. 12.

33 John McGivering, Notes to "Mrs. Hauksbee Sits Out," <http://kiplingsociety.co.uk/rg_sitsout1.htm>.

34 Martin Seymour-Smith, *Rudyard Kipling* (New York: St. Martin's Press, 1989), p. 70.

35 David Gilmour, *The Long Recessional: The Imperial Life of Rudyard Kipling* (New York: Farrar, Straus and Giroux, 2002), p. 33. See also Jad Adams, *Kipling* (London: Haus Books, 2005), p. 40.

36 Kipling, "Three and—an Extra," *Plain Tales from the Hills,* The Writings in Prose and Verse of Rudyard Kipling (New York: Scribner's, 1898), vol. 1, p. 11.

37 Lycett, *Rudyard Kipling*, p. 133.

38 Lycett, *Rudyard Kipling*, p. 133.

39 Kipling, "A Second-Rate Woman," *Under the Deodars, The Story of the Gadsbys, Wee Willie Winkie,* The Writings in Prose and Verse of Rudyard Kipling (New York: Scribner's, 1898), vol. 6, p. 66.

40 Kipling, "Mrs. Hauksbee Sits Out," *Under the Deodars*, p. 72.

41 Kipling, *Something of Myself*, p. 121.

42 Letter of 28 February 1925. *Rudyard Kipling to Rider Haggard: The Record of a Friendship*, Morton Cohen, ed. (London: Hutchinson, 1965), p. 140.

43 Ecclesiasticus 24:21.

44 Kipling, "Fairy-Kist," *Limits and Renewals: The Writings in Prose and Verse of Rudyard Kipling* (New York: Scribner's, 1932), vol. 33, p. 190.

45 Kipling, *Something of Myself*, p. 33.

46 Years later, he wrote "The Children of the Zodiac" (1891), one of his most accomplished stories in which the language is markedly like that of *Parables from Nature*. After failure earlier, this story proved that he had, like Margaret Gatty and Juliana Ewing before him, mastered the style of artistic duplicity. A comparison of the opening of the two works reveals his success. Gatty's "Night and Day" begins as follows: "In old times, long long ago, when Night and Day were young and foolish . . . " Kipling's "The Children of the Zodiac" begins: "Thousands of years ago, when men were greater than they are today . . . " Throughout "The Children of the Zodiac," the language is that of a myth, strikingly similar to that of *Parables from Nature*.

47 Kipling, "The Last of the Stories," *Abaft the Funnel* (New York: Doubleday, 1909), p. 317.

48 Juliana Ewing, *Jackanapes* (London: Society for Promoting Christian Knowledge, n.d.), p. 58.

49 A. W. Yeats, "The Genesis of the Recessional," *Texas Studies in English*, 31 (1952), pp. 97–108. The poem, "Forget not Yet the Tried Intent," by Sir Thomas Wyatt, is reproduced below:

> Forget not yet the tried intent
> Of such a truth as I have meant;
> My great travail so gladly spent,
> Forget not yet.
>
> Forget not yet when first began
> The weary life ye know, since whan
> The suit, the service, none tell can;
> Forget not yet.
>
> Forget not yet the great assays,

The cruel wrong, the scornful ways;
The painful patience in denays,
Forget not yet.

Forget not yet, forget not this,
How long ago hath been and is
The mind that never meant amiss;
Forget not yet.

Forget not then thine own approved,
The which so long hath thee so loved,
Whose steadfast faith yet never moved;
Forget not this.

Chapter 1

[1]   Horatia K. F. Eden, *Juliana Horatia Ewing and Her Books* (London: Society for Promoting Christian Knowledge, n.d.), pp. 138–43.

[2]   Eden, *Juliana Horatia Ewing*, p. 105.

[3]   In a letter of 2 January 1868, Ewing wrote her mother in regard to "Reka Dom," a part of *Mrs. Overtheway's Remembrances*: "I mean to compress it very much." Eden, *Juliana Horatia Ewing*, p. 169.

[4]   This supposition is based on the fact that the novel was published in 1861, when Ewing had turned twenty.

[5]   Juliana Horatia Ewing, *Monsieur the Viscount's Friend: A Tale in Three Chapters, Melchior's Dream and Other Tales* (London: Society for Promoting Christian Knowledge, n.d.), pp. 134–6. All page references to *The Viscount's Friend* are to this edition and are hereafter given in the text.

[6]   The final chapter begins with a description of the château after the damages it sustained during the Reign of Terror. Clearly, the narrator is speaking not only of the château but also of the Viscount: "It is the château once more. It is the same, but changed" (p. 184). So it is with the Viscount. In the depth of his being, he is the same person as that boy referred to in the first chapter who had a certain haughty way about him but whose eyes revealed a soft,

compassionate nature, an "underlying expression of natural amiability" (p. 136). There is no question, however, that though he is on the one hand the same, on the other he is changed, as is also the château, of which Ewing writes: "The unapproachable elegance, the inviolable security, have witnessed invasion. The right wing of the château is in ruins, with traces of fire upon the blackened walls; while here and there, a broken statue or a roofless temple are sad memories of the Revolution" (p. 184). Inside the chateau, however, as deeply within the Viscount, "all looks well," and there all is well. He has gone through intense tribulation and because of that has reached the conclusion that beauty (or what he once thought was beauty) is not necessarily truth, and ugliness can be truth. Therefore, he has taken steps to be sure that he never forgets the ugliness that has taught him a greater truth than beauty ever did.

7   The two poems in their entirety are given below:

The Passionate Shepherd to His Love (Christopher Marlowe, 1599)

Come live with me and be my love,
And we will all the pleasures prove
That valleys, groves, hills, and fields
Woods or steepy mountain yields.

And we will sit upon the rocks,
Seeing the shepherds feed their flocks
By shallow rivers to whose falls
Melodious birds sing madrigals.

And I will make thee beds of roses
And a thousand fragrant posies,
A cap of flowers, and a kirtle
Embroidered all with leaves of myrtle;

A gown made of the finest wool
Which from our pretty lambs we pull;
Fair lined slippers for the cold;
With buckles of the purest gold;

A belt of straw and ivy buds,
With coral clasps and amber studs;
And if these pleasures may thee move,
Come live with me and be my love.

The shepherds' swains shall dance and sing
For thy delight each May morning:
If these delights thy mind may move,
Then live with me and be my love.

The Nymph's Reply to the Shepherd (Sir Walter Raleigh, 1600)

If all the world and love were young,
And truth in every shepherd's tongue,
These pretty pleasures might me move
To live with thee and be thy love.

Time drives the flocks from field to fold,
When rivers rage and rocks grow old;
And Philomel becometh dumb;
The rest complain of cares to come.

The flowers do fade, and wanton fields
To wayward winter reckoning yields;
A honey tongue, a heart of gall,
Is fancy's spring, but sorrow's fall.

Thy gowns, thy shoes, thy bed of roses
Thy cap, thy kirtle, and thy posies,
Soon break, soon wither, soon forgotten,
In folly ripe, in reason rotten.

Thy belt of straw and ivy beads,
Thy coral clasps and amber studs
All these in me no means can move
To come to thee and be thy love.

> But could youth last and love still breed,
> Had joys no date nor age no need,
> Then these delights my mind might move
> To live with thee and be thy love.

8   From "God Moves in a Mysterious Way," a hymn of 1774 by the English poet William Cowper (1731–1800). The fourth verse reads:

> Judge not the Lord by feeble sense,
> But trust Him for His grace
> Behind a frowning providence
> He hides a smiling face.

The concept of providence working in the life of an individual through supreme adversity to bring about a long-range good—the theme of *The Viscount's Friend*—is nowhere better illustrated than in the life of Joseph in the biblical Old Testament. It is hard to imagine anyone ever having a rougher part of his life than Joseph in the biblical book of Genesis, yet he sees the working of providence in the murderous intentions of his brothers toward him and says to them as he forgives them: "But as for you, ye thought evil against me; but God meant it unto good, to bring to pass, as it is this day, to save much people alive" (Genesis 50:20).

9   That he has also lived a noble and courageous life since his survival of the Reign of Terror and has fought for and sacrificed an arm for his country is implied in Chapter 3 as he is walking with Valerie on the grounds of the château: "It is evening, and Monsieur the Viscount is strolling along the terrace with Madame on his arm, He has only one to offer, for where the other should be an empty sleeve is pinned to his breast, on which a bit of ribbon is stirred by the breeze" (p. 185). It is, perhaps, the same arm and hand with which he once intended to slay a toad in his garden. Ewing thus leaves it up to her readers to perceive and to appreciate the appropriateness of the Viscount's having lost the arm with which as a boy he intended to kill a harmless toad.

10   William Cowper. See note 8.

Chapter 2

1   *Canada Home: Juliana Horatia Ewing's Fredericton Letters, 1867–1869*, Margaret Howard Blom and Thomas E. Blom (eds) (Vancouver: University of British Columbia Press, 1983), p. 256.

2   This is her sister's phrase. Horatia K. F. Eden, *Juliana Horatia Ewing and Her Books* (London: Society for Promoting Christian Knowledge, n.d.), p. 16.

3   Blom and Blom (eds), *Canada Home*, p. 256.

4   That is, written while the writer is grinning.

5   Eden, *Juliana Horatia Ewing*, p. 35.

6   Eden, *Juliana Horatia Ewing*, p. 105.

7   Eden, *Juliana Horatia Ewing*, p. 105.

8   Eden comments: "It amazes me now to realize how unreasonable we [Juliana's siblings] were in our impatience, and how her powers of invention ever kept pace with our demands." *Juliana Horatia Ewing*, p. 15.

9   Eden, *Juliana Horatia Ewing*, p. 16.

10 Eden, *Juliana Horatia Ewing*, p. 28.

11 Quoted in Eden, *Juliana Horatia Ewing*, pp. 28, 30.

12 U. C. Knoepflmacher, *Ventures into Childland: Victorians, Fairy Tales, and Femininity* (Chicago: University of Chicago Press, 1998), p. 391.

13 Rudyard Kipling, *Something of Myself: For My Friends Known and Unknown*, The Writings in Prose and Verse of Rudyard Kipling (New York: Scribner's, 1937), vol. 36, p. 9.

14 Richard Wagner (1813–83).

15 Quoted in Christabel Maxwell, *Mrs Gatty and Mrs Ewing* (London: Constable, 1949), pp. 179–80.

16 "Christmas Crackers," *The Brownies and Other Tales* (London: Society for Promoting Christian Knowledge, n.d.), p. 168. All page references to "Christmas Crackers" are to this edition and hereafter are given in the text. The daughter no doubt means Godpapa Drosselmeier of E. T. A. Hoffmann's *The Nutcracker and the Mouse King* (1816). He is a magician who creates toys and is godfather to Clara and Fritz.

17 Blue Beard secreted the bodies of his ex-wives in a certain room in his castle. As he is about to go on a journey, he gives the keys to the castle rooms to his current wife and instructs her that she may go into all the rooms she wishes with the exception of that one room; she must not enter that particular room.

When he leaves on his journey, his wife cannot resist her curiosity and visits the forbidden room thus precipitating her own demise.

Chapter 3

1   One reason for the autobiographical reading of "Madam Liberality" is that the story stands out among Ewing's writings as puzzlingly different from her other works. It cries out for some sort of explanation as to why the author wrote it, what she had in mind. Ewing was adamant about the importance of morals in fiction, her point being that without an important message to readers, stories were pointless. What confuses about "Madam Liberality" is that the protagonist is treated sympathetically and yet her characterization is at the same time unsympathetic. That unusual authorial tone seems to cancel out any clear message or moral emerging from the story and invites the theory that the author may well be writing about herself and her own personal contradictions.

2   Horatia K. F. Eden, *Juliana Horatia Ewing and Her Books* (London: Society for Promoting Christian Knowledge, n.d.), pp. 12–13.

3   Marghanita Laski, *Mrs. Ewing, Mrs. Molesworth, Mrs. Hodgson Burnett* (London: Arthur Barker, 1950), p. 31.

4   Eden, *Juliana Horatia Ewing*, p. 13.

5   Gillian Avery, *Mrs Ewing* (New York: Walck, 1964), p. 17.

6   Christabel Maxwell, *Mrs Gatty and Mrs Ewing* (London: Constable, 1949), p. 194.

7   Later in her discussion of "Madam Liberality," Maxwell finds that in various places of the story, Ewing "became personal" when describing the main character and events in the life of Ewing that parallel those in the life of Madam Liberality: "There was, for example, the terrible Christmas of 1861 when Julie had worked so hard to make the festival a happy one, and a few days before had been forced by a quinsy to keep to her room and miss all the fun that she had contrived." Maxwell, *Mrs Gatty and Mrs Ewing*, p. 196.

8   Maxwell, *Mrs Gatty and Mrs Ewing*, p. 194.

9   Juliana Horatia Ewing, "Madam Liberality," *A Great Emergency and Other Tales* (London: Society for Promoting Christian Knowledge, n.d.), p. 257.

All page references to "Madam Liberality" are to this edition and hereafter are given in the text.

10 Laski, *Mrs. Ewing*, pp. 31, 32.

11 In modern psychology, Madam Liberality would probably be diagnosed as suffering from a mental disorder. Karen Kleiman describes this particular disorder, "Over-Giving," in terms that apply strikingly to Madam Liberality:

> Generous giving comes from a generous place, which implies that you have taken care of your own needs and can put forth energy toward others. It comes from a full heart. Over-Giving, on the other hand, is not the ultimate form of selflessness. Instead, it essentially comes from the inability to receive. That means that you give, give, give because you think (or hope) it will be appreciated, or because it makes you feel good about yourself, or because you feel morally obliged to.

The article goes on to indicate that one is an "Over-Giver" if the following feelings (among others) are present, all of which apply to Madam Liberality:

> It feels so good and important for you to be the giver in almost every relationship. You put the needs of others before your own. You find that you give because you want to feel loved, liked, or admired.

Karen Kleiman, "Are You an Over-Giver?" <http://www.psychologytoday.com>, 26 March 2014.

12 Juliana Horatia Ewing, "Brothers of Pity," in *Brothers of Pity and Other Tales of Beasts and Men* (London: Society for Promoting Christian Knowledge, n.d.), p. 19.

13 Ewing, "Brothers of Pity," p. 19.

Chapter 4

1   Christabel Maxwell, *Mrs Gatty and Mrs Ewing* (London, Constable, 1949), p. 215.

2 <http://victorianweb.org/authors/ewing/jackanapes.html>.

3 Horatia K. F. Eden, *Juliana Horatia Ewing and her Books* (London: Society for Promoting Christian Knowledge, n.d.), p. 109.

4 Eden, *Juliana Horatia Ewing*, p. 109.

5 Quoted in Marghanita Laski, *Mrs. Ewing, Mrs. Molesworth, and Mrs. Hodgson Burnett* (London: Arthur Barker, 1950), p. 11.

6 Eden, *Juliana Horatia Ewing*, p. 124.

7 Maxwell, *Mrs Gatty and Mrs Ewing*, p. 197.

8 Jennifer Litster, "'One Wing Clipped': The Imaginative Flights of Juliana Horatia Ewing," *Popular Victorian Writers*, Kay Boardman and Shirley Jones (eds) (Manchester: Manchester University Press, 2004), p. 155.

9 Eden, *Juliana Horatia Ewing*, pp. 217–18.

10 Eden, *Juliana Horatia Ewing*, p. 169.

11 Juliana Horatia Ewing, *Jackanapes and Other Tales* (London: Society for Promoting Christian Knowledge, n.d.), p. 10. All page references to *Jackanapes* are to this edition and hereafter are given in the text.

12 Letter of 1 September 1879. Eden, *Juliana Horatia Ewing*, p. 214.

13 *Yours Pictorially: Illustrated Letters of Randolph Caldecott*, Michael Hutchins (ed.) (London: Frederick Warne, 1976), p. 7.

14 The word *Jackanapes* is used most often to describe a saucy, conceited, impertinent person, but it also is used to describe an unusually active, mischievous child. It is this latter sense that the doctor who delivers Jackanapes obviously has in mind. He is asked right after the birth takes place: "Will he live, Doctor?" The doctor answers in such a way as to recall the distinction between slow living and fast living, between always playing it safe and being a "racer." "Live?" responds the doctor, "God bless my soul, ma'am! Look at him! The young Jackanapes! (p. 20).

15 Laski, *Mrs. Ewing*, p. 51.

16 For a discussion of Billy Budd as a kind of unfallen Adam, see William B. Dillingham, *Melville's Later Novels* (Athens: University of Georgia Press, 1986), pp. 365–99.

17 Herman Melville, *Billy Budd, Sailor (An Inside Narrative)*, Harrison Hayford and Merton M. Sealts, Jr. (eds) (Chicago: University of Chicago Press, 1962), p. 44.

18 Melville, *Billy Budd*, p. 78.

19 Melville, *Billy Budd*, p. 94.

20   Melville, *Billy Budd*, p. 123.

21   For an exhaustive treatment of the process by which *Billy Budd* was composed and published, see Hayford and Sealts (eds), *Melville, Billy Budd*, pp. 1–39.

22   See Merton M. Sealts, Jr., *Melville's Reading*, revised and enlarged edition (Columbia: University of South Carolina Press, 1988).

23   "The political men declare war, and generally for commercial interests; but when the nation is thus embroiled with its neighbours the soldier . . . draws the sword, at the command of his country . . . One word as to thy comparison of military and commercial persons. What manner of men be they who have supplied the Caffres with the fire-arms and ammunition to maintain their savage and deplorable wars? Assuredly they are not military . . . Cease then, if thou would'st be counted among the just, to vilify soldiers." W. Napier, Lieut.-General, November, 1851[Ewing's note].

24   "The Mail Coach it was that distributed over the face of the land, like the opening of apocalyptic vials, the heart-shaking news of Trafalgar, of Salamanca, of Vittoria, of Waterloo . . . The grandest chapter of our experience, within the whole Mail Coach service, was on those occasions when we went down from London with the news of Victory. Five years of life it was worth paying down for the privilege of an outside place." Thomas De-Quincey [Ewing's note].

25   "Brunswick's fated chieftain" fell at Quatre Bras, the day before Waterloo, but this first (very imperfect) list, as it appeared in the newspapers of the day, did begin with his name, and end with that of an Ensign Brown [Ewing's note].

Chapter 5

1   Juliana Horatia Ewing, *Six to Sixteen: A Story for Girls* (London: Society for Promoting Christian Knowledge, n.d.), p. 179.

2   Horatia K. F. Eden, *Juliana Horatia Ewing and Her Books* (London: Society for Promoting Christian Knowledge, n.d.), pp. 200–1.

3   It was reported that the children's game, "The Game of the Earthly Paradise," was "received with great delight by the readers of the story; one family of children adopted the word 'Mary-meadowing.'" Horatia K. F. Eden, Preface, *Mary's Meadow and Other Tales of Fields and Flowers* (London Society for Promoting Christian Knowledge, n.d.), p. ix.

4   Saxon is probably based on a dog that Ewing knew while she was living in Canada. In a letter of 29 September 1867, to her sister Horatia K. F. Gatty, she wrote: "I have fallen head over ears in love with another dog. Oh! Bless his nose! . . . His name is Hector. He is a *white* pure bull-dog. His face is more broad and round—and delicious and ferociously good-natured—and affectionately ogreish—than you can imagine. The moment I saw him I hugged him and kissed his benevolence bump . . . " Eden, *Juliana Horatia Ewing*, p. 167.

5   Elizabeth S. Tucker writes: "Dogs were her [Ewing's] special favorites, and nothing was too good for them to eat, and no place too clean to be climbed on by their muddy paws. She was always most tender of hurting their feelings . . . Once when she was calling at the house of a friend . . . she was asked by her hostess to leave her dog . . . out on the steps. She did so, but was compelled to go out several times during her visit, and whisper words of apology and condolence in the ear of her big banished pet." Elizabeth S. Tucker, *Leaves from Juliana Horatia Ewing's "Canada Home"* (Boston: Roberts Brothers, 1896), pp. 30–1.

6   Juliana Horatia Ewing, *Mary's Meadow and Other Tales of Fields and Flowers* (London: Society for Promoting Christian Knowledge, n.d.), pp. 113–14. All page references to *Mary's Meadow* are to this edition and are hereafter given in the text.

7   Eden, *Juliana Horatia Ewing*, p. 207.

8   Eden, *Juliana Horatia Ewing*, p. 207.

9   In her letter of 10 April 1880, to her husband, Alexander (Rex), Juliana writes that at dinner she sat with Alfred Hunt, whom she describes as "a water-colour painter to whom Ruskin is devoted." Sitting on her other side was "that dear old Arctic Explorer, old Ray," who revealed to her certain weaknesses in his fellow explorer Sir John Franklin. There is no mention in this letter of the subject of her conversation with her hostess, Jean Ingelow. Eden, *Juliana Horatia Ewing*, pp. 227–8.

10   To understand the nature of the river's appeal (and that of the meadow), it is helpful to recall a concept of one of Ewing's favorite poets, William Wordsworth (1770–1850). Ewing was familiar with his idea of "spots of time," which he defines in Book 12 of his long poem, *The Prelude*: "There are in our existence spots of time, / That with distinct pre-eminence retain/ A renovating virtue, whence, depressed / By false opinion and contentious thought, / Or

aught of heavier or more deadly weight, / In trivial occupations, and the round / Of ordinary intercourse, our minds / Are nourished and invisibly repaired; / A virtue, by which pleasure is enhanced, / That penetrates, enables us to mount, / When high, more high, and lifts us up when fallen" (Book 12, ll. 208–18, 1850 edition). As an epigraph for her story "Our Field," Ewing quotes several lines from Wordsworth's "Intimations of Immortality from Recollections of Early Childhood" among which are the following: "And, O ye fountains, meadows, hills, and groves, / Think not of any severing of our loves! / Yet in my heart of hearts I feel your might" (ll. 92–4). Since the quotation included "meadows" as an example of that which forms the kind of image from nature that remains in the mind and is recalled both at times of happiness and when the spirit is low and in need of lifting, it would have been equally appropriate for *Mary's Meadow*. Wordsworth's treatment of the "spots of time" idea is also to be found in "Lines Composed a Few Miles above Tintern Abbey": "These beauteous forms,/ Through a long absence, have not been to me / As is a landscape to a blind man's eye: / But oft, in lonely rooms, and 'mid the din / Of towns and cities, I have owed to them, / In hours of weariness, sensations sweet, / Felt in the blood, and felt along the heart; / And passing even into my purer mind / With tranquil restoration" (ll. 23–31).

[11]   Thomas Berry, *The Great Work: Our Way into the Future* (New York: Bell Tower, 1999), pp. 12–13.

[12]   <http://www.greenmountainmonastery.org/thomas-berry-sanctuary/the-meadow-thomas-berry-burial-site/>.

[13]   Juliana Horatia Ewing, "Our Field," *A Great Emergency and Other Tales* (London: Society for Promoting Christian Knowledge, n.d.), p. 253.

[14]   Christabel Maxwell, *Mrs Gatty and Mrs Ewing* (London: Constable, 1949), p. 202.

[15]   Dedication, Juliana Horatia Ewing, *Six to Sixteen*, p. v.

[16]   The term *paradise* as used in the title of Parkinson's book (*Paradisus*) does not refer to heaven but simply denotes a beautiful area such as a park or elaborate garden.

[17]   Henry David Thoreau, *Walden; or, Life in the Woods* (Garden City, NY: Anchor Books, 1973), p. 8.

[18]   Alphonse Karr, *A Tour Round My Garden*, ed. and trans. by J. G. Wood, illustrated by William Harvey (London: Routledge, 1855), pp. 283–5.

[19] Rudyard Kipling, "Fairy-Kist," *Limits and Renewals, The Writings in Prose and Verse of Rudyard Kipling* (New York: Scribner's, 1932), vol. 33, p. 190.

[20] Oddly enough, the ending of *Mary's Meadow* is strikingly like the concluding words of Voltaire's *Candide*. It could well be Mary speaking instead of Candide, who in replying to his long-time mentor's statement of the strange workings of the world, says: "All that is very well, but let us cultivate our garden." Francois-Marie Arouet ("Voltaire"), *Candide* (New York: Dover, 1991), p. 87.

Chapter 6

[1] Christabel Maxwell, *Mrs Gatty and Mrs Ewing* (London: Constable, 1949), p. 158.

[2] Quoted in Maxwell, *Mrs Gatty and Mrs Ewing*, pp. 234–5.

[3] "The Fleshly School of Poetry" is a term created by Robert Buchanan in an article in *The Contemporary Review* in October 1871 in which he accuses this group, consisting of Dante Gabriel Rossetti, William Morris, and Algernon Charles Swinburne, of immorality.

[4] Horatia K. F. Eden, *Juliana Horatia Ewing and Her Books* (London: Society for Promoting Christian Knowledge, n.d.), p. 254.

[5] U. C. Knoepflmacher, *Ventures into Childland: Victorians, Fairy Tales, and Femininity* (Chicago: University of Chicago Press, 1998), p. 387.

[6] Quoted in Maxwell, *Mrs Gatty and Mrs Ewing*, p. 198.

[7] Quoted in Maxwell, *Mrs Gatty and Mrs Ewing*, p. 198.

[8] Eden, *Juliana Horatia Ewing*, p. 34.

[9] Margaret Howard Blom and Thomas E. Blom (eds), *Canada Home: Juliana Horatia Ewing's Fredericton Letters, 1867–1869* (Vancouver: University of British Columbia Press, 1983), p. 256.

[10] In her book about her sister, Horatia Eden describes the poem "A Sweet Little Dear" as merely "the personification of a selfish girl" and "Master Fritz" similarly as merely the story of "an equally selfish boy," ignoring completely the wider thematic significance of the poems. Eden, *Juliana Horatia Ewing*, p. 88.

[11] Eden, *Juliana Horatia Ewing*, p. 181.

12 Two well-known stories illustrate this point: the myth of Midas teaches the destructiveness of greed; the myth of Narcissus, the destructiveness of excessive self-love.

13 This theme is fairly common in myths. Below is a myth of "The Coyote" from the Sahaptin/Salishan Tribes of Western America, retold by S. E. Schlosser. <http://americanfolklore.net>.

The Coyote and the Columbia

One day, Coyote was walking along. The sun was shining brightly, and Coyote felt very hot.

"I would like a cloud," Coyote said. So a cloud came and made some shade for Coyote. Coyote was not satisfied.

"I would like more clouds," he said. More clouds came along, and the sky began to look very stormy. But Coyote was still hot.

"How about some rain," said Coyote. The clouds began to sprinkle rain on Coyote.

"More rain," Coyote demanded. The rain became a downpour.

"I would like a creek to put my feet in," said Coyote. So a creek sprang up beside him, and Coyote walked in it to cool off his feet.

"It should be deeper," said Coyote. The creek became a huge, swirling river. Coyote was swept over and over by the water.

Finally, nearly drowned, Coyote was thrown up on the bank far away.

When he woke up, the buzzards were watching him, trying to decide if he were dead.

"I'm not dead," Coyote told them, and they flew away.

This is how the Columbia River began.

14 She handled these frequent bouts of illness with patience, grace, and courage. It is thus disturbing that someone who knew her casually and for a relatively short time should write for public consumption a statement that depicts her as a boring hypochondriac. Ethel Smyth writes that Ewing "enjoyed bad health," and charges that her letters are rife with "references to her poor back, her wretched head, the air-cushions people lent her, the number of hours spent

on the sofa after each journey, and so on." *The Memoirs of Ethel Smyth* (New York: Viking, 1987), p, 50.

15   For example, in Browning's famous "My Last Duchess," the Duke not only defines himself as he speaks about his former wife but also characterizes her, not so much in the way he means to present her but as she really was. Consequently, she becomes nearly as important in the poem as the speaker if not equal to him.

EU GPSR Authorized Representative:

LOGOS EUROPE, 9 rue Nicolas Poussin, 17000 La Rochelle, France

contact@logoseurope.eu

www.ingramcontent.com/pod-product-compliance
Lightning Source LLC
Chambersburg PA
CBHW031359160426
42814CB00040B/393/J